T0297014

Other Books by Paul Krassner

*How a Satirical Editor Became a Yippie
Conspirator in Ten Easy Years*

Best of The Realist [Editor]

Tales of Tongue Fu

*Confessions of a Raving, Unconfined Nut:
Misadventures in the Counterculture*

*The Winner of the Slow Bicycle Race:
The Satirical Writings of Paul Krassner*

Impolite Interviews

*Sex, Drugs & the Twinkie Murders:
40 Years of Countercultural Journalism*

*Murder at the Conspiracy Convention
and Other American Absurdities*

*One Hand Jerking:
Reports From an Investigative Satirist*

*In Praise of Indecency:
Dispatches from the Valley of Porn*

*Who's to Say What's Obscene?
Politics, Culture, and Comedy in America Today*

Pot Stories for the Soul

pot stories
for the soul
An Updated Edition for a Stoned America

compiled and edited by
Paul Krassner

Foreword by Harlan Ellison

True tales by and about
Ken Kesey, Hunter S. Thompson,
Allen Ginsberg, Michelle Phillips,
Wavy Gravy, Jack Herer,
Mark Mothersbaugh, John Sinclair,
Abbie Hoffman, Jerry Rubin,
Robert Anton Wilson, Stephen Gaskin,
Carolyn Garcia, Harry Shearer,
Lynn Phillips,
Michael Simmons,
Kate Coleman,
Jonah Raskin,
Tommy Chong,
and many more.

SOFT SKULL PRESS
NEW YORK

Library of Congress Cataloging-in-Publication
Data is available.

ISBN: 978-1-59376-444-9

Soft Skull Press
New York, NY
www.softskull.com

Interior design by Gopa & Ted2, Inc.
Cover design by Ann Weinstock

Printed in the United States of America

For Peter McWilliams, whose creative and compassionate leadership in the medical marijuana movement has continued to inspire and invigorate

"Marijuana is not a medicine. It is a drug that makes people think they feel better."

—Art Croney, a lobbyist for the Committee on Moral Concerns

"I admit I experimented with drugs in college. What I don't say is the experiment was a success."

—Steve Coppage, satisfied smoker

Contents

pot stories
for the soul

Foreword by Harlan Ellison

T'ANKS BUT NO T'OKES

Basically, fuck dope. No offense, dude, but fuck dope.

This has virtually nothing to do with the subject at hand, but as deep background, permit me this brief preamble: I ran away from home at age thirteen. I'd already been earning my living for three or four years prior to that, apart from mooching off my parents in Painesville, Ohio.

I mean, I was nine or ten, fer chrissakes, so when I say "I was earning my own living," I mean I was paying for everything a kid of nine or ten in the early forties would need money for: ten cents for admission every Saturday afternoon to the Lake Theater; the latest issue of *Big Shot Comics* featuring Skyman and Tony Trent as The Face; an occasional Grosset & Dunlap hardcover of a Lone Ranger novel ($2 each) bylined by Fran Striker, who had created the radio show and the character, but actually ghostwritten by the unsung Gaylord DuBois; a new pair of U.S. Keds high-tops with the big red ball on the side; a Tom Mix "nuclear bombardment chamber" radio premium ring for ten cents and two Ralston Purina box tops; a bottle of Teel tooth drops; some Fleer's Dubble Bubble . . . I earned the money for such staples by selling the Sunday edition of Cleveland's *The Plain Dealer* every Saturday night at the corner of State and Main streets, by shining shoes at that same excellent location, by mowing lawns, raking leaves, shoveling snow, catching flies, cleaning garages and attics. Back in the days before the discovery of Cultural Guilt and the advent of the Victim Society, that was how us lower-middle-class white boys paid our way. It was a hardscrabble existence for Clark Bars.

And then I ran away. And began to earn my keep for real. No mommy bargaining that if I'd eat my peas and carrots, I could stay up an hour later to hear *Big Town* or *The Hermit's Cave*. No father saying if I cleaned my room, I could come downtown after he closed the store on Saturday night and we'd have hot roast beef sandwiches and French fries at Jerry & Bert's. It was *La Strada*, dude. I was on the road, sans bucks, sans mommy/daddy, sans even Kerouac—who wouldn't be published yet for another decade. I worked on farms and in orchards, picking crops. I bluffed my way into truck-driving jobs on construction sites. I worked in a lumber camp, on tuna boats, as a door-to-door salesman, a short-order cook, a printer's devil and slag-bucket carrier in a lithographing plant, a garbage collector. I worked in a carnival, on a road gang, in a quarry, standing by the side of the road selling bouquets of flowers. I lied to farmers' wives and told them I could repair (or mangle) the busted washing machine (or stove or hot plate) out there rusting in the side yard in exchange for a meal. I rode the rods, I drank gypsy coffee out of a tin can with Princes of the Road under railroad trestles in ten different states, I had my ass saved a hundred times by men of many other colors, and I was locked up in the old Kansas City slam with a carny geek who had gone "wet-brain" so long ago that the scent of rancid sour mash came out of his pores when he sweated.

I saw what liquor and dope had to offer. I have been around drugs all my life. I came back with Chinese food one night to a sleazy railroad flat I was sharing with a beautiful girl and found her dead, naked, OD'd in the tub. The water was still warm. One night, I actually heard Charlie Parker blow at a $1 admission rent-and-spaghetti party up on 101st and First Avenue in Harlem; and he went into the can, went Charlie "Bird" Parker, and he fixed, and he came out, and he blew . . . crap. Discordant shit. I heard the great legend Bird blow, only that once, a year or two before he died, and he sounded like shit. From the dope.

Here is the subject at hand: I have been on the street since I was thirteen. I have learned important stuff about staying alive. I have learned that sneaky bastards and kindhearted slobs come in all colors. I have learned that you're never as smart as you think you are. I have learned that love is rare but cowardice is plentiful. I believe that anything not nailed down is mine—and anything I can pry loose ain't nailed down.

All through the '60s and '70s, going to parties and just hanging, this one or that one would offer me a hit of this or a lid of that. Drop one of these, stick this in your instep, shove this spansule up your ass, honk a line of this, inhale a vape of this . . . I always said, "No thanks."

I wasn't afraid. Ask anyone who knows me. I don't scare. Simply put, I didn't want any part of that crap. When someone would thrust a doobie the size of a Macanudo cigar under my nose and intone the magic word "toke?" I'd reply with a sweet smile, "Not till I come down." Theodore Sturgeon (if you don't recognize the name, go look it up, you ignorant asshole) once wrote that he'd seen studies of people who allegedly produced psilocybin in the bloodstream. He opined that I was like that . . . always high. Otherwise, how do I explain all the weird stuff I've done in my life?

The subject at hand is Krassner asking me to write my "dope story" for his idiot book.

Here it is.

Fuck dope.

Oh, and . . . have a nice day.

Introduction

PAUL KRASSNER

Pot Stories for the Soul was first published by High Times Books in 1999.
It won the Firecracker Alternative Book Award and also became a Quality
Paperback Book Club selection. All rights have since been reverted back
to me, and this is an expanded and updated edition of that collection.

The original concept was a trilogy of true dope tales—*Pot Stories for
the Soul, Acid Trips for the Soul,* and *Magic Mushrooms for the Soul*—but
attorneys for the *Chicken Soup for the Soul* publisher sent a letter to High
Times Books demanding that it "cease and desist."

Thus, the first sequel was retitled *Acid Trips for the Mind,* but the dis-
tributor insisted that it be changed to *Psychedelic Trips for the Mind.* The
second sequel was retitled *Magic Mushrooms for the Body,* but I changed
that to *Magic Mushrooms and Other Highs: From Toad Slime to Ecstasy.*

I sent a copy of the latter book to contributor/friend Todd McCormick,
but the warden rejected it "because on pages 189–190, it describes the
process of squeezing toads to obtain illicit substances, which could be detrimental to the security, good order, and discipline of the institution."

This was pure theater of cruelty. Federal correctional facilities do not
have a toad problem, and outside accomplices have not been catapulting
loads of toads over barbed wire fences to provide the fuel for a prison
riot.

But the moral of this story is, although theologians and scientists
agree that the soul cannot be located, it *can* be copyrighted.

In order to counteract the negative propaganda about marijuana, I
began collecting the material in *Pot Stories for the Soul* by contacting 250
friends and acquaintances, requesting their accounts of experiences with
marijuana. Then I put announcements in *The Realist, High Times,* and
Funny Times and on Roy of Hollywood's midnight show on KPFK and
Bob Fass's midnight show on WBAI in New York.

The stories were chosen because they're funny, whimsical, bizarre, poignant, informative, and, yeah, soulful—you got a problem with that? The styles may be different, but all reveal snippets of an essentially good-natured subculture. One correspondent wrote, "I'm sure that I have some funny dope stories, but I can't remember any." Another confessed, "I expanded my mind so many times I've got stretch marks on my brain."

The priorities are insane. Cigarettes are legal—subsidized by the government, in fact—and kill more than 1,200 people a day in this country alone, whereas marijuana is illegal and the worst that can happen is the blind munchies might lead you to raid your neighbor's refrigerator.

Voter support for the total legalization of marijuana has risen from 29 percent in 1999 to an all-time high of 50 percent today. That includes parents—tokers or not—ranging from those who want to protect their children from the perils of prohibition to those who are anticipating that time when the kids are off to college and they can fill their empty nests with the latest stash.

And yet, between 1965 and 2000, there were more than twelve million marijuana busts in America. In 2009, over half of all drug arrests in the United States were for marijuana. A FBI report concluded that police prosecuted 858,408 individuals for marijuana violations that year. Currently, almost half of all drug prosecutions nationwide are for simple possession.

As former *High Times* editor Peter Gorman told reporters at the magazine's Tenth Annual Cannabis Cup in Amsterdam,

> While we would never dismiss or diminish the suffering of any group at the hands of another—and if we could stop their suffering somehow, I hope that we would have the courage to work towards that end—there are in fact several hundred million marijuana and hashish smokers worldwide being prosecuted, jailed, and sometimes put to death in more than one

hundred separate countries simply for their use of cannabis. There is no other group, no religious organization, no single kind or color of people who are persecuted in such numbers in so many different places anywhere on the globe.

Which does not diminish the suffering of anyone. It is not a contest. Certainly the threat of being sentenced to a year in jail in the U.S. or France or England does not compare to the threat of marauders killing an entire village's inhabitants simply for their having religious beliefs. But neither should your persecution go unnoticed. And it is precisely because there are so many of us being threatened, beaten, jailed, losing our property and denied our rights, so many of us who are suffering for our belief in this gentle and healing herb that we have become the single largest persecuted minority on the planet.

So, the next time you see antimarijuana propaganda from the Partnership for a Drug-Free America, just remember that it was founded and funded by legal drug pushers—the tobacco, alcohol, and pharmaceutical industries—that have a vested interest in keeping illegal drugs unpopular.

The Partnership received $150,000 each from Philip Morris (Marlboro cigarettes), Anheuser-Busch (Budweiser), and R.J. Reynolds (Lucky Strike and Camel cigarettes). Other contributors included Beam Inc. (Jim Beam), PepsiCo, and the Coca-Cola Company. Contributing pharmaceutical companies included Bristol-Myers Squibb, Dow Chemical Company, DuPont, Novartis, GlaxoSmithKline, Hoffmann-La Roche, Johnson & Johnson, Merck & Co., Pfizer, and Schering-Plough. Publishers Hachette Book Group (Time Warner), Dow Jones, and the Reader's Digest Association also contributed funds.

As long as any government can arbitrarily decide which substances are legal and which are illegal, those victims of victimless crimes who remain behind bars for the possession of illegal substances are actually political prisoners. Significantly, unlike dangerous and addictive legal drugs, marijuana has long been sold solely on the basis of word-of-mouth. That's the purest form of advertising, and it's free. All together now, let us chant: "We don't need no steenkin' Joe Camel!"

When this book was originally published in 1999, one pop-culture sign of a changing climate concerning marijuana was the movie *Half Baked,* a sort of *Dumb and Dumber* for potheads, cowritten by and starring stand-up comic Dave Chappelle. In the process of promoting *Half Baked*, he was a guest on the *Late Show with David Letterman.*

Letterman asked him outright if he smoked marijuana. Chappelle hesitated, milking the silent tension. Then he said, "Yes," pausing for effect before adding, "but only for medicinal purposes." Laughter and applause ensued, although that joke is a truism according to the gospel of Dennis Peron, coauthor of Proposition 215, who has stated *seriously* that *"All* marijuana use is medicinal."

In *Details* magazine, John Brodie wrote,

> *Half Baked*'s journey from Chappelle's head to theatrical release shows that weed—after a fifteen-year absence wrought by Nancy Reagan and the timidity of studio execs—may no longer be anathema in Hollywood. Tommy Chong believes a cultural shift is already at hand. "I could not even get a meeting during the Reagan years," he says. "One of the reasons that Cheech and I broke up is that Universal offered him a movie without me based on the fact that it wouldn't be a pot movie. That was *Born in East L.A.*"
>
> Chong, who is bullish enough on pot comedies to be self-financing his own, *Tommy Chong's Best Buds*, maintains that things are about to change because a silent stoner majority, who do not subscribe to the "pot will rot your brain" theory, have come of age, and those kids who grew up watching his movies are now in positions of power in Hollywood. "There are," he says in a conspiratorial tone, which suggests he may

be keeping a list, "potheads in charge of the studios and the networks."

In December 2011, Matt Diehl wrote in the *Los Angeles Times*,

> The Discovery Channel's series *Weed Wars* offers unprecedented access into the medicinal-cannabis universe. Though groundbreaking, *Weed Wars* may be just an opening salvo in what is shaping up to be a growing reality subgenre devoted to illicit substances. The show has scored well with key demographics, averaging just under a million viewers a week . . . And later this spring, National Geographic Channel will present the new series *American Weed*, focusing specifically on the marijuana-legalization movement of Colorado.

Chuck Braverman, the executive producer of *Weed Wars*, admits that it's taken a while for television to catch up. "The irony is, two years ago I had a marijuana-related project, and every network passed on it."

And Shirley Halperin, coauthor of *Pot Culture: The A-Z Guide to Stoner Language and Life*, says that the wave of pot-based programming jump-started with the surprise success of CNBC's 2009 documentary special *Marijuana Inc.: Inside America's Pot Industry*. "The ratings are there, advertisers are there. Weed's place in pop culture is at critical mass."

I'll smoke to that.

When sitcom cancer patient Murphy Brown smoked medical marijuana to relieve her chemotherapy-induced nausea, Thomas Constantine, then head of the Drug Enforcement Administration (DEA), announced that he was checking to see "if any laws were broken."

Well, not the First Amendment, anyway.

Back in real life, in November 2011, Cedars-Sinai Medical Center in Los Angeles denied a liver transplant to a patient with inoperable liver cancer because he used medical marijuana, which had been approved by his oncologist at the same hospital despite the fact the facility had a "substance abuse" contract.

Studies have concluded that marijuana use does *not* affect liver transplants adversely, but the patient, scheduled for a transplant in two months, was delisted. He was to abstain from marijuana for six months while attending weekly substance-abuse counseling sessions in order to be reinstated at the bottom of the list.

In October 2011, Apple cofounder Steve Jobs died after a seven-year battle with pancreatic cancer. In 2009, he *did* have a liver transplant, but cannabis activist Steve Kubby, who is chief officer of the "Regulate Marijuana Like Wine" initiative campaign in California and a cancer survivor, told *CelebStoner*,

> One of Jobs' closest friends, Daniel Kottke, talked with Jobs about using our medical marijuana lozenges to treat his illness. We provided Jobs with a peer-reviewed study on the cancer-fighting properties of cannabis, for which I am, literally, living proof. Unfortunately, Jobs was told if it didn't work and he tested positive for cannabis, he would be denied a liver transplant, which his physicians told him was his only other option.
>
> Steve Jobs decided against using medical cannabis to treat his cancer, not based on science or medicine, but upon the consequences for him if he used this legal medicine, because of prohibition and a federal government that puts policy above lives. The loss of this visionary pioneer is a loss for the entire planet. Tragically, it appears it might have been prevented.

Meanwhile, in the midst of the nation's catastrophic economy and in the face of government crackdown, the medical marijuana industry has blossomed. By 1999, voters in six states and Washington, D.C., had opted for medical marijuana in the previous election. Now there are more than 1,500 growing operations and dispensaries across the country. So far, sixteen states and Washington, D.C., have accepted medical marijuana, and more than a dozen other states are also considering that possibility.

However, between January 2010 and May 2011, federal agents staged more than ninety raids on medical marijuana dispensaries and growers. In November 2011, the *Drug War Chronicle* reported that the governors of two medical-marijuana states—Lincoln Chafee of Rhode Island and Christine Gregoire of Washington—"called on the federal government to reschedule marijuana. In a joint 106-page petition to DEA Administrator Michele Leonhart, they said marijuana needs to be classified as a drug with accepted medical uses so that states that have passed medical marijuana laws can regulate its distribution without fear of federal prosecution."

In December 2011, according to *AlterNet,* "Less than two months after California's U.S. Attorneys announced plans to initiate a federal crackdown on the state's medical marijuana distributors and patients, hundreds of California's medical marijuana dispensaries have been forced to close their doors."

That same month in San Diego, a federal judge turned down a request from medical marijuana advocates that sought to halt the government crackdown against dispensaries and collectives. Almost two-thirds of the roughly 220 dispensaries in San Diego have closed voluntarily under threats of federal property seizures and city lawsuits.

And *The Sacramento Bee* reported,

> Only eight of ninety-nine dispensaries remain open in Sacramento County, and twenty-five of thirty-eight have closed in Sacramento city. Even more have closed out of fear of federal prosecution against business operators and their landlords . . .
>
> The United Food and Commercials Workers Union, which launched a drive to unionize pot workers during the California dispensary boom, estimates 20 percent of marijuana stores statewide have gone out of business in less than a month.

Dan Rush, who directs the union's medical cannabis division, said letters from four U.S. Attorneys threatening dispensary landlords with loss of their buildings put a chill on the trade. "There is a high rate of people closing voluntarily," Rush said. "They didn't want to cause trouble for their landlords or they're closing to get a chance to figure out how to come back in compliance."

California's Proposition 19, which would have legalized pot, failed to pass in November 2010, but a year later, *Time* magazine ran a cover story with this headline: "Legalization Went Up in Smoke, but 'Medicinal' Pot has Gone Mainstream." And, on the inside pages, *Time* noted: "In some parts of California—where marijuana is the biggest cash crop, with total sales of $14 billion annually—medical pot has become such an established part of the commercial base that cities are moving toward taxing it."

Even the DEA is in favor of such a plan—but only to benefit big pharmaceutical companies—which explains why drug czar Gil Kerlikowske stated that "the federal government is the largest source of funding for research into the potential therapeutic benefits of marijuana, and every valid request for the use of marijuana for research has been approved by the Drug Enforcement Administration."

Awareness of medical marijuana has also wiggled its way into the syndicated comic strips. In *Pardon My Planet* by Vic Lee, a doctor tells his patient, "I recommend you work up to the medical marijuana—so I'm going to start you on medical nachos with cheese and then on to a quart of medical Chunky Monkey ice cream with Doritos sprinkles." In *Candorville* by Darrin Bell, one character says to another, in reference to why he doesn't want to take his prescription for an antipsychotic drug, "Is it 'cause it's all a scam perpetrated by big pharmaceutical companies who don't want you to know you could get antipsychotic effects for free if only *WEED* were legalized?" And a cartoon by David Sipress depicts a doctor instructing his patient, "This marijuana is for medical purposes only. Call me immediately if you start having fun."

Meanwhile, it's been anything but fun for the medical marijuana movement. In April 2012, the DEA and IRS raided Oaksterdam University, the first pot trade school in the country. According to Americans for Safe Access, more than 170 raids of dispensaries nationwide have been conducted by federal agents since 2009.

A letter to the editor of the *Los Angeles Times* once stated, "I go to a Marijuana Anonymous meeting twice a week . . . Those rooms are full of young people, many in their teens and already struggling with an addiction just as real as alcoholism."

"Wrong," I responded. "Many of these so-called addicts are going to such rehab places only because it's an alternative to prison. Faking addiction is a viable option to spending time behind bars for a victimless crime that is unconstitutional. 'An addiction just as real as alcoholism'? Hey, it was beer drinkers, not pot smokers, who were so viciously violent at the Dodgers Giants game."

Over 37 percent of the estimated 288,000 people who entered rehab in 2007 for marijuana "addiction" had *not* reported using it in the entire thirty days previous to their admission. Another 16 percent said that they had used marijuana only three times or less in the month prior to their admission.

And so it has come to pass that progressive organizations have been launched, including the following:

Students for Sensible Drug Policy: A network with more than 150 chapters in universities, colleges, and high schools around the world, SSDP promotes student and teacher activism and has been officially recognized by the United Nations as a drug policy consultant.

Moms for Marijuana: Launched by single mother Serra Frank in 2006, Moms for Marijuana's purpose is to reach out to mothers who seek cannabis relegalization, not just for medical use, but also as a safer recreational substance than alcohol, which kills 37,000 Americans every year, not including alcohol-related auto accidents.

Law Enforcement against Prohibition: With a membership of thirteen thousand—including police officers, judges, prosecutors, prison wardens, and others—LEAP's mission is to legalize and regulate all drugs. It's a cause LEAP's members believe in after having witnessed and participated in the horrors and injustices resulting from prohibition.

The FBI's Crime in the United States report shows that in 2008 there were 1,702,537 drug arrests, or one every eighteen seconds. Jack Cole, a retired undercover narcotics detective who heads LEAP, said, "If we legalized and taxed drug sales, we could actually create new revenue in addition to the money we'd save from ending the cruel policy of arresting users."

Namely, we could generate $77 billion a year.

At the fortieth annual National Organization for the Reform of Marijuana Laws (NORML) Conference in April 2011, Congressman Jared Polis (D-CO) told an overflow crowd in his keynote speech,

> I am optimistic that we will reach a day when America has the smart, sensible marijuana policy that we deserve. But it could go either way. We could return to the dark ages of repression, or we could be on the eve of a new era of marijuana legalization.
>
> Your efforts will help determine which route this country takes and the legacy of this generation of activists on what marijuana policy looks like. Together, we can accomplish this. Marijuana policy is really coming of age. In my last two elections, even my Republican opponents were for legalization. It's become a very mainstream value.

In the June 2011 issue of *High Times*, associate publisher Rick Cusick wrote, "It is no longer a question of *whether* marijuana will be legalized, but rather of how and when." Colorado and Washington State and national drug-reform groups have announced that they plan to put a legalization initiative on the ballot for 2012.

A family in the syndicated comic strip *Pardon My Planet* by Vic Lee explains why legalization has been taking so long. The father says, "Marijuana is very dangerous because you could get hooked on it." The young son sitting on his lap asks, "Why's that dangerous?" And his mother responds, "Because it leaves fewer people to get hooked on alcohol and tobacco."

More than a dozen years have passed since *Pot Stories for the Soul* was first published. Things change. In 1999, over ten million Americans enjoyed smoking marijuana. Now, according to government statistics, there are twenty-five million annual pot smokers in the United States. That includes an ever-increasing number of baby boomers as well as young people who have been toking away on their favorite weed.

In the following pages of this updated edition of *Pot Stories*, there's a section of my latest writing entitled "One Toke over the Century: Krassner's New Stuff," all of which appeared in *High Times*, except for "Lenny's Last Laugh," a shorter version of which was published in *Playboy*. Also, several new pieces that have been written by others in the interim are scattered throughout. (Wherever there's a story with no byline, it means that the writer requested to remain anonymous.)

However, there's one particular story that's missing, written by my friend John Cochran, who is currently in prison. I had invited him to contribute a piece to this book, and he was delighted that he would be included. But a prison form (the "Notice of Rejection/Disposition of Mail") rejected his "attempt to send contraband out of any DOC [Department of Corrections] operated or contract facility," and the handwritten disposition stated: "Homemade bookmark (wooden)—Envelope rejected in TOTAL."

"Well," Cochran wrote to me, "I sent you my story—last Saturday. I sent that and a really cool Xmas gift I made you out of a piece of the stump that was the old hanging tree here back in the mid-1800s—the territorial days. They didn't like that—not a bit. Declared it contraband, the gift, the story, the letter, the package & postage—all—and destroyed it. Anyway, I'm so disgusted I can't even bring myself to sit down & write the motherfuckin' thing again. I wrote it, rewrote it, and then wrote it a third time legibly—eight pages. Piss on it."

So *that's* his story.

"Sorry," he continued, "you had a very unique gift coming your way. I imagine it is now on some Jack's [a guard's] desk at home. And you would've liked the pot story. Selah [a Hunter-Thompsonism, meaning 'So there it is']. I've always had difficulty with mail between me & you since way back at the very beginning in 2001. You sent me a copy of *The Realist* where you had perverted a Rockwellian scene to such a degree that they 'investigated' you & placed your name on a watch list. Ha!"

Norman Rockwell's paintings on the covers of *The Saturday Evening Post* were always synonymous with saccharine wholesomeness. But then his son Peter, speaking at the National Press Club, mentioned that his father's long-standing ambition was to visit an opium den. Ultimately, he was dissuaded from taking any such trip by the advertisers in the magazine.

When I learned that on C-Span, I immediately assigned versatile illustrator Kalynn Campbell to capture the venerated artist's secret vision. (You can see that cover by Googling "*The Realist* Archive Project.") I thought that such an under-the-surface image of American culture would serve as an appropriate metaphor for the final issue of *The Realist*.

And that's *my* story.

Here come the rest of 'em now . . .

One Toke over the Century:

Krassner's New Stuff

Remembering Scott Kelman

Scott Kelman had seen me perform stand-up at Town Hall in New York in 1962, and again twenty years later at the L.A. Stage Company in Hollywood. He moved to Los Angeles and in 1984 launched an alternative theater in the grungy, old, industrial skid-row area of downtown. He named it the Wallenboyd (at the corner of Wall and Boyd) Theater and invited me to open there as soon as it was completed. In fact, on the first night of my performances, the crew was still banging in the final nails.

At the time, I was living in San Francisco, so Scott slept at his office and I stayed at his apartment in Venice Beach. A year later, I moved to an apartment on that same block. Scott became my producer and my close friend. We never had any need for a signed contract. As my producer, he would occasionally give me suggestions and I would follow those that I felt worked for me.

"It doesn't matter if you fuck up," he'd say in his distinctive gravelly voice—he was addicted to cigarettes—"it's how you recover." That was theatrical advice, but it also applied to life. And it was a two-way street. For Scott, whatever happened in life automatically became grist for his theatrical mill. And he was an exemplary explorer.

Knowing I was an unbeliever, he once asked me, "What do atheists say during sex when they come?"

"Oh, *no*-God!" I responded, interspersing those words with moans and groans. "Oh, *no*-God! Oh, *no*-God! Oh, *no*-God!"

He suggested that I expand that concept into a stage piece, and it evolved into a ten-minute meditation on the relationship between religion and orgasms.

Scott conducted theatrical workshops, and one of his students was John Densmore, the former drummer for The Doors. "I stumbled into the downtown art scene," Densmore told me, "after a big peak in rock 'n' roll. It felt as creative as the '60s. I now get off on the *process*, and it doesn't matter if it's fifty people at the Wallenboyd or twenty thousand at Madison Square Garden, it's the work that rings my bell."

Scott also produced Peter Bergman, of the Firesign Theatre. Scott thought that *Peter, Paul and Harry* would be a great title for an evening of political satire at the Museum of Contemporary Art. He asked the curator if she knew of an appropriate performer named Harry. She suggested Harry Shearer. Scott asked me about him. "He's brilliant," I said, "let's do it." And so he produced a completely sold-out series that was extended for two weekends. But if Harry had been named after his *other* grandfather, there wouldn't have been a *Peter, Paul and Harry*.

Each of us prepared to perform in our own particular way. Peter stared at himself in the mirror and made strange sounds to exercise his vocal cords. Harry sat in a separate room where his makeup woman, who had flown in from Iowa, transformed him into Derek Smalls from the mockumentary *Spinal Tap*. And I was off hiding behind some boxes, toking away on a joint of the marijuana that served as my creative fuel.

Scott was sure that I performed better when I wasn't high, and he was under the impression I was straight when he told me one night, "That was the best show you've ever done." I confessed that I had smoked a giant doobie before I went onstage. The irony was that Scott sold pot to help pay the rent, and that was exactly the stash that got me stoned that night.

Who Killed Peter McWilliams?

Enjoy. That was his favorite word. He always signed his e-mails with it, even if he was bringing bad news. And Peter McWilliams, a Los Angeles-based author and publisher, was living with bad news every day. In 1996, he was diagnosed with cancer and AIDS, yet he was bursting with enthusiasm. His other favorite word was *consent*. His license plate said CONSENT, and his self-published, best-selling book was titled *Ain't Nobody's Business If You Do: The Absurdity of Consensual Crime in a Free Society.*

McWilliams survived cancer and controlled the AIDS with pills that nauseated him. Ironically, if he threw up his lunch, that regurgitation would also include the nausea-producing pills he needed to stay alive. But if he smoked marijuana, it not only increased his appetite, it also counteracted the nausea.

That same year, California Proposition 215 was passed, legalizing marijuana for medical use when recommended by a physician. It had been recommended to McWilliams by *four* physicians. Cannabis clubs opened up where AIDS patients could purchase marijuana. McWilliams devised a plan to supply marijuana to these buyers' cooperatives that were providing a legal service for their sick and dying customers at reasonable prices in a pleasant setting.

He hired Todd McCormick—a cancer patient since the age of nine—to research and write the book *How to Grow Medical Marijuana.* McCormick proceeded to grow four thousand plants in a house known as the Cannabis Castle. But the DEA insisted that federal law superseded state law, and he was arrested in 1997. Federal prosecutors obtained an order forbidding a medical-marijuana defense—leaving McCormick with no defense at all—and, in order to avoid a mandatory ten-year minimum sentence, he pleaded guilty and served five years behind bars.

In 1998, McWilliams was arrested as the kingpin of this conspiracy to cultivate and distribute medical marijuana. In *Ain't Nobody's Business If You Do*, he had chronicled the cruelty of putting people in prison who had not harmed anyone. Now, not only had McWilliams not harmed anyone, he was trying to *help* others. But, like McCormick, he wasn't allowed a medical-marijuana defense and ultimately pleaded guilty for the same reason as McCormick.

Without a medical-marijuana defense, he too had no defense at all. He would be considered the godfather of an insidious cartel. Furthermore, a federal judge prohibited him from smoking his medicine while he awaited sentencing, which was scheduled for August 15, 2000—the second day of the Democratic National Convention in Los Angeles, so it was unlikely there would be any media coverage of his incarceration.

Anthropologists of the future will look back upon these times and wonder how legislators could have been so uncivilized. Although eight states and Washington, D.C., had already passed initiatives to legalize medical marijuana, then–Indiana Congressman Mark Souder (known as "Mad Mark") claimed in July 2000 that any effort to make medical marijuana legal "is just a phony excuse to be a pothead."

In an interview in 1998, McWilliams told me,

> I agree that medical marijuana will eventually lead to the legalization of marijuana use for all adults, but not for the reasons the drug warriors paint. There is no "massive, well-funded conspiracy" to legalize marijuana that General Drug Czar McCaffrey and his drug warriors maintain. Certainly the few million spent each year by all the marijuana legalization groups combined becomes an ineffective drop in the ocean when compared to the fifty-billion-dollar annual drug-war budget.
>
> Medical marijuana will lead to recreational marijuana legalization through the natural process of experience and education. Once people personally discover how benign marijuana is, the next logical question is simply no reasonable, factual

response to that question. As [marijuana activist] Jack Herer pointed out, once enough people ask, "Why isn't the emperor wearing any clothes?" the game is over. All it takes is enough people asking the question.

Enter medical marijuana. Once in general use, tens of millions of Americans will be asking that question. How many people? Well, let's consider pain relief alone. In 1997, the National Academy of Neuroscience determined, based on studies from four major universities, that ninety-seven million Americans each year could benefit from the use of medical marijuana to treat pain. Once those ninety-seven million—half the adult population of America—realize that the horror stories they have heard about marijuana are simply not true, there will be a chorus of "Why isn't the emperor wearing any clothes?" It will shake the narco-prison-industrial complex to its very foundations.

Something that a lot of people don't realize is that when you smoke marijuana regularly—several times a day—it loses its euphoric effect. The medical benefits continue—relief of nausea, pain (physical or emotional), spasticity, excessive eye pressure (glaucoma), and so on—but the euphoric effects go away. While I was using marijuana to treat my nausea, I can't tell you how much I missed getting high. Although I'd smoke it several times a day, the average high school student was getting high more times a month than I was. That's because after the first month, I never got high, and I really enjoy marijuana's high. Simply put, recreational marijuana you use to get high; medical marijuana you use to get by.

Marijuana is the country's fourth-largest cash crop after corn, soybeans, and hay. There are eighty million Americans who have smoked pot. Eleven million still smoke it every month, and half of them smoke it every day. And they inhale. And they enjoy it. But marijuana arrests accelerated during the '90s. In federal prisons, average drug offenders spent more time behind bars (82.2 months) than rapists (7.3 months). In California, more inmates are doing life terms for possession of marijuana than for murder, rape, and robbery combined.

In the larger prison outside those walls, more and more companies are requiring employees to submit to random drug tests, and their privacy goes down the drain while their urine is sent to the lab. *The New York Times* and *Rolling Stone* are among the publications that have such a policy. When a *Times* employee takes a drug test, the faucets are removed from the sinks in the bathroom so that employees cannot dilute their urine with water.

Peter McWilliams was subject to random drug tests for two years while his sentencing date was postponed over and over. His AIDS medications caused nausea, but he couldn't smoke marijuana to keep it down. And he vomited, and vomited, and vomited again. Every day. With a touch of mordant humor, he told me,

> The stomach acid that comes up along with everything else with the regularity of Old Faithful has eroded my teeth into spiky little remnants of their former selves—my mouth resembles a photograph from *The Amazing Ozark Mountain Book of Dental Oddities.*
>
> Over time, I tried various techniques to keep the AIDS medications down a little longer before vomiting. In addition to large doses of Marinol [synthetic marijuana prescription], which is essential, I added herbs, lying in hot water, curling up in a fetal position in bed, and two electric massagers— a smaller one to stimulate the acupuncture points for anti-nausea and a larger one for my stomach.
>
> Gradually, over many months of trial and mostly error, I was able to increase the length of time I could hold down my medications from thirty minutes to one hour and fifteen minutes. That forty-five-minute increase is apparently enough

for the medications to get into my system. The procedure of keeping them down is agonizing, exhausting, and debilitating, and I must do it three times a day. It is entirely unnecessary if I could use medical marijuana.

Peter was hoping to be sentenced to home detention with an electronic monitoring ankle bracelet while simultaneously trying to prepare himself for the possibility of five years' incarceration in a federal prison. On June 14, 2000, two months before he was due to be sentenced, he was found dead in his bathtub. He had died from asphyxiation. He had choked to death on his own vomit. He had been murdered—but by whom? And for what reason?

I accuse President Bill Clinton for coming out against medical marijuana during his term. By doing so, it's as if he said, "I feel your pain; I just don't want to help you relieve it." I accuse former Drug Czar Barry McCaffrey, who proclaimed, after medical-marijuana initiatives were passed in Arizona and California, "There is not a shred of scientific evidence that shows that smoked marijuana is useful or needed."

I accuse former California Governor Gray Davis for opposing recommendations by his own Attorney General's Task Force on Medical Marijuana. I accuse Assistant U.S. Attorneys Jackie Chooljian and Mary Fulginiti, the pair of prosecutors who sought to prevent the use of a medical-marijuana defense. I accuse Federal Judge George King, who denied Peter McWilliams—slumping in his wheelchair in the courtroom—not only the right to a medical-marijuana defense, but also his legal right to *smoke* medical marijuana.

These individuals participated in an unspoken conspiracy, all for the same reason. And what was it they had in common? They all wanted to keep their jobs. They all wanted to advance in their careers. They all wanted prestige. They all wanted to live in a nice house. They all wanted to send their kids to college. They all wanted to be responsible to their families. And the price was simply their own humanity.

McWilliams's death at the age of fifty occurred the same day the governor of Hawaii signed into law a medical-marijuana bill passed by the state legislature. His signature made Hawaii the first state in the United States to authorize the medical use of marijuana through the legislature rather than by a vote of the people. A vote had been attempted twice in California, and although the legislature passed the bill in each case, then-Governor Pete Wilson vetoed it both times, which caused the people to eliminate the middleman and pass a referendum.

A few politicians have had the compassion and courage to speak out against the insanity of the war on drugs. I mean the war on *some* people who use *some* drugs *sometimes*. Among such heroes are: former New Mexico Governor Gary Johnson (a presidential candidate in the 2012 Republican primaries), who stated, "We're trying to get tougher with things that *we* got away with. And there's a hypocrisy to that, in my opinion," and former California State Senator John Vasconcellos (a Democrat), who introduced legislation to implement recommendations whereby persons legally possessing ID cards would be immune from arrest under state law for possession, transportation, delivery, or cultivation of medical marijuana. In July 2000, the bill was passed.

That same month, the DEA—forced by recent scientific evidence— began legally binding procedures that could conceivably result in the end of marijuana prohibition. Meanwhile, like a pair of dinosaurs trying to survive, both major presidential candidates were drowning in chickenshit. Al Gore and George Bush both took public anti-medical-marijuana positions. Another presidential candidate, Social Democrat David McReynolds, came out publicly as a pot smoker.

At the Green Party convention, Ralph Nader's opponents—Jello Biafra (the lead singer of The Dead Kennedys and a political activist) and Stephen Gaskin (founder of The Farm commune and author of *Cannabis Spirituality*)—each preceded Nader with a ten-minute speech. Biafra called the war on drugs "ethnic cleansing, American style." Gaskin, sad and angry over Peter McWilliams's death, spoke with great passion, declaring that it was "as if Barry McCaffrey came out with a pistol like that South Vietnamese general and executed him."

Nader watched this on the TV monitor, and during his own ten-minute speech—clearly influenced by Gaskin's tribute to McWilliams—he proclaimed, "We've got to stop this drug war that does these horrible things to our people." Later, in his lengthy acceptance speech, he said:

> At home, our criminal justice system, being increasingly driven by the corporate prison industry that wants ever more customers, grossly discriminates against minorities and is greatly distorted by the extremely expensive and failed war on drugs. These prisons often become finishing schools for criminal recidivists. At the same time, the criminal justice system excludes criminally behaving corporations and their well-defended executives.

At the National Libertarian Party Convention—where presidential candidate Harry Browne came out firmly for the decriminalization of marijuana—Peter McWilliams became the first posthumous winner of their Champion of Liberty Award. Peter was the victim of a political assassination, but his legacy lives on.

I e-mailed this piece to a few friends and received the following responses.

From Robert Anton Wilson: "Nobody except Tim Leary ever faced oncoming death with as much bravery and *hilaritas* as Peter. He will be missed by multitudes. I do not think you exaggerate in using the word *murder*. Depriving the ill of the medicine they need ranks as 'depraved indifference' or Murder Two in most states."

From retired Congressman John Vasconcellos: "I am deeply saddened, deeply angered. Poor Peter! Poor each and all of us in this crazed society we inhabit! What shall we do next?"

And from Ken Kesey, with his uncanny ability to cross-fertilize compassion and irreverence: "Well, I would rather choke on my own vomit than on somebody else's."

My immediate instinct was to forward Kesey's little message to Peter, whose particular sense of humor would have enabled him to really appreciate such a sardonic observation. And, of course, I would have signed that e-mail with *Enjoy*.

Checkmating with Pawns

It was a hot day at the chess tournament in Phoenix, Arizona—103 degrees, to be exact—and fourteen-year-old Nathaniel Dight was elated over his custom-made chess set. The carved wooden pieces had been weighted precisely for the smooth moves he liked to make. Each one had been lacquered and, for this extreme heat, carefully protected by matte acrylic spray. But before the game could begin, young Nathaniel was ordered to take a urine test.

"I know why you're doing this," he snarled. "It's because I've won three tournaments in a row, isn't it?"

"No, son, that's just a coincidence. This is a *random* drug test."

"I don't do any drugs. I mean, like when I get a headache from playing chess too long, I won't even take an aspirin."

"Look, here's a cup. I need you to go fill it, right now . . . "

All right, I confess, I made all that up, but consider the implications of something that I *haven't* made up:

America's former Drug Czar Barry McCaffrey wrote in an article published in *Chess Life* magazine: "Research proves that mentoring youngsters and teaching them games like chess can build resilience in the face of illegal drug use and other destructive temptations. Drug testing is as appropriate for chess players as for shot-putters or any other competitors who use their heads as well as their hands."

Accompanying the television image of a couple of eggs sizzling in a frying pan, the phrase *This is your brain on drugs* has always carried negative connotations, but apparently General McCaffrey has changed his mind about that. He now seems to believe that drugs can actually *improve* the way your the brain functions.

There was an infamous chess player named Alexander Alekhine, who held the world championship longer than anyone else. His games often had superb surprise endings, known in chess circles as "brilliancies."

For instance, he would checkmate with a pawn move that no sane and sober mind could ever imagine. However, he was a notorious alcoholic, and McCaffrey was only referring to illegal drugs.

"Just when I thought I'd heard it all from McCaffrey," said Allen St. Pierre, executive director of NORML. "Drug testing for chess players? What's next from this overreaching drug czar? Drug testing for tiddly-winks players? How about bingo players?"

Moreover, McCaffrey's proposal smacks of subliminal racism. Social psychologist Walli Leff told me, "I think most of the movement to involve young people in chess is directed toward the African American community, and the assumption is, if the kids are black, they're going to be drug users. I think white middle-class suburban parents would have a fit if their kids had to take drug tests for their extracurricular activities. Or am I out of it and am I missing a new white middle-class suburban submissiveness?"

McCaffrey had been influenced by Chesschild, a group sponsored by the Office of National Drug Control Policy (ONDCP). Chesschild is a substance abuse prevention program conducted in libraries and schools, promoting a combination of drug-free lifestyles and chess.

"Policy recommendations like this one from ONDCP," said St. Pierre, "demonstrate a deep and disturbing pathology that goes well beyond opposing drug-law reform efforts."

Maybe the drug-law reformers should follow the example of gay-rights activists by having celebrities come out of the pot-smoking closet. Already, veteran stand-up comic George Carlin—in an interview with *The Daily Show*'s Jon Stewart following Carlin's HBO special—admitted that he smoked a joint to help him "fine-tune" his material. "One hit is all I need now and it's punch-up time."

At the Shadow Convention that took place while the Democrats were in Los Angeles in 2000, Bill Maher revealed to the audience, "I'm not just a pot reformer, I'm a user"—something ABC forbid him from saying on *Politically Incorrect*. Then he quickly added, "Just making a light remark there, federal authorities."

Actor and hemp activist Woody Harrelson has stated, "I do smoke." Willie Nelson confirmed in his autobiography that he smoked pot in the White House. And on talk show host Michael Jackson's radio show on KRLA, Michelle Phillips, actress and former member of the Mamas and the Papas, said that she still enjoys smoking marijuana.

Just as Ellen DeGeneres appeared on the cover of *Time* magazine saying, "Yep, I'm gay," there might come a day when a presidential candidate will appear on the cover of *Newsweek* saying, "Yep, I'm stoned." Isn't that what young pot-smokers need—good role models, so they won't be ashamed of their private pleasure seeking?

Meanwhile, then–Drug Czar McCaffrey continued his crusade, not only against illegal substances, but perhaps also against certain food supplements, such as a popular herbal mixture with a reputation for aiding memory and concentration. Who could ever have dreamed that chess players might get in trouble for using ginkgo biloba as a performance enhancer?

The Ballad of Tommy Chong

Jonathan Shapiro, who was a writer and executive producer of the 2006 Fox TV series *Justice*, reviewed Tommy Chong's book *The I Chong: Meditations from the Joint*, for the *Los Angeles Times*. Shapiro wrote,

> Being incarcerated for resisting imperial power or because of Bone's sexual preference or getting sent to the gulag for dissenting opinions are searing human tragedies that inspired brave acts of artistic resistance. Selling bongs over state lines just doesn't carry the same moral weight.

Hey, Jonny boy, *whoa!* You'd better buy a new state-of-the-art apocryphal scale if you're going to compare the moral weight of prison sentences.

In February 2003, Tommy Chong was among fifty-five people who were arrested in raids across the country as a culmination of the DEA's Operation Pipe Dreams, named after one of Cheech & Chong's stoner movies. Agents forced their way through the door of his home at six o'clock in the morning with automatic weapons drawn. Chong, who was the only one who served time—nine months at a federal prison—paid a $20,000 fine, not to mention the $103,000 that was seized when he got busted.

The reason he became an exception and received such punishment was precisely *because* of his "dissenting opinions" and "artistic resistance." It simply would not have happened otherwise.

The DEA wanted to get him really bad. Traditionally, local law enforcement has the discretion to decide what priority should be given to prosecuting cases involving drug paraphernalia. Because both Pennsylvania and Ohio make that a top priority, the DEA chose to open a decoy head shop in Pennsylvania. Four times in one year, these sting-meisters tried to buy a pipe autographed by Chong online, but his Nice Dreams Enterprises would not fill any orders coming from either of those two states.

However, a request from a different return address easily passed through a new employee who acted as a fake firewall. Chong said he suspected that the employee was sent to infiltrate his company. I asked why he suspected that. He responded that it was a very strong suspicion, based on the fact that the employee left the company a couple of days before the bust, giving no reason.

In a deal with the authorities, Chong agreed to plead guilty in exchange for his wife and son not being indicted. Ironically, he was sentenced on September 11, the second anniversary of the *real* terrorist attacks, rather than a business run by an actor in such Cheech & Chong movies as *Up in Smoke* and, more recently, a recurring role on a popular sitcom, *That '70s Show*, where he continued to play the part of a dedicated pot smoker.

The prosecutor, U.S. Attorney Mary Beth Buchanan—ignoring all relevance of the First Amendment in favor of her professional career—had the audacity to introduce Chong's fictional character in the courtroom as evidence of his "frivolous" attitude toward the enforcement of drug laws. Chong said this was "like jailing all of the *Police Academy* people for making fun of cops." Furthermore, he had joked with reporters about putting this criminal case in his next movie with Cheech. The prosecution insisted that such a comment indicated that Chong was making light of the case and might exploit it for money.

Behind bars, Chong said, "I'm a doper comedian, and I'm in here because I made a stupid joke about the bongs being the only weapons of mass destruction that the Bush administration had found." Chong, who is half Scottish-Irish and half Chinese and was raised in Canada, added, "When I became an American citizen, I took a vow to uphold the Constitution of the U.S. Doing anything less than exercising my right of free speech in defense of pot and against its prohibition would be a violation of my vow."

So listen, Jonathan, if your show *Justice* ever returns to TV, how about considering a story line revealing the basic *in*justice of arresting 830,000 individuals every year for the "crime" of possessing marijuana? It may not get you high, but hopefully your consciousness will be raised in the process.

As for Prosecutor Buchanan, *her* career had been inadvertently boosted by the terrorist attacks of 2001 when a United Airlines plane crashed inside her jurisdiction (sixty miles southeast of Pittsburgh), catapulting her to prominence in the law enforcement community and enabling her to instigate the yearlong undercover sting. Three days after 9/11, she became the first woman and the youngest person in Pennsylvania history ever to be named a U.S. Attorney, and for her first major operation, she chose Tommy Chong as her priority target because *his* career had "glamorized" the use of marijuana.

Meanwhile, the cruel absurdity of antiparaphernalia laws continues to be underscored by such creative substitutes as apples, soda cans, toilet-paper cardboard tubes with aluminum foil, tweezers used as roach clips, and don't forget those plain old regular *tobacco* pipes.

In Fulton, Kentucky, police investigating a marijuana-smoking complaint found pot burning on a backyard grill with a large fan on the other side of the house that was sucking the smoke throughout the home—in effect, said the police chief, it turned "the house into a large marijuana bong." Seize it immediately, boys!

Bong Hits 4 Jesus

The Supreme Court sucks so badly that it finally turned itself inside out. In 2007, their outrageous five-to-four ruling made it acceptable to suspend a high school student for the off-campus act of holding a fourteen-foot banner reading BONG HITS 4 JESUS. That harmless bit of incongruity became a federal case ending with a dangerous precedent for suppressing free speech.

Chief Justice John Roberts agreed with the school principal that "the banner would be interpreted by those viewing it as promoting illegal drug use, and that interpretation is plainly a reasonable one." What a ton of bullshit. Justices Samuel Alito and Anthony Kennedy voted with him but also stated that the their decision didn't address "political or social issues such as the wisdom of the war on drugs or of legalized marijuana for medical use." Ironically, this is the same Supreme Court that upheld the illegality of medical marijuana by falsely denying the existence of positive research.

Studies have concluded that cannabis is effective for relieving muscle spasticity and chronic pain in AIDS patients. The miracle weed can both increase hunger in HIV patients and suppress hunger to fight obesity. It can help those with glaucoma, Alzheimer's disease, asthma, hepatitis, diabetes, epilepsy, osteoporosis, arthritis, insomnia, sleep apnea, migraine headaches, scoliosis, hypertension, depression, shingles, PMS, menopause, Parkinson's disease, and multiple sclerosis. Cannabinoids can inhibit the proliferation of cancer cell lines, including breast, prostate, colon, pancreatic, and brain cancer.

As for the "concern about the health effects of smoking marijuana," it was reported at the 2005 meeting of the International Cannabinoid Research Society that smoking marijuana—"even heavy long-term use"—does not cause cancer of the lungs, upper airways, or esophagus. As for recent claims of psychosis, the rate of psychosis has remained unchanged since 1950, while the rate of marijuana use has increased 10,000 percent since then.

Medical marijuana is already legal in many states, yet it is prohibited—and trumped—by federal law. But cynical critics treat the legalization of medical marijuana as though it were intended to be a gateway leading to legalization of nonmedical marijuana. So this is really about the war on pleasure. In the past forty years, twenty million Americans were arrested for violating antimarijuana laws, primarily for simple possession.

The New York Times even editorialized about the importance of medical marijuana: "Although there are other prescriptions that are designed to relieve pain and nausea, and there is concern about the health effects of smoking marijuana, there are some truly ill people who find peace only that way." But those "other prescriptions" are pushed by the pharmaceutical industry, which spent a record-breaking $155 million to lobby the government from 2005 to mid-2006. Altogether, prescription drugs killed over thirty thousand Americans in 2008. In 2009, more than a million emergency room visits resulted from prescription-drug overdoses, and fifteen thousand of prescription-drug OD's resulted in death.

The World Health Organization spent three years working out an agreement with 171 countries to prevent the spread of smoking-related diseases, particularly in the developing world, but the United States opposed the treaty, which included a minimum age of eighteen for sales to minors. Around the globe, tobacco now kills almost five million people a year. Within a generation, WHO predicts the premature death toll will reach ten million a year. Anthropologists of the future will surely look back upon these times as incredibly barbaric.

Former Drug Czar John Walters insisted that pot growers are "violent criminal terrorists who wouldn't hesitate to help other terrorists get into the country with the aim of causing mass casualties." But syndicated columnist Clarence Page—referring to the Wo/Men's Alliance for Medical Marijuana (WAMM)—wrote about the DEA raiding "a legitimate health cooperative that was treating more than two hundred patients, some of them terminally ill, in Santa Cruz, California. Snatching medicine out of the hands of seriously ill patients sounds like terrorism to me. In this case, it was federally sponsored and taxpayer-financed."

WAMM, founded by Valerie and Mike Corral, has been helping people dying of cancer and AIDS for nineteen years. Learning that such patients couldn't afford the high cost of marijuana, WAMM established a communal garden where medicine is grown for patients who have a doctor's recommendation; they may take what they need and give what they can, even if that is nothing.

The late Robert Anton Wilson, a prolific countercultural author, told me,

> I never thought I would become another WAMM patient. My post-polio syndrome had been a minor nuisance until then. Suddenly, two years ago, it flared up into blazing pain. My doctor recommended marijuana and named WAMM as the safest and most legal source. By then I think I was on the edge of suicide—the pain had become like a permanent abscessed tooth in the leg. Nobody can or should endure that.

After the DEA raided WAMM's garden and arrested its founders, outraged Santa Cruz city and county officials sponsored WAMM's medical marijuana giveaway on the steps of city hall and joined WAMM's lawsuit against the DEA, the attorney general, and the Office of National Drug Control Policy. WAMM is considered the most likely organization to ultimately sway the Supreme Court at the time. According to Federal Judge Jeremy Fogel, "WAMM is the gold standard of the medical marijuana movement."

Meanwhile, what ever happened to Joseph Frederick? He was the eighteen-year-old student in 2002 who, when the Olympic torch passed through Juneau, Alaska, seized upon the opportunity to hold up that banner that said BONG HITS 4 JESUS. He is currently learning Mandarin and teaching English in China. He's proud that he stood up for his rights, with the aid of the ACLU, but regrets "the bad precedent set by the ruling." However, his case was settled at the state level in November 2008, winning him $45,000 and forcing the school to hold a forum on free speech.

If only that banner had said BONG HITS 4 WAMM, then, by the Supreme Court's own language—that their decision did not address "political or social issues such as the wisdom of the war on drugs or of legalized marijuana for medical use"—the "Bong Hits 4 Jesus" student would not have been punished. He would've been protected by the First Amendment because *blasphemy is protected* by the First Amendment. But the prejudiced Supreme Court justices rationalized that "Bong Hits 4 Jesus" was "promoting illegal drug use," even though such promotion is also protected by the First Amendment.

The Great Hippie Debate

At the Winnipeg Comedy Festival, I participated in a fake debate—
"Whereas they were mostly disheveled, disorganized, and doped up,
be it resolved that the hippies of the '60s accomplished nothing"—
played strictly for laughs. Comedian Bruce Clark took the affirmative
position:

> Don't get me wrong, I like hippies. Some of my best friends
> are squeegee kids. In fact, it would be a better place if hippies
> were running the world. And when I say "running the world,"
> what I really mean is harvesting the marijuana. It would be a
> kinder, gentler society, but let's be honest, nothing would ever
> get done. Unless you think it's an accomplishment to stare at
> your own hand for an hour or tie-dye your cat.
>
> Hippies often give their children names associated with
> hippie culture. Names like Sky, Rain, Sunshine, and Autumn.
> I thought it was because of their respect for nature. But it's
> actually something else that's associated with hippies—being
> homeless. I didn't figure that out myself, I heard it from
> the son of hippie parents and a good friend of mine, Spare
> Change. He's not happy with the name, but his sister Dump-
> ster Diver is livid.
>
> Hippies justify their counterculture lifestyle by pointing
> to the man they call the original hippie, Jesus. I gotta say,
> I agree. Jesus had long hair, he wore sandals, he was anti-
> establishment, and he hung around with a dozen other guys
> who never seemed to have a job. And he must have been
> stoned to hang around with all those lepers. I'll concede the
> fact that Christ was a hippie—but I doubt that Jesus made his
> wine out of bong water.

Unless we employ revisionist history, there's no evidence to suggest hippies accomplished anything. Grace Slick, the lead singer of Jefferson Airplane, said it best when she said, "If you remember the '60s, you probably weren't there." And if you *were* there, you're probably too old to remember them. Hippies have added little to the world. It would be a great Master-Card commercial: Used Volkswagen bus, $600. Incense, $10. Collection of Grateful Dead eight-tracks, $6. Being a hippie: Useless.

Then came my rebuttal:

In the aftermath of the repression and blandness of the 1950s, hippies exploded onto the scene, deriving their entire philosophy from Celestial Seasonings tea bag boxes. At its core, the counterculture was a *spiritual* revolution. The holy trinity was sex, drugs, and rock 'n' roll. But the fundamental accomplishment of hippies was that they cared for each other. This characteristic was crystallized at Woodstock by an announcement warning the audience: *Do not take the brown acid.*

Timothy Leary, a cheerleader for the hippie movement, was the guru of LSD, a chemical compound that he considered to be a vehicle for expanding consciousness. Leary even wanted to experience consciousness after his death. He planned to have his head frozen so that someday technology would enable him to be cloned from his own cells. And if that didn't work, his head could always be used on *Celebrity Bowling.*

After I took my first acid trip, I told my mother about it. She was very concerned. She said, "It could lead to marijuana." My mother was right. She cautioned me, "And marijuana could become a habit." Indeed, when *High Times* published a questionnaire, one of the questions was, "Is it possible to smoke *too much* pot?" And a reader responded, "I don't understand the question."

Socrates said, "Know thyself." Norman Mailer said, "Be thyself." And the hippie movement said, "Change thyself." Many hippies changed their names as a symbolic act of their independence from mainstream society. The editor of a psychedelic paper, *The San Francisco Oracle*, changed his name to Siddartha and he joined a commune, where they all called him Sid. They thought his name was Sid Arthur.

Hippies not only developed a humane value system, they also *lived* their alternative, based on cooperation rather than competition. They served as harbingers of organic farming, alternative medicine, women's liberation, environmental proactivity—and hippie theme parks.

That old hippie maxim of the 1960s, "make love, not war," is as relevant today as it was then. Literally. Aging male hippies don't seem to have any problem with erectile dysfunction. They just worry that it's *really* rigor mortis setting in on the installment plan.

I imagine myself emceeing the Geezerstock Festival, standing on an outdoor stage, looking out at a vast audience of gray-haired hippies with paunches and wearing granny glasses. "Are you having fun? I can't hear you! No, I mean *I really can't hear you!* And now I'd like to introduce the Rolling Stones before they gather any more moss. Oh, wait, I've just been handed an announcement: *Warning: Do not take the brown antacid.*"

Judging by audience applause, the moderator declared me the winner of the debate.

Lenny's Last Laugh

Fifty years ago, Lenny Bruce predicted: "Pot will be legal in ten years. Why? Because in this audience probably every other one of you knows a law student who smokes pot, who will become a senator, who will legalize it to protect himself. But then no one will smoke it anymore. You'll see." But Lenny's premature ejaculation could finally become a reality in November 2010, when California voters consider ballot initiative Proposition 19 to legalize and tax marijuana for personal use.

California Assemblyman Tom Ammiano—who introduced a similar bill, not only to address the state's economic crisis, but also to begin a discussion about how best to regulate its largest cash crop at $14 billion a year—is optimistic. He told me,

> This is landing in the hottest places. Milton Friedman and all these conservative economists and *The Wall Street Journal* said this needs to be done. There's a big libertarian streak here, too. So it might be the perfect storm: a political will, bipartisan, populist, economic concerns, and the feds are lightening up. The best scenario would be, make it a states' rights issue.

"Ah, yes," I observed, "'states' rights—it's not just for racists anymore."

The State Board of Equalization estimates that the bill's proposed $50-per-ounce sales tax could raise $1.3 billion a year. It's a matter of doing the right thing for the wrong reason. Nevertheless, lame duck Governor Arnold Schwarzenegger said it's "time for debate" on whether the state should legalize and tax the sale of, well, a *weed*. And that debate is now in full swing, with utterly strange bedfellows on both sides.

For example, here's what loose-cannon reactionary Glenn Beck has to say about it:

It's about time we legalize marijuana. We have to make a choice in this country. We either put people who are smoking marijuana behind bars or we regulate it. This little game we're playing in the middle is not helping us, it is not helping Mexico, and it is causing *massive* violence on our southern border. We need to—how can I say this?—do something or get off the pot.

That sounds a lot like NORML's stance:

While NORML supports cannabis medicalization and decriminalization efforts, we also recognize that these efforts fall woefully short for many Americans. The *only* way to fully protect our citizens from abhorrent police raids is through the legalization and regulation of marijuana for *all* adults.

Conversely, in Humboldt County, where the entire economy depends on the sale of their only cash crop   superb weed—*growers* were actually displaying KEEP POT ILLEGAL bumper stickers, concerned that legalization would drive down prices. Rumors abounded about corporate cannabis copyrights, that Philip Morris and other firms were buying acres and acres of cropland, and that Wal-Mart was on the bandwagon to sell yet another product for mass consumption. Bloggers predicted that tobacco companies would crush small farmers if the legalize-and-tax-pot initiative passed.

"If residents don't act," local radio host Anna Hamilton warned, "we're going to be ruined."

Not surprisingly, John Lovell, a lobbyist for the California Narcotics Officers Association—whose members wouldn't benefit from having fewer people to arrest—rationalizes that "we have alcohol, tobacco, pharmaceuticals. Why on earth would any sane person want to add another mind-altering substance to the available legal array?"

Surprisingly, Dennis Peron—coauthor of California's Proposition 215,

which legalized the use of medical marijuana with a doctor's recommendation—is *opposed* to legalizing "recreational" use. Reciting a startling
litany of medical uses for marijuana, he told me, "By definition, marijuana provides efficacy to such a broad spectrum of human maladies
and conditions, from anxiety to heart disease, that one can safely say *all*
marijuana is medical." Thus, recreational use is a myth, and passing
Ammiano's bill or the ballot initiative would perpetuate that myth.

Peron had other reasons for his opposition to Proposition 19:

> It's too restrictive. Only a five-by-five area can be cultivated,
> which would increase the cost of marijuana. It makes a whole
> new class of criminals by creating a felony for smoking with
> and/or furnishing marijuana to minors, including eighteen- to
> twenty-one-year-olds. Not to mention the tax of $50 an ounce
> will make the product prohibitively expensive, and the taxes
> will be used to prosecute people.

Meanwhile, activists in two other states were also proposing pro-pot
initiatives. Neither campaign would obtain enough signatures to qualify.
Phillip Dawdy, coauthor of the Washington initiative, explained:

> This state has a "single subject rule" for initiatives, and it's very
> strictly applied by the courts. So, literally, all we could do was
> just end criminal penalties to a straight repeal of all criminal
> penalties connected with marijuana, for adults eighteen and
> over. Since we're not doing any taxation and regulation in our
> initiative, it would be kind of difficult for the feds to come in
> and argue federal preemption to *anything* we're doing because
> all we're doing is repealing state [criminal] laws; we're not talk-
> ing about the federal government and any of their laws. In the
> conservative eastern half of the state, marijuana legalization
> polled at 52 percent in favor, in an area that sends Republicans
> to Congress and to the legislature. It's a cross-cultural thing,

a cross-racial thing, a cross-class thing. We're finally in the view.

And Paul Stanford, primary author of the Oregon Cannabis Tax Act, envisioned taking legalization one step further, agreeing with my position that there should be amnesty for anyone convicted of possessing or growing marijuana. He told me,

> We did look at the amnesty provision. We found that it made us lose about 15 percent of the vote. There were polls that 15 percent is crucial to being able to win. As a past marijuana felon myself, I would like nothing better than to let our people pretty much go and grow, but politically it's just not going to fly right now at the same time. So that clause is not in there: "Get out of jail." But hopefully, once it's legal, then the parole boards of all different prisons will look at it in a different light.

Leland Cole, leader of the International Cannabis Clemency Project, asks this rhetorical question: "Do you really think you can legalize marijuana for some, while others remain on the inside, without making any provisions for those that have lost their liberty?" Furthermore, he points out, "Most of the people presently being held for cannabis charges in California are from one racial minority group or another, or are of poor economic status, or both. No equal protection there. This is a federal civil rights lawsuit waiting to happen."

I may be slightly jaded, but I was shocked that 15 percent of Oregon citizens who support legalizing pot would hold such an illogical and unjust antiamnesty position—thereby allowing simple compassion to go right down the drain—as though people should no longer be arrested for pot, yet it's okay to leave behind all those who are *already* living in cages.

America's puritanical political process serves as a buffer between the status quo and the force of evolution. For instance, in order to get

Republican votes for the children's health care bill, Democrats agreed to fund $28 million to the *Republican* abstinence-only sex-education program.

Also, during the 2008 presidential campaign, Barack Obama admitted, in the context of health care reform, that the multinational insurance conglomeration is so firmly entrenched that he would be unable to dispense with it. And so there would have to be compromises. Now, amnesty is the single-payer system of marijuana reform, and growing your own pot with no reservations is the public option.

Nationally, between 1990 and 2005, there have been more than 7,200,000 marijuana-related arrests. One out of every eighteen felony convictions resulted from pot busts. In California alone, 70 percent of the 150,000 state prisoners are currently serving time for drug-related convictions. With that in mind, I decided to return to Tom Ammiano for a follow-up. He assured me,

> While I understand the desire to have the initiative provide clemency for marijuana convictions, it simply cannot accomplish everything that people want.
>
> Undoing the damage of thirty years of the war on drugs will take more than one ballot initiative. Sentencing reform is an integral part of that, and it is crucial that those in the movement see the forest through the trees. The initiative is simply the next step in the struggle for a rational public policy towards marijuana, but it will not be the last.

Meanwhile, a report by the American Bar Association's Law Student Division claims that "chronic use of marijuana allows the user to block out pain, frustration, and confusion. The THC affects the brain's pleasure center, providing the illusion of feeling good." What the fuck were *they* smoking?

Obviously, these were not the same law students that Lenny Bruce had in mind.

A Letter to Barack Obama

Since California's Proposition 19 was defeated, the bottom line remains, as so eloquently put by author/activist Harvey Wasserman: "[Here's] the simple truth about America's marijuana prohibition: Any law that allows the easy incarceration of any citizen any time those in power want to do it is the ultimate enemy of democracy. With eight hundred thousand annual arrests over an herb used by tens of millions of Americans, it is the cornerstone of a police state."

Shortly before the midterm election in 2010, I wrote the following letter to Barack Obama, and a journalist friend faxed a copy directly to him:

> It seems that the theme emanating from the White House is "Eat, Pray, Be Disappointed." And yet, whenever I feel disappointed, I always realize that the alternative was John McCain, with Sarah Palin just one Halloween *"Boo!"* away from the presidency, and then I always feel a sense of relief. But you promised to end the raids on medical marijuana dispensaries. They haven't stopped.
>
> [In 2009, Attorney General Eric Holder issued a memo ordering an end to federal raids of medical marijuana dispensaries. In March 2011, there were twenty-eight such raids in twenty-four hours.]
>
> Bob Woodward writes in *Obama's Wars* about Colin Powell's status as an adviser to you. Powell has finally changed his mind about gays in the military. As a stand-up satirist, I used to conduct an imaginary dialogue with him: "General Powell, you're the first African American to be head of the Joint Chiefs of Staff, and you come from the tradition of a military family. So you know that blacks were once segregated in the army

because the other soldiers might feel uncomfortable if blacks slept in the same barracks. And now that's what they say about gays, that other soldiers might feel uncomfortable about gays sleeping in the same barracks." "Well," he replied, "you have to understand, we never told anybody we were black."

And, Mr. President, that was the forerunner of the same "don't ask, don't tell" policy that you promised to rescind, only you haven't been acting like a commander in chief. Those who serve in the military are trained to follow orders. If they can follow orders to kill fellow humans, they can certainly follow orders to treat openly gay service people with total equality.

Not only is the current guideline counterproductive, but also this display of trickle-down immorality must, on some level of consciousness, serve as a contributing factor to enabling the antigay bullying and torturing of innocent victims. The ultimate irony is that gays in the military are fighting, being maimed, and dying unnecessarily, supposedly to protect the freedom their own country is denying them . . .

Gay rights and marijuana-smokers' rights are both constitutional civil rights. Yet, Attorney General Holder—having been pressured by nine former DEA chiefs, plus the president of Mexico—warned that if Proposition 19 was passed, the federal government would not look the other way, as it has done with medical marijuana. Holder (who had refused to prosecute the Bush administration for promulgating torture) explained:

Let me state clearly that the Department of Justice strongly opposes Proposition 19. If passed, this legislation will greatly complicate federal drug enforcement efforts to the detriment of our citizens. We will vigorously enforce the [law] against those individuals and organizations that possess, manufacture, or distribute marijuana for recreational use, even if such activities are permitted under state law.

In a truly free society, the distinction of whether marijuana is used for medical or recreational purposes would be as irrelevant an excuse for discrimination as whether the sexual preference of gays and lesbians is innate or a matter of choice.

Newt's Noxious Nuttiness

What do Barack Obama and Newt Gingrich have in common? They were both pot-smokers.

"When I was a kid, I inhaled frequently," Obama said. "That was the point."

Gingrich said, "That was a sign we were alive and in graduate school in that era."

What else do Obama and Gingrich have in common? They have both flip-flopped on the issue of medical marijuana.

In 2011, the Obama administration issued a memo approving federal prosecution of anyone in the business of growing or supplying marijuana for medical patients and ordering the Justice Department to crack down on dispensaries even if they complied with state law.

But Obama had promised in 2008 that he would let states set their own policies. Could this change of position possibly be related to the fact that during his presidential campaign he received $2.1 million from pharmaceutical companies, many of which develop synthetic marijuana products?

In 1991, then-Congressman Gingrich introduced pro-medical-marijuana legislation. In 2011, he changed his position.

"What has changed is the number of parents I met with who said they did not want their children to get the signal from the government that it was acceptable behavior," Gingrich explained, adding that Americans who need medical marijuana will simply have to cope with the inconvenience of debilitating pain and nausea.

"[My] supporters," he continued, "were prepared to say as a matter of value, it was better to send a clear signal on no drug use at the risk of inconveniencing some people than it was to be compassionate toward a small group at the risk of telling a much larger group that it was okay to use the drug. It's a change of information. Within a year of my original support of that bill, I withdrew it."

Mixing political pandering with drug control is an established practice in the fear-mongering disinformation business. In 1998, an antidrug booklet with a foreword by Senator Orrin Hatch informed parents that among the warning signs their children are using marijuana or other drugs is "excessive preoccupation with social causes, race relations, environmental issues, etc."

That same year in Mississippi, anyone found guilty of possessing marijuana for any reason could face the removal of a limb if proposed legislation became law. Then-Congressman Bobby Moak (R-Lincoln County) introduced a bill, which authorized "the removal of a body part in lieu of other sentences imposed by the court for violations of the Controlled Substances Law."

Keith Stroup, then-executive director of NORML, called the measure "political posturing at its most extreme. This is a truly barbaric proposal that shocks the conscience."

A provision in the bill mandated that a convicted person and the court "must agree on which body part shall be removed." Yes, you would have been required to choose between sacrificing an arm or a leg. And even that seems humane in comparison to Newt Gingrich's sponsorship of federal bill HR 41, which would require the death penalty for individuals convicted of importing illegal drugs into the United States—including marijuana. Capital punishment could conceivably apply to someone who imported more than fifty grams of pot. That's less than two ounces.

And yet, in 1981, Gingrich introduced a bill that sought "to provide for the therapeutic use of marijuana in situations involving life-threatening illnesses or sense-threatening illnesses and to provide adequate supplies of marijuana for such use." In 1982, he wrote the following passionate letter to *The Journal of the American Medical Association*:

> The American Medical Association's Council on Scientific Affairs should be commended for its report, "Marijuana: Its Health Hazards and Therapeutic Potential." Not only does the report outline evidence of marijuana's potential harms, but it distinguishes this concern from the legitimate issue of

marijuana's important medical benefits. All too often the hysteria that attends public debate over marijuana's social abuse compromises a clear appreciation for this critical distinction.

Since 1978, thirty-two states have abandoned the federal prohibition to recognize legislatively marijuana's important medical properties. Federal law, however, continues to define marijuana as a drug "with no accepted medical use," and federal agencies continue to prohibit physician-patient access to marijuana. This outdated federal prohibition is corrupting the intent of the state laws and depriving thousands of glaucoma and cancer patients of the medical care promised them by their state legislatures.

On September 16, 1981, Representative Stewart McKinney and I introduced legislation designed to end bureaucratic interference in the use of marijuana as a medicant.

We believe licensed physicians are competent to employ marijuana, and patients have a right to obtain marijuana legally, under medical supervision, from a regulated source. The medical prohibition does not prevent seriously ill patients from employing marijuana; it simply deprives them of medical supervision and denies them access to a regulated medical substance. Physicians are often forced to choose between their ethical responsibilities to the patient and their legal liabilities to federal bureaucrats.

Representative McKinney and I hope the Council will take a close and careful look at this issue. Federal policies do not reflect a factual or balanced assessment of marijuana's use as a medicant. The Council, by thoroughly investigating the available materials, might well discover that its own assessment of marijuana's therapeutic value has, in the past, been more than slightly shaded by federal policies that are less than neutral.

Flash ahead to 1996: In an interview with Hilary Stout for *The Wall Street Journal*, Gingrich rationalized his ass off. "See," he told her, "when I smoked pot, it was illegal, but not immoral. Now, it is illegal *and* immoral. The law didn't change, only the morality . . . That's why you get to go to jail and I don't."

Ultimately, the bottom line is that Newt Gingrich's ability to look the other way and dehumanize people suffering because of the war on weed enabled him to claim that child labor laws are "truly stupid," suggesting that poor children should work as school janitors and later declaring that they don't understand work unless they're doing something illegal.

And, as for President Obama, his ability to look the other way and dehumanize people suffering because of the war on weed enabled him to fight to keep cluster bombs, as reported on AllGov.com:

> American diplomats are lobbying for changes to the international treaty banning cluster bombs so the U.S. and other major military powers can join the protocol without actually giving up the deadly weapons. Cluster munitions are designed to burst open in midair and release anywhere from dozens to hundreds of smaller munitions that explode tiny fragments of metal, frequently injuring or killing civilian noncombatants.
>
> Representatives from about one hundred countries are discussing the U.S.-backed proposal at the Fourth Review Conference of the Convention on Conventional Weapons (CCW) in Geneva. The U.S. is not a party to the Convention on Cluster Munitions.
>
> The agreement currently bans the weapons, requires destruction of stockpiles within eight years, and mandates clearance of areas contaminated by cluster munitions within ten years and assistance to victims. The U.S.-backed amendments to the CCW would allow ongoing continued use, production, trade, and stockpiling of cluster munitions.
>
> At various times, the United States has used cluster bombs in Vietnam, Cambodia, Laos, Lebanon, Grenada, Libya, Iran, Iraq, Kuwait, Saudi Arabia, Bosnia and Herzegovina, Serbia, Montenegro, Kosovo, Afghanistan, and, most recently, Yemen.

U.S. companies, with the permission of the federal government, have sold cluster munitions to at least thirty nations,
most recently to the United Arab Emirates (2006), India
(2008), and Saudi Arabia (2011).

The U.S. maintains a stockpile of an estimated five million
cluster munitions and seven hundred million submunitions.
Zach Hudson, coordinator of the United States Campaign to
Ban Landmines for Handicap International, told Inter Press
Service that the changes sought by the Obama administration
represent a "backslide" and are "really unacceptable." Hudson
added that the new draft "essentially undermines" the effort
to rid the world of the destructive weapons.

So, then, what else do Obama and Gingrich have in common? They
both need a compassion transplant.

The Kesey Papers

The Bust at Kesey's Place

LEE QUARNSTROM

Exhausted by several days of Prankster foolishness that we were call-ing "space travel," I was napping one evening in a back bedroom of Ken Kesey's cabin in the forested mountains above Palo Alto on the San Francisco Peninsula, when I heard Michael Hagen's voice shouting something about a search warrant. Search warrant? We'd been expecting something like this, but I was in no mood to stick around to see what this search warrant business was all about. It sounded like Hagen was out front somewhere, so naturally I was up and heading out back. I was halfway to the door in the back bedroom before I was even awake.

As I dashed into the darkness of the back bedroom, someone tossed me the mayonnaise jar with all the pot in it. Expecting a raid, we'd con-solidated all the dope into a single quart jar so it could be more easily disposed of in an emergency such as the one we were now apparently encountering.

The jar was about two-thirds full. It was enough for two or three days.

I scrambled across a bed and started out the door, hoping to hustle the few yards down to edge of La Honda Creek and, under cover of the total darkness you find at night in a redwood forest, toss the stash as far as I could into the stream. Hopefully, I was thinking as I stumbled toward the door, the mayo jar would smash on one of the boulders in the creek and the evidence would be washed away westward to the Pacific, a few miles down La Honda Road.

The trouble was, as I scooted out the door I ran straight into the barrel of an automatic pistol that was pointed directly at my forehead! I could feel the gun at the bridge of my nose. It was cold! It was hard! It was scary!

"Stop or I'll shoot," the gunman shouted, displaying no originality, I thought as I turned.

Foolheartedly, I didn't believe he'd actually shoot me over something as benign as a little illegal weed, so I ran back into the room. The cop, probably as confused and scared as I, stumbled into the blackness behind me. He grabbed my ankle as I started to crawl back across the bed, the mayonnaise jar still in my hand. Realizing that the room was pitch black, I understood in that instant that he'd never be able to recognize me in the light.

On the other hand, of course, he could have shot me! So I kicked him in the chest and tried to break loose. Another Prankster, Hagen I think, dashed into the bedroom and headed toward the door into the bathroom—which had two entrances, the other off the kitchen. I lobbed the mayo jar to Hagen and followed him into the john.

What a sight! There was Kesey, who'd been dabbing yet another touch of Day-Glo paint to the constantly expanding mural-montage that covered the walls, the porcelain, and every other surface of the bathroom. Only now he was busy with the more pressing business of flushing the grass down the toilet. The Best Foods jar was empty! At the same moment, a fat Asian man, who turned out to be the late federal drug agent Willie Wong, ran into the bathroom from the kitchen, smacked Kesey's balding head with a huge flashlight, then jumped onto his back.

Now, Kesey had been a championship wrestler during his college days at the University of Oregon. He was strong, agile, and just then operating on adrenaline. He stood up from the swirling toilet bowl, agent Wong clinging to him. With a terrific shrug, Kesey tossed him from his back onto Page Browning, a.k.a. Des Prado, who was standing frozen at the sink where he had been shaving. Somehow, despite the chaos going on around him, Page was still applying the razor to his skinny face.

Wong, still armed with the huge Rayovac, landed on Page like a sumo wrestler as he was tossed from Kesey's back. The pair of them, Wong and Page, tumbled into the bathtub.

Page still held the razor in his hand. Suddenly, a huge automatic pistol shattered the bathroom window and extended into the room.

"Stop or I'll shoot," the gunman shouted from outside. "You're under arrest!"

Wong, who'd regained his footing, shouted that he was charging Page and Kesey with resisting arrest.

"What else was I going to do?" Kesey later asked a judge. "I was raised during World War II. What would you have done? A big Jap jumped on me. I didn't know what was happening. I tossed him off."

The judge didn't buy it. Neither did he buy Kesey's claim, as Ken looked at the good, well-dressed citizens of San Francisco sitting in the courtroom, that they had failed to impanel a jury of his peers.

After Kesey and Page had been subdued and handcuffed, we were led at gunpoint into the living room. There were fourteen of us—Kesey, Neal Cassady, Des Prado, Ken Babbs, Gretchen Fetchin the Slime Queen, Hermit, Mountain Girl, Jerry Anderson—whose bride-to-be, Signe Tolle, sang with a band called The Matrix (soon to change its name to Jefferson Airplane)—Hagen, a woman named Rosalie I was spending time with, myself, and three others. We were handcuffed and charged with violating California's Health and Safety Code restrictions against the possession of illegal drugs, specifically *cannabis sativa*.

We weren't Boy Scouts, that's for sure. But since we had known—or suspected or, at least, feared—that the authorities were set to raid our little scene in La Honda, our motto in the previous few days had been "be prepared!" So when the squad of federal, state, and county narcs and deputies came across Kesey's bridge armed with search warrants and automatic pistols on the night of April 23, 1965, we were ready. At least, naïve and simple pot- and acidheads that we were, we *thought* we were ready.

Faye, Kesey's wife, had gone over the place with the housekeeping equivalent of a fine-tooth comb before leaving with their three kids and the dogs: Schnapps, a mean little dachshund bitch Faye asked me to

take to the pound a year later when we were living in Santa Cruz—Kesey
has never forgiven me for taking Schnapps on her final journey—and
Lion Dog, the wire-haired Airedale that had never been the same, really,
since the time she ate a handful of LSD someone had carelessly left
lying around.

(Kesey, when you read this, I was only following Faye's orders. But
yes, you're right, I probably would have done it on my own if I'd have
thought about it; Schnapps was a nasty little bastard!)

Faye had vacuumed stray marijuana flakes from the rugs. She had
rounded up all the alligator clips and hemostats and Squirkenworks
devices that might be considered roach clips. She had even picked errant
pot seeds from between the boards of the floor in the house. We swallowed or smoked or otherwise ingested or got rid of all the DMT, Obetrol,
DET, Dexamil, Dolophine, hashish, and other stimulants, depressants
and psychotropics, legal or otherwise, that we found stashed around the
place.

As far as I knew, the only grass in the place was in the jar—and that
had come from my cabin when I had been sent out on a "tether" a couple
of days earlier.

Let me explain. We were under what we called "spaceship conditions."
Just as Kesey insisted you were either on the bus or off the bus, for
this spaceship endeavor you were either on the spaceship or off it. The
front gate on our side of the raggedy bridge across La Honda Creek was
locked; no one could go in or out. That gate, welded out of old tools, car
parts, bucksaws, and odd pieces of metal by sculptor Ron Boise (of the
infamous *Kama Sutra* statues that blue-nosed San Francisco cops had
confiscated the prior year from the Vorpal Galleries), was the "airlock"
between our spaceship and the rest of the universe—at least until the
narcs invaded. We were, in our drug-sparked protoscientific way, trying
to discover what life would be like isolated on a spaceship, cut off from
the rest of humankind, fueled only by a little food and a little dope,
knowing that alien life forces were out there ready to pick us off. We had

shut off the phones, told friends to stay away, and put up signs shooing visitors away from the premises.

Of course this smacked of cult behavior, although none of us, Kesey included, ever considered the possibility that we were engaging in such activities. We were experimenting. We were, in the words of our pal Hunter Thompson, riding this weird torpedo out to the end to see where it exploded. We were, in Kesey's own words, exploring inner space without the slightest damned notion of whether we'd get back to home base without going crazy.

Often, in the years since La Honda, I've thanked Cosmo, as I call God, that Kesey was more or less a benign Prankster leader. Had the chief, as Cassady called him, asked or ordered us to do some thing evil, would we have done it? I doubt it, but jeez, you never know, do you?

We knew that April day in 1965 that we might get busted: We'd seen sheriff's deputies watching us, including one up on the hill across La Honda Road. We could watch him keeping tabs on us through his binoculars. Mountain Girl kept turning on the microphone for the exotic sound system we'd spread across our hillside and inviting the deputy down for coffee. The lawman later testified during our preliminary hearing that, as a graduate of an antidrug course at some police academy, he was able to swear that we were observed walking about in a "floating" manner "indicative of people high on marijuana." He also testified that he had seen us using "heroin, maroin, and peynotty." The prosecutor blanched.

Also, during the day of the raid, some neighbors had stopped across the creek to shout at us that there were squadrons of deputy sheriffs gathering not far up the road. The neighbors, who tolerated us even if they didn't invite us in to spike their water supplies, were genuinely concerned for our welfare. But we were still those simpleminded potheads who couldn't quite believe that cops would really break into the home of a famous writer and his pals just because we were weird, looked funny, and used marijuana. (Remember, LSD—and we had enough Owsley

Acid in the refrigerator to disable a major city—was still legal in April 1965.)

Not all that many people wanted to be aboard our spaceship if we were going to be busted, or if there was a chance we were in for a brush with the law. Those fourteen of us "acid-nauts," who'd stayed had spent three or four days, most of it awake, on the last of the house "white cross" Benzedrine stash, watching the bus movie *Intrepid Traveler and His Merry Band of Pranksters Look for a Cool Place,* and smoking the pot parceled out by Babbs from the mayo jar.

It might have gotten weird in there, fourteen of us locked up together, not sleeping, barely eating, taking lotsa bennies, smoking lotsa grass, destroying other pharmaceutical evidence at a rapid clip. I don't know: It was always pretty weird at Kesey's, so how would we have been able to tell?

When we ran out of grass, I was dispatched up the road to the tiny shack I had rented on a nearby muddy mountain road aptly named Redwood Terrace. I was on a "tether" (i.e., I talked into a portable tape recorder—remember, technology was fairly primitive in 1965—during my ten-minute round trip from Kesey's, up to the cabin, and back). It was our version of walking in space, I guess.

The marijuana I brought from my place was the stuff in the mayo jar, and it went into the septic tank when Kesey flushed just as Willie Wong rudely hopped onto his back. So I was sort of surprised, after we'd been officially arrested and were milling around the living room in handcuffs, waiting to be transported down to the county jail in Redwood City, when I heard Babbs ask Gretchen, "Would you care to eat some joints, Miss Fetchin?" She nodded and he passed her a couple from a personal stash in his pocket that he had, as was his wont, hidden from the rest of us. Babbs and Gretch proceeded to eat the remaining evidence.

The narcs did confiscate the acid, though, along with a jar of roaches they said they found. But I can assure you that they didn't really find any roaches; we ate our roaches or, occasionally, when several joints were going at once, jammed a bunch into the end of what Kesey had dubbed a "nose-cone," a cardboard tube from a roll of toilet paper, and smoked the whole shebang.

Under the watchful eyes of the deputies and narcotics agents who had set up shop at the huge, round, redwood-slab dining room table into which we'd all carved our initials and anything else that had come to mind, I tried to act cool. I wasn't cool, of course, and sort of squeaked when they asked me my name and occupation.

Like most of my fellow prisoners, I described myself as an employee of Intrepid Trips, Inc., not mentioning that just a couple of weeks earlier, after many months of life in La Honda with Kesey and the Pranksters, I had quit my job as a reporter for the *San Mateo Times*. I knew that the managing editor down there, a guy who'd disliked me, my politics, my lifestyle, and my friends, would be tickled pink when he learned that I'd been busted. Subsequently, I was quoted in newspaper accounts of the raid in my role as the "public relations director" for Kesey's Intrepid Trips, Inc., including a story that reported that "Kesey seemed queasy" when booked into the county jail. I made it sound like Intrepid Trips was one of your run-of-the-mill big-time corporations.

I was cuffed to Cassady and put in the back seat of a sheriff's squad car along with Kesey, who was surprisingly quiet. In fact, we all seemed pretty reflective as we were rushed down to the county seat; we were facing time behind bars, and that, we were all concluding, was hard to laugh at.

At the jail, where photographers from the San Francisco newspapers waited to snap our pictures, we were all booked on marijuana-possession charges. Kesey was also charged with resisting arrest, operating a disorderly house—an archaic way of saying he owned the place where the drugs were found—and for possession of narcotics paraphernalia, which was actually a hypodermic syringe full of machine oil we used to lubricate hard-to-reach gears in our armory of movie cameras, tape recorders, and film projectors.

We were locked into a couple of cells. I was in the drunk tank, along with about five other Pranksters, a few winos, and a big black guy who had commandeered half of the space for himself after revealing that he'd just slit his wife's throat with a butcher knife. The Hermit, who was completely cuckoo on speed by this time, took over another quarter of the cell by acting crazy, climbing on the bars, making hideous screeching noises, and generally scaring everyone except the wife-killer and his fellow not-so-Merry Pranksters.

We were bailed out by Brian Rohan and Paul Robertson, Zonker's brother-in-law, around six in the morning. The highlight of our release was Hermit's mother's confrontation with Kesey.

A nurse at the same veteran's hospital where Kesey had worked when he got the idea for *One Flew over the Cuckoo's Nest*, Hermit's mom threw a copy of that novel in its author's face.

"Go back to your cuckoo pad," she screamed at him. "You should have stayed in the nest instead of flying over it, you big cuckoo!"

Kesey deftly snatched the book out of the air, signed it, and handed it to one of our jailers, who gratefully accepted the autographed novel by the famous local writer.

By the time we were on our way back home to La Honda, we were in pretty good spirits again. For one thing, we were out of jail. For another, our arrest was front-page news in the *Chronicle, The Examiner,* and the *Mercury News,* where I now work as a reporter and columnist, and we were basking in the limelight. Several dailies ran a photo of me handcuffed to Cassady while being escorted with Kesey into the jail in the company of a pair of nattily dressed sheriff's deputies.

We were already, though, considering the downside of the situation. We could end up in jail or prison. Neal Cassady and Jerry Anderson, who had prior convictions on drug charges—Neal for marijuana, Jerry for harder stuff—faced life sentences for being third-time losers, an early version of the now popular "Three Strikes and You're Out" deal. That wasn't until after Ken's second pot bust a few months later, though, and until after we'd all split to Mexico—Kesey, a fugitive from American justice—and until we'd returned and he'd been nabbed by the FBI.

After spending five months at the San Mateo County jail farm not far up the road from his home, Kesey—who'd agreed, ironically, as part of his guilty plea, to stay away from La Honda—told me he'd never cop a plea again, ever, to anything, no matter what the consequences were to anybody.

Actually, both Kesey and Page Browning pleaded guilty. Charges were dropped against the rest of us. But the narcs were not going to brook any arrest-resisting, even by a hapless Prankster whose only resistance consisted of falling in the tub when Willie Wong flew into him.

We started to think about our lawyers' fees. Rohan and Robertson said they'd work for free, both knowing their reputations would soar among dopers and long-haired acidheads if they defended the country's most prominent apostle of psychedelic drugs. But we still would need some money, and none of us, Kesey included, was bringing in any income at the moment.

One day a $7,000 royalty check for the Italian translation of *Cuckoo's Nest* arrived in the mail. "I didn't even know there was an Italian translation, Kesey admitted as he handed the check to Faye, who handled the money. That was shortly after the night that Kesey had drunk the last of the milk in the sparsely larded refrigerator. Faye, the outraged mother of three little kids now deprived of milk until more cash came our way, picked up a skillet and beaned her famous husband with it as we sat at the dinner table. (When he recovered, Kesey suggested that maybe it would be politic if we were more helpful to Faye, more polite and less demanding.)

Kesey suggested that one way to make money was to sell articles, stories, novels, or anything else with his name on it. He suggested that I call his agent, Sterling Lord, and see if he could make any deals.

"You can write it and put my name on it," Kesey told me. "Write anything you want. We can probably make more money if they think I wrote it."

I tried, but Sterling Lord wasn't enthusiastic about making any quick deals for Kesey, and, frankly, the publishing business in those days was pretty stuffy. If Kesey was using drugs, he must be a burned-out head case, they figured.

Paul Krassner later told me he saw Kesey's suggestion that I write and use his nom de plume as "very Zen. He had no ego. Kesey saw that the Pranksters could use his name as a tool" to raise money. Frankly, aside from my inability to agree that Kesey has no ego, I think it was merely a case of Kesey the Writer having decided he wasn't going to write anymore. I remember the day our lawyer friend, Jim Wolpman, took him to meet a banker. Kesey wanted to borrow some money. As usual, he wore a bright shirt cut from an American flag and his light-colored jeans with Pentel-pen doodlings all over them.

"I love your novels, Mr. Kesey," the banker told him. "What are you writing these days?"

"I'm writing on my pants," the famous author replied.

Which, of course, reminds me of a story. One evening, taking a nap on the living room floor while the endless bus movie was showing—we had forty hours of film, forty miles of film, that Kesey and Mountain Girl were trying to fashion into a coherent, feature-length picture (at least that's what they said they were doing in the backhouse next to Hagen's infamous "screw shack")—I awoke with my head under a little end table. I gazed up and saw that someone, probably someone who'd eaten a few Benzedrine tabs, had used Pentel pens in a variety of bright colors to completely cover the underside of the piece of furniture with doodles and drawings and designs. The artist had not signed his or her work, which was not visible unless you were lying beneath it, but had entitled it the *Sistine Table*.

By the way, I realize that it doesn't sound all that outrageous these days to know that Kesey wore an American flag shirt down to the bank. But you gotta remember, in those days the flag was still . . . well, I guess you could say it was still sacred. When Kesey and the Pranksters started to wear flag shirts, or when Kesey in his bus-movie role as Swash Buckler (Ken Babbs was the Intrepid Traveler of the title) tied Old Glory around his head like a pirate's bandanna, he was truly doing something extraordinary. No one had yet designed flag-patterned rugby shirts, let alone burned American flags to protest anything. I mean, when folks saw Kesey with the Stars and Stripes draped around his neck like a scarf, they didn't know whether to salute or call the cops.

Kesey had a knack for coming up with things that someone else would quickly popularize and cash in on. It never occurred to him, nor to any of us, for instance, to make money by selling flag shirts. We never even suspected that anyone else would ever want to slap a Day-Glo paint job on their old buses! I remember during the Great Duck Storm, as we cruised, high as kites, along some Mendocino County highway one night, duck feathers from a torn comforter blowing so thickly into the dark that the car behind us had to turn its windshield wipers on, that I turned to Zonker and Hassler, who were sitting with me atop the bus, and laughingly asked, "Hey, what would we do if we suddenly saw another painted bus pass us going in the other direction?" It was such an absurd thought that we just giggled.

Modestly, I'll claim credit here for inventing the peace sign. We didn't pass any psychedelic buses in those days, but every once in a while we'd pass another vehicle with long-haired passengers with crazy looks in their eyes. I started flashing them the V sign, thinking of it as the old Winston Churchill "victory" symbol. It caught on. Pretty soon it was the peace sign. This is the truth; ask Zonker.

There soon followed—we're back, here, to the La Honda raid and notorious drug bust—a half dozen or more court appearances as our arraignment and preliminary hearings got underway in the old courthouse down at the San Mateo County seat in Redwood City. Sometimes we'd spend the whole day in court, with lunch breaks at noon and marijuana breaks midmorning and midafternoon.

Oh, they weren't *called* pot breaks. They were officially called ten-minute recesses. And we didn't carry grass into court with us, as we did previously. We might have been goofy, but we weren't stupid. Instead of holding the weed, we all chewed gum when we made our first appearance before the judge, then stuck it under the courtroom benches. While the Juicy Fruit wads were still gooey, we affixed joints to the undersides of our seats and were always able to reach down to get something to smoke whenever we went to lunch or on a recess. We figured they'd never search us when we *left* the courtroom.

Excerpted from a memoir-in-progress, When I Was a Dynamiter.

Halloween 1970

LENNY LIPTON

Behind me lay the Sacramento Valley, the A&W Root Beer Drive-In in Redding, a hash joint in Weed, the ever-looming Mount Shasta, the Siskiyous, Ashland, and the long glide downward into Oregon. Before me, across the road, that Halloween moonlit night, I heard the sounds of a rock band coming from the big old house with the Jeffersonian columns. The house sat on a knob of land formed by a bend in the Mohawk River, just a few miles outside of the town of Marcola. They said it had been used in the Jimmy Stewart movie *Shenandoah*, and true or not, the story lent an air of glamour to the downtrodden manor.

I parked next to the pasture and apple trees where Chief and Apache daily grazed and, after fourteen hours on the road, emerged from my fire truck–red Volvo 544. The music grew louder as I walked across the cold hard lawn, opened the door under the columned porch, and feasted my eyes on a mob of laughing, singing, dancing, howling, hooting, and jumping fiends—what we used to call long-haired freaks—people with names like Sunshine, Nixy Knox, Belle Donna, Tangerine, Sky, One-Eyed Joe, Pink Cloud, Oxygen, and Gentle Waters. They wouldn't be put off if you called them freaks. They'd like it because freaks were what they were—hippie freaks.

Zigzagging through the throng, I came upon Ken Kesey, Master of the Mystic Arts, who had learned the secret of clouding men's minds from Dr. Strange et al, sitting at a round table doing five-and-dime magic tricks. He was fooling with decks of cards, little paddles, shining metal cups, and colored balls, amusing a dozen friends. Piled next to the tricks were what I assumed to be uppers and downers sprawled in a colorful heap. At first glance you couldn't tell the pills from the magic apparatus, and as you will learn, it is this and the Master's sleight of hand that kept him out of the joint.

I had only moments to drink in the scene when a hippie jumped into the room, raving: "The pigs! The pigs are coming! We're surrounded by the pigs!" My first thought—an attempt at denial, I admit—was that this was a brother's paranoid fit, but alas, within moments we got another such report from near-naked people who had been steaming in the nearby sweat lodge perched upon the banks of the Mohawk. Bummer! The police, we were told, had surrounded us and, sure enough, when I looked out a windowpane frosted with patterns of crystalline lace, I saw three police cars parked on the lawn like panthers ready to pounce. But the music, dancing, and magic tricks continued—the threat taken in stride, for these partying fools were psychedelic commandos: veterans of acid tests, bad acid, newspapers and television, Jerry Rubin speeches, Timothy Leary declaring victory again and again, police riots, teargas-sings, Jerry Lewis telethons, and their parents' scorn.

In clumped a couple of properly costumed and armed cops; you couldn't tell them from the real thing. One of them sauntered up to Kesey's magic round table.

"What are you doing here, Officer Doogle?" asked Ken. Maybe "Doogle" was what Ken said, and maybe it wasn't. If it wasn't, that's the only thing I've made up.

"We believe there are minors present in a place where alcohol is being consumed," said Doogle, "and we want to look around."

"Where is your warrant?" asked Ken, who, without so much as a moment of hesitation, continued on with his magic act. He told Doogle that this was police harassment, for this very Doogle was the same officer who had arrested Kesey a few months before for the crime of walking a dog without a license through the streets of Eugene. At that instant, Kesey proved that he was indeed a Master of the Mystic Arts; his was the greatest magic act I've witnessed, dwarfing the disappearance of a stage full of elephants, for right before Doogle's eyes, Ken hid the dope. The argument between the two of them had so diverted Doogle that Ken's manipulation of the pills looked like part of his magic act. He vanished the stash.

Other policemen entered the Marcola house and began to slowly scan each room—looking for crime. I went upstairs and found a scene of panic and chaos, for it was in these quarters that the serious offenders had been medicating themselves. Word of the raid had created a panic, and I saw one man leap out a second-story window into the night. Others, like my friend Terry, were frantically attempting to dispose of their dope. He had impulsively dumped the contents of his baggie into a toilet bowl in order to flush it into the void. Some of those who survived the glorious countercultural revolution learned a lesson: You can't flush grass down a john.

As the police came up the stairs, Terry disappeared, leaving me gaping into a toilet bowl. I had a flash born of desperation, and I bent over the toilet making the raucous sounds of vomiting. How much better it would have been had I something to throw up, I thought, as I stared at the leaves and seeds floating inches from my face. No matter how I tickled my throat with my fingers, I could not barf and by this means conceal the contents floating on the waters below. I made all manner of retching sounds, but it was noise without substance. I sank to my knees to perfect my performance.

"Too much of a good thing," said a compassionate cop as he watched me through the open bathroom door. He wasn't getting paid enough to look into that toilet bowl.

After their search, the police decided that this was a proper Halloween party; they saw no crimes in progress. Don't ask me to explain it— nothing is as nutty as the truth. They had had their little Halloween prank; they had come without saying hello, and they left without saying good-bye.

The magic had reached a peak when they were present. It was a more exciting party when they were there, but we didn't miss them after they'd gone.

Thinking about that Halloween night, after almost thirty years have passed, makes me wonder about what's happened to the playfulness, the foolishness—the magic in the world. Today, the long-haired freaks have short hair and the crew-cut police have let theirs grow. The hippies have gone straight; they've become lawyers, stockbrokers, and college professors. And the police, who, after all, are only following orders and still doing their thing—steadfast guardians, with fidelity transcending comprehension.

Mouse Power

PAUL KRASSNER

I moved from New York to San Francisco in 1971, having accepted an invitation by Stewart Brand to coedit with Ken Kesey *The Last Supplement to the Whole Earth Catalog*. Hassler (Ron Bevirt), a veteran Prankster, served as our managing editor, chauffeur, photographer, and general buffer zone. A ritual developed. Each morning, Kesey and Hassler would come by the psychodrama commune where I was staying. We would have crunchy granola and ginseng tea for breakfast. Then, sharing a joint in an open-topped convertible, we would drive up winding roads sandwiched by forest, ending up at a large garage that was filled with production equipment.

Kesey and I would discuss ideas, pacing back and forth like a pair of caged foxes. Gourmet meals were cooked on a potbellied stove. Sometimes a local rock band came by and rehearsed with heavy amplification, drowning out the noise of our electric typewriters.

Kesey had been reading a book of African Yoruba stories. The moral of one parable was "he who shits in the road will meet flies on his return." With that as a theme, we assigned R. Crumb to draw his version of *The Last Supper* for our cover of *The Last Supplement*.

One day, two black women from Jehovah's Witnesses stopped by the garage, and within ten minutes Kesey convinced them that in Revelations where there's talk of locusts, it was really a reference to helicopters.

Kesey threw the *I Ching* every day as a religious ritual. When his daughter Shannon was invited out on her first car date, he insisted that she throw the *Ching* in order to decide whether or not to accept.

Once he forgot to bring his family *I Ching* to the garage, and he seemed edgy, like a woman who had neglected to take her birth control pill, so I suggested that he pick three numbers, then I turned to that page in the unabridged dictionary, circled my index finger in the air, and it came down to the word *bounce*. So that was our reading, and we bounced back to work.

After a couple of months, we finished *The Supplement* and had a party. Somebody brought a tank of nitrous oxide to help celebrate. Kesey suggested that in cave-dwelling times all the air they breathed was like this.

"There are stick figures hovering above," he said, "and they're laughing at us."

"And," I added, "the trick is to beat them to the punch."

Later on, in an interview for *The Realist*, I asked him, "What do you think is the meaning of a lyric like 'One toke over the line, sweet Jesus'?"

It was obviously from a song about marijuana by Brewer & Shipley, with Jerry Garcia on steel guitar. Although banned on some radio stations, it was performed by a naïve couple on *The Lawrence Welk Show*, and Welk described it as a "modern spiritual."

Kesey replied, "I think they are singing about that state when you've gone and got so high that you're forced to operate mostly on faith."

We hung around La Honda for a while. We were smoking hashish in a tunnel inside a cliff, which had been burrowed during World War II so that military spotters with binoculars could look toward the ocean's horizon for incoming ships.

All we spotted was a meek little mouse right there in the tunnel. We blew smoke at the mouse until it could no longer tolerate our behavior. The mouse stood on its hind legs and roared at us: "*Squeeeeeeek!!!*" This display of mouse assertiveness startled us and we almost fell off the cliff. The headline would've read, "Dope-Crazed Pranksters in Suicide Pact."

Goofy Macho

KEN KESEY

A couple of years back, a woman from East Germany came by the farm. She was an absolutely beautiful woman, an Olympic pentathlete, about six feet two inches. She was traveling across the country and was actually studying the '60s. She'd been wined and dined the entire way. This was during the Gulf War—Desert Storm—and she'd attended all of these conventions and honorary dinners that were being given for East Germans and ex-Communists.

Because of the war, these functions had been heavily laden with military traffic—a lot of army people. Also a lot of bad roast beef. She confided to us that there seemed to be a lot of machismo evident at these affairs—that it reminded her of what she'd read about Germany in the 1930s.

Anyway, Ken Babbs and I were driving her around, showing her places around Oregon. I got out a joint, passed it, and immediately she said, "Oh, no! Oh, no! I don't do the dope! I don't do the dope!"

I said, "My God! You're over here studying the '60s and you haven't smoked dope? That's like being a downhill skier and hating snow. This is one of the things the '60s ran on."

She hesitated and said, "Oh, okay."

She was competitive and started taking some good hits of this stuff. Gradually, you began to see this stern, grim, Germanic face of hers change. Everything dropped. You saw fear come into her eyes, and her mouth open and go wide.

After sitting awhile, her face began to return to shape. You could see her mouth pulling up into a smile. Her eyes were now squinty and merry. She looked over at Babbs and me and said, "All over America I have been. I have seen every kind of macho. But I did not know there was a goofy macho!"

Celebrities

I Was Allen Ginsberg's Accountant

I started smoking in my late twenties. My wife, Linda, and I enjoyed an occasional puff. In 1969, we went to Allen Ginsberg's farm in Cherry Valley, New York, and I had to bring the stash. I actually became Ginsberg's supplier for a while. Me. Mild-mannered accountant and professor at St. John's University. When Linda died in 1971, I began smoking with a vengeance.

On my fortieth birthday, my then-girlfriend threw a party for a bunch of my friends. George, who had never smoked before, had a gay old time. He left for his home in Putnam County at about 11:00 PM (an hour's ride from our home in Brooklyn). He returned at 12:00—and again at 1:00 and again at 2:00 and again at 3:00. He was so stoned that he kept riding around the block unable to negotiate the ride home.

We, of course, laughed all night at poor George. But, of course, everything was funny that night. We awoke the next day to find all of the stereo equipment stolen. Burglars. I had to go back to the store where I had bought the stuff—Crazy Eddie's first store on King's Highway in Brooklyn—to get receipts for insurance.

Went to Allen's funeral. It took place in a Buddhist temple in New York (actually a temple in an office building). Mostly a turnoff:

"Is that Yoko over there?"

"He looks famous. Is it Dylan?"

I left at noon, and when I hit the street, I was faced with a bunch of reporters and TV cameras. Their gleeful smiles, resulting from getting someone to interview many hours before the service was over, froze on their faces when I said I was Allen's accountant. Luckily for us all, a stretch limo pulled up and a rock-star-looking dude with incredible cowboy boots oozed out of the car with a bimbo in tow. The paparazzi turned on a dime and left me before I could enjoy my ten minutes of fame.

Kidnapping Jerry Rubin

LESLIE MEYERS

Jerry Rubin asks me if I'll roll some joints for him. I tell him I don't know how but would love a lesson. After all, learning from a guy with Jerry's history would be like having Betty Crocker teach me how to bake a cake. Jerry puts a piece of rolling paper on the counter, dumps a pile of pot in the middle, pats it a bit, then turns to me and says, "Roll it like a carpet." He then licks the ends and hands it to me with a flourish.

"Now, Jerry, I realize I don't know much about this, but aren't you supposed to remove the seeds and sticks?"

He shakes his head and says, "Oh, no—I mean, you can if you really want to."

The following day, my friend Alison and I smoke this masterfully rolled joint and decide to kidnap Jerry at his office. We go to the toy store, buy water guns, and wait outside his office building. As he walks out, we jump from either side and announce our abduction plans. Jerry immediately sees through our elaborate disguises (sunglasses) and tells us that we have to take him to the Daily Grill to pick up his to-go order.

Being kinder, gentler kidnappers, we allow for this change in plans— he pushes it with the stop at Flair Cleaners and the drugstore, though I must say I find triple-protection Aqua Fresh to be the funniest thing I've ever seen—and with our arrival at the restaurant, Jerry looks at us and exclaims, "Go look in the mirror, both of you. I've never seen two more stoned people in my entire life!"

Alison cannot let go of this concept. "Hey, he's seen a lot of stoned people." She asks Jerry to repeat his comment, then has to know if he really means it. With each saying of yes, Alison counters with another comparison—i.e., "The most stoned this decade or all decades inclusive?" I suggest that she allow for hyperbole, but Alison won't give up until with certainty we are deemed "most stoned ever seen."

Jerry then begs for freedom, or maybe he tells us to drive him home, but either way we feel our kidnapping is a wild success.

Heath Ledger and the Tragedy of Marijuana Prohibition

LANNY SWERDLOW, RN

Over the last twenty years, prescription pharmaceuticals caused the death of between fifteen thousand and twenty-seven thousand Americans each year, but you don't hear about it unless a famous person has died. Whitney Houston, Michael Jackson, Anna Nicole Smith, Elvis Presley, Judy Garland, and Marilyn Monroe are just a few of the famous who have died from prescription pharmaceuticals. Recently, Heath Ledger's passing was one of the most tragic high-profile deaths.

Ledger's death galvanized the public's attention, but the underlying cause of his death has not been recognized. Insights into this can be found in the January 23, 2009 issue of *Entertainment Weekly*, which prominently featured the posthumous Academy Award–winning actor on its cover with an eight-page spread that recounted his life and death.

Not shying away from the circumstances of his death, the article reported, "There was immediate speculation he had overdosed on illicit drugs, but autopsy reports ruled his death an accidental toxic combination of prescription painkillers, antianxiety medication, and sleeping pills."

What had happened was the prescription pharmaceuticals Ledger was taking for pain, mental agitation, and insomnia reacted with each other to produce a deadly combination that killed him. Heath Ledger died directly from what was an entirely appropriate use of legal prescription pharmaceuticals prescribed to him by his doctor.

Shining a light on Ledger's short but extraordinary rise to stardom, the article included personal and poignant stories from many of Ledger's closest friends and associates. One of them was Terry Gilliam, a close friend and director of *The Brothers Grimm*, one of Ledger's early starring roles, and his last film, *The Imaginarium of Doctor Parnassus*.

Gilliam told of his work and relationship with Ledger and, revealing a rather intimate knowledge of the actor's life, commented that "marijuana was no longer in his life, which he had enjoyed a bit." Gilliam did not say why Ledger stopped using marijuana, but for some unknown reason he stopped using it even though *he had enjoyed it a bit*. Other than it was illegal, there was no problem associated with his use of marijuana, so why he stopped remains a mystery.

It was a fatal decision. Ledger was given multiple prescription pharmaceuticals to treat his pain, reduce his anxiety, and relieve his insomnia. He didn't need all of those prescription pharmaceuticals when he was using marijuana.

Dating as far back as five thousand years ago, marijuana was used all over the world for pain relief, mental agitation, and insomnia. When Grandma was tossing and turning and unable to fall asleep, she would go to the medicine cabinet for a bottle of tincture of cannabis, place a few drops under her tongue, snuggle back into bed next to Grandpa, and drift off to sleep.

Today, those symptoms continue to be safely and effectively treated with cannabis by millions of Americans—some legally, most illegally. By reducing some of the problems associated with insomnia such as pain, depression, anxiety, stress, and nausea, cannabis can help induce sleep. Even without any underlying problems, cannabis can help you get a good night's rest.

If Heath Ledger had *not* stopped using marijuana, he would not have needed as many, if any, of the prescription pharmaceuticals that killed him. If he had not stopped using marijuana, he would have lived to accept his Academy Award for best supporting actor and would be alive today, continuing to make blockbuster motion pictures.

Although Ledger died from a toxic combination of prescription pharmaceuticals, what really killed him was our nation's marijuana prohibition laws because his doctor could not prescribe him cannabis. For the ailments that ailed Ledger, his doctor could only prescribe the prescription pharmaceuticals that kill so many Americans every year.

The Institute of Medicine, which advises Congress on health policy, reports that Americans spend nearly $3 billion a year trying to get to sleep. *Consumer Reports* warns readers that all these medications can cause dependency and a host of other problems. Ambien—one of the most popular insomnia medications, with physicians writing twenty-six million prescriptions a year—was reported by *The New York Times* to make the top-ten list of drugs found in impaired drivers.

Due to prohibition hysteria and a rational fear of government saber rattling, no one draws the line between Ledger's death from prescription pharmaceuticals and his discontinued use of marijuana.

This is a tragedy that continues to play out every day in the lives of not just celebrities, but also in the lives of millions of Americans who have no choice but to use the far more dangerous, generally less effective, and arguably more costly prescription pharmaceuticals.

Protecting their bottom line, America's giant pharmaceutical corporations—along with those other stalwarts of American business, the alcohol and tobacco companies—spend millions of dollars every year hiring lobbyists and providing funds in support of law enforcement's insatiable feeding frenzy at the taxpayer-funded pig trough of marijuana law prohibition.

Until marijuana is once again restored to its rightful place in our nation's medicine cabinets, thousands of Americans, like Heath Ledger, will continue to needlessly die every year from prescription pharmaceuticals because they were denied the choice to use marijuana. Millions of others will continue to have their health jeopardized and their lives destroyed because of our nation's marijuana prohibition laws.

[*Originally published in* Culture *magazine. Lanny Swerdlow, a registered nurse, is director of the Marijuana Anti-Prohibition Project, a medical-marijuana patient support group and law reform organization. To subscribe to his free newsletter, send a request to lanny@marijuananews.org.*]

Under the Counterculture

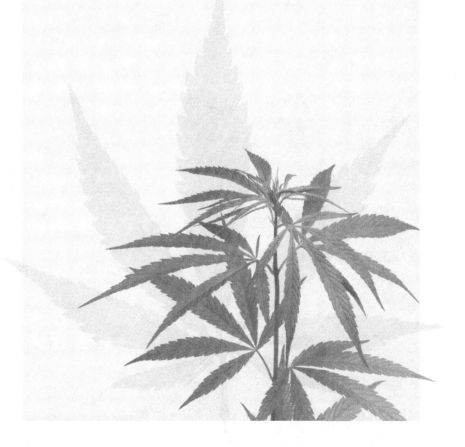

Turning on Newsweek

KATE COLEMAN

I just love it when people in high places quit their jobs and then expose the fancy people they used to work for. I devoured every word penned by Jackie Kennedy's former secretary, Mary Gallagher, when she disclosed to the world her boss's finicky demands to have her nylons hand-ironed after laundering and her penchant for selling her hardly worn clothes to discreet secondhand shops rather than giving them to her maids the way most rich women do. Ex-establishment people have a real fascination for me. I myself am an ex-establishment person, and this is my exposé. I worked for three years at *Newsweek*, half a block from St. Patrick's Cathedral. I quit the magazine in October 1968 and fled the country for a year to regain my sanity.

I came to *Newsweek* after five and a half years at the University of California at Berkeley, armed with a BA sloppily attained in English and a political education and lifestyle carefully nurtured through years of demonstrating, organizing, arguing, turning on, and free loving. I had been busted once, for ecstatically sitting in as a fanatical adherent of the free speech movement (FSM). My sentence was a light one, due to the recommendation of my probation officer. She was favorably impressed with me for no other reasons than liking a CBS documentary on the FSM, entitled *The Berkeley Rebel*, in which I had appeared. I was the archetype of the Berkeley liberated woman, and like Joan of Arc, I cut off all my long, black hair and headed for the big city and the real world to act out my destiny. In this state, I fell upon *Newsweek*.

For the full three years I was at the magazine, I was always startled by people's reactions to my working there. Old politico friends from Berkeley whom I would see from time to time looked askance at me and mumbled under their breaths that I had sold out. Maybe my Berkeley friends were right. From the free speech movement to *Newsweek*?

Was I or was I not co-opted? At *Newsweek* I was the house Freako-Doper-Lefty and I was tolerated, later even indulged, because I carefully cultivated the illusion that I knew everything about drugs and which buildings would be taken over next at which school. Men and women alike at *Newsweek* cultivated a knowing air of sophistication about everything in the world. After all, the magazine touched on everything in the world within its covers. They prided themselves on their "hip" ability to assimilate anything that might take place—as long as the impact was first tempered by being filtered through *Newsweek*.

For the first eight months I was a "clipper," brandishing my "rip-stick" (a yard-long piece of metal with a single-edged razor on one side) at eleven newspapers a day, searching for stories for the Nation Department to rewrite at the end of the week. Omigod, every day clipping out pieces of newsprint and filing them in little cubbyholes for writers who worked wedged into coffin-size cubicles—and all the while congratulating myself for having landed a glamorous New York job, outcompeting five hundred other identically qualified liberal arts, Betty Co-ed graduates.

I can't tell you how thrilling it was to work in such an important place. I took home $65 a week for the privilege and was even supplied with a khaki uniform smock denoting my status. Ostensibly, the smock was utilitarian rather than an indication of caste, to save the clippers' clothes from newsprint smudge. In my case, however, it hid the fact that I had to wear the same clothes every day because my salary only permitted such luxuries as toilet paper and lunch.

When I was hired, there was no such thing as a male clipper. Later, the whole system was altered and girls were hired directly as researchers. Clippers were hired on a permanent basis and did not have to have a college degree. But during my early employment, I developed a hatred of all the young hotshots coming out of Harvard and other Ivy League holes who held degrees identical to mine, but who, because of their penises, were automatically sent to one of the bureaus and paid $120 a week to become writer-reporter trainees.

But besides career promises, there was a wonderful lack of formality about the place that belied the stigma of my drab smock. Everyone was on a first-name basis. I could call Editor Osborn Elliott "Oz." Writers would talk to me and call me by my first name. Very early in my clipper days, I established myself as an authority on hippies, drug addicts, and leftists. And it was smoking dope that got me my first reporting assignment, liberating me from the clip desk. It was unheard of for a clipper to do reporting, but I had a special background.

The Nation Department was doing a story on the scene in Greenwich Village—drugs, runaways, lifestyles. Despite the fact that they had New York–based reporters and some half dozen researchers sitting there, Senior Editor John Jay Iselin (a thirty-six-year-old, short, dark-haired man who always appeared in shirtsleeves and wore suspenders) decided to make use of the magazine's Berkeley freak for an undercover assignment. I dressed up like a hippie and hung out on MacDougal Street and in Washington Square, asking teenagers from Queens if they turned on or fucked. While there, I met a very hip and talkative dealer, went to his apartment, interviewed him, and bought a tiny chunk of hash, which I duly brought into Iselin's office the following morning to show him. He peeled back the tinfoil as delicately as a demolition expert, asking all kinds of dumb questions about how you smoke it, what the high was like, and if it was addicting. When I told him I'd had to buy it so that my dealer friend would trust me, he instructed me to fill out an expense account form. Did he want the hash?

"Oh, no," he said quickly. "You keep it."

"How do I write it up?" I asked naïvely. "$15 for hashish?" (I had never filled out an expense account form before.)

"Put it down as entertainment," said the great-great-great-great-grand-child of America's first chief justice.

In the summer of 1967, Newsweek indirectly bought enough grass and paraphernalia to warrant a felony sentence of one to fifteen years in New York. Only three years behind the times, it was decided to do a cover story on marijuana, and, naturally, I was assigned to the story. The cover designer, Bob Engels, uncertain of what he wanted, allowed me to hunt up paraphernalia and other material for a cover photo.

I went down to the Lower East Side's psychedelicatessen and purchased two beautiful water pipes, a hash pipe, roach holders, a dozen packets of cigarette papers, and a few little psychedelic toys. What a haul! I also bought two ounces of Acapulco Gold and one ounce of Panama Red from my favorite exclusive downtown dealer.

Newsweek footed the whole bill without a ripple, and I got the payola of a lifetime. But it didn't end there. The fact that marijuana was to be legitimized twixt the pages of *Newsweek* gave rise to unexpected curiosity on the parts of both the senior editor and the writer of the piece, both of whom decided, independent of each other, that their respective editing and writing would lack verisimilitude unless they tried the stuff. The writer, Paul Zimmerman, a graduate of Amherst with a masters from Berkeley, was a chubby, dark-haired, easygoing fellow in his early thirties who was quickly ascending the *Newsweek* hierarchy. He played it safe and took the dope and my instructions home with him to share with his wife. Liking it, he nevertheless castrated his story, balancing the viewpoint to be exactly in the wishy-washy middle—even before he was edited.

Ed Diamond, the forty-five-year-old senior editor, wanted atmosphere as well as dope. He asked me in conspiratorial tones if he couldn't come down to my place to try it out. For a moment I was panicked, as my past proselytizing for the weed included my testimony that it enhanced lovemaking. But I was mistaken in my fears, for he quickly added that he would like me to invite some of my pot-smoking friends. And so I invited some of my more respectable dope-smoking, ex-Berkeley friends to be good Samaritans to my boss.

Frantically, I cleaned my West Village apartment, borrowed chairs and colored lights from the gay man next door, and bought all kinds of head food to delight the palate of the stoned. On the afternoon before the engagement, Diamond called me into his office. He looked worried. Uh, he paused, would ... uh ... I mind if ... uh, his wife, Adelina, came too?

Ed had compulsively confessed what he was doing, and his suburbanite wife insisted on coming. I didn't mind at all. The family that smokes together goes on to better things. Ed and my friends came on schedule; the wife came later. I had the best of all possible dope rolled and set out on the table. We all began smoking and conversing in awkward tones.

The senior editor, however, didn't know how to inhale (shades of Bill Clinton), as he was not a smoker, thus necessitating the use of special paraphernalia to ensure his getting high. Adelina, quiet and withdrawn, smoked and smoked and never said a word but later sat there with a weird smile on her drawn face. Ed conversed as energetically as he would at any cocktail party, while my friends and I got so high our tongues stuck to the roofs of our mouths. The rest of us had had enough, but Ed wouldn't smoke unless we continued, so we kept on going. I staggered into the kitchen to prepare the goodies and was swept by a tidal wave of dizziness.

Blackness encroached along the edges of my vision, and I realized with horror that I was about to pass out—I had OD'd in my zeal to get that maniac high. I lurched toward the living room. "Heh . . . heh . . . ha, ha . . . I . . . uh . . . hmmmm, ah . . . smoked a little too much hash . . . don't . . . uh . . . judge by me . . . be with y'all in a sec . . . " I lay down on my bed and listened to the screaming silence from the next room. I blew it, I thought. I recovered shortly and fed them, but Diamond wouldn't smoke any more and he and his wife soon left, thanking me profusely for a wonderful time. Later he told me his wife had loved the stuff, but that he only got a slight "buzz." I made a vow never to play guru again.

After the cover story came out with the only piece of actual writing I was ever allowed to do for the magazine—it was so heavily edited that all statements that seemed to emanate from my own personal knowledge of grass were deleted and substituted with phony quotes from people who didn't exist; Oz was fearful lest *Newsweek* readers get the idea that a staffer smoked the stuff with the magazine's approval—I was approached by people from all over the magazine, asking me to get them some pot. They all wanted to try it but were afraid of buying it from some shady dealer.

Me they trusted, and for a week I toyed with the idea of increasing my meager earnings by being *Newsweek*'s exclusive dealer, but in the end I decided I didn't want to deal with the notorious suspiciousness of novice smokers who see any dealer as someone who's out to burn them. And they were so straight, too.

During the marijuana issue, I came to work with some Japanese incense and lit it in the office I shared with Zimmerman. The smell went all the way down the drab, institutional corridors, prompting editors and researchers to come banging on my door to verify their suspicions that, at last, they had smelled the sinister weed. Amazing. They not only had never smelled pot, but also didn't even know what incense was. I was ordered to stop burning the stuff.

To be fair, I wasn't the only one at *Newsweek* who had ever turned on. A few of the researchers had occasionally imbibed, but only one of them could be classified as a head, and she was circumspect about it. I was pleased that one ex-Harvard writer whom I initiated became a confirmed head. It led, I am convinced, to his leaving *Newsweek* and eventually heading for hip San Francisco and a television job.

One late Friday night, while a blizzard raged outside, he and I sat in my office with the window wide open and the snow pouring in, furtively puffing away at three joints in a row, giggling hysterically, and half hoping we would be discovered. I am sad to say it was the only time that I turned on at work. It was my choice; I could have done it easily enough. But I hated the sterility of the place. The walls were the same color as my discarded clipper's smock, and the lights were naked fluorescent fixtures. Only the senior editors on up rated a carpet and a colored wall.

To prevent retina regurgitation, I bought rose-colored glasses for my myopic eyes and plastered my side of the office walls with offensive collages of LBJ, Vietnam atrocities, naked balling couples, and Fillmore art-nouveau posters. Zimmerman's side of the room was bare, and he bitched to me that he didn't want to have to look at napalmed babies every day when he worked. Other visitors also complained that my choice of wall art was tasteless and offensive, but I was the self-appointed scourge of *Newsweek* and believed it was good for them. When I appeared on a CBS network documentary on marijuana, urging viewers to turn on, CBS disguised my identity by saying I worked for an unnamed major magazine and left it at that, so *Newsweek* didn't care.

[*Excerpted from an article in* Scanlan's *magazine.*]

Ash Valley

GUY MAYNARD

It was always only a rumor of a possibility when the dope would come. We were in the midst of a near-snowbound winter on our "ranch" in the foothills of the Cascade Mountains, ten miles from the nearest other private property, eighteen miles from the nearest store. The snow was piled high on the forest access road that ran through our property, but we could get out if we could coax one of our old pickups into running and scrape together enough money for some gas and whatever needed supplies could justify a trip to town.

But that combination of circumstances didn't come together often, so mostly we huddled close to our wood stoves, which struggled to cough up some heat with the wet wood we managed to scrounge up when winter came too fast and too hard. Reading, dreaming over seed catalogs, macraméing, figuring out what combination of canned tomato products, potatoes, onions, and lentils we'd eat that day, plotting the revolution. And waiting for the dope.

There were about fifteen of us left after the peak of around thirty in the glorious days of our first Oregon summer—and only ten of us were actually physically on the land most of the time in through the dark cold winter, the others off somewhere on some personal or collective mission. Refugees from the political and cultural battles of the early '70s, we had moved on to this spectacular place—a 135-acre box canyon surrounded by virgin fir forests—as blue skies nudged out the gray spring, full of hope and conviction that we could create an island where we could live lives that made sense to us and become strong enough to stand up against— one way or another—the death culture we had left behind.

A core group from Boston had been filtering west for almost a year, like-minded folks who had also somehow found their way to a tiny river town in the Oregon hinterlands, joined us. The land, like so much in those days, seemed to come to us magically. Folks wandering the back roads stumbled onto it. Low down payment. Big balloon payment after a year. We could get on the land and then figure it out.

It was a ranch in the sense that the hard-crusted Oregonian we bought it from kept his cattle on it. The cows calmly watched our comings and goings but kept on chewing their cud, unfazed. We grew a decent garden that first year and had varying degrees of success—and failure—raising chickens, goats, turkeys, and pigs. We picked from nearby farms (forty or fifty miles away) lots of potatoes, onions, and tomatoes. We supplemented the two existing houses on the property (one sort of modern, one shack) with houses built from salvaged materials and converted some outbuildings into dwellings.

In addition to our earnest attempts at real work, we partied through the summer. We were a popular destination for friends and friends of friends, and lots of strangers, too, who heard about us somehow on the hippie grapevine. We all shared lots of pot and plenty of psychedelics.

But when the smoke cleared and we got down to the nitty gritty chores of living together, we found gaping differences in what we all wanted and what we were willing to do. Doing your own thing and being part of a working commune—especially one with some still-vague political intent—were vastly different and often downright contradictory undertakings. We had people at all points of that individualist-to-collectivist continuum, even within the group that had come out of Boston, which at least shared intense personal history. But a divide quickly developed between most of us and the new folks we'd met just before moving onto the land.

Most of them were from California, a little older, a tad religious (in a hippie kind of way), and not really into group decision-making. That and the awkward gender and sexual demographics of nine couples (plus three kids), eight single men, and, eventually, one single woman—and we were a long way from anywhere one might meet a prospective romantic partner—made for a series of psychosexual and group-dynamic dramas. We lost about a third of our original group before summer ended, with others soon to follow.

We got more serious as the rain came and the constant flow of visitors stopped. We established clear expectations about work and chores: rotating cooking duty, cleanup crews, firewood gathering. We built a structure of responsibilities for the ongoing running of the ranch: managing our funds and budgeting expenses, education and correspondence, garden planning, food supplies and nutrition. We talked about gender roles and how couples fit into the group. We planted cover crops and laid out plots for hay and vegetables and an orchard. We started thinking about how we would raise the money for our balloon payment, due at the beginning of the next summer: Raising pigs? Selling hay? Leasing space for others to run cattle?

Somewhere during those early gray days, one of our members, more given than most of us to the restlessness that can come from being cooped up miles from the nearest hamburger or TV or other faces, was off being not-on-the-ranch, when he discovered a connection for Columbian pot in his home state of Florida—and suddenly solutions to two fundamental problems seemed possible: money for the looming $20,000 balloon payment and a steady source of dope, an undeniable glue that held us together, part shared sacrament, part communal celebration.

Pot didn't solve—or cause, for that matter—the craziness of the ranch. But it gave us a break from it. One of our common beliefs was *The Fabulous Furry Freak Brothers* declaration that "dope will get you through times of no money better than money will get you through times of no dope."

We needed both dope and money, so that meant going into the dealing business, especially for the restless one and his closest friend, who shared his feelings about loving the ranch in small doses. Both of them had dabbled in dealing, but small-time retail stuff, ounces of pot, grams of hash. This was a whole different level. But it suited them, gave them a good reason to be off the ranch and a way to serve the people that didn't involve chainsaws or killing chickens. And they still had the ranch to come home to.

So they were off in Florida, moving pounds, staying in hotels. Communication was spotty. One of the women on the ranch—the only ostensibly single woman—did transportation, suitcases, and buses, so there must have been some kind of regular phone contact (nearest phone booth, eighteen miles away), but for most of us the dope-dealing was taking place in an entirely different realm of time and space. Every once in a while, though, our two fundraisers would come home bearing the fruits of their labor. But we never knew exactly when—a week or two or three, plus or minus, around some vague date.

When they showed up in the deep white darkness of that winter, though, it didn't take long for word to spread to the various dwellings around the valley. Shouts of "Eddie and Jeffrey and the Columbian" filled the night air, and we all made haste to the Main House. It had been weeks since we'd had any pot. It's not like we were climbing the walls or freaking out or anything like that. I'd been holed up in our little octagon at the far end of the ranch, reading Kim Il-Sung and Marx, taking notes, making plans. The short days and thick snow made for a quiet, thoughtful time, free for a while from the drama of the summer, but also missing the celebratory joy that had swept us into this life and onto this land.

Eddie and Jeffrey had been far from that quiet and had traveled 3,300 miles to snap us out of our near-hibernation, the last mile or so on foot after their car gave out trying to plow its way up the steep road to the ranch.

What a thrill it was cracking open the bundle of the rich gold-tinted green buds, handfuls spread over a newspaper on the central table in the Main House, the dozen of us huddled around it like kids on Christmas morning, half of us rolling fat joints as fast as we could, lighting them up, sending them around—joints colliding in the circle, people smoking two at once, the deep embedded chill of the house chased away by the clouds of smoke swirling around us.

We laughed, merry and full. We cranked up the generator—used sparingly to stretch our thin supplies of gasoline—and blasted tunes: the Dead, Jethro Tull, Traffic, Jefferson Airplane. Dancing in the smoke, we intermingled tales of Miami drug-dealing and the quotidian winter life on this place where everything was different from anything we had imagined it might be. It all blended, fit together; we were all together, together in all the senses that word carried in those days.

It was real, that joy, that togetherness, as real as the petty squabbles, wet wood, endless lentils, sexual triangles, dead vehicles, and widely divergent dreams that each of us carried for that land. We had all triumphed in some way to be gathered around that table, getting stoned out of our minds, feeling the love that held us together in spite of everything. Those big, fat endless joints helped us to forget everything but each other for a few hours, and it was each other that had brought us and held us there. It was each other that we celebrated long into that cold dark night.

Everything, eventually, overcame us. That slow winter of involuntary contemplation convinced some of us that there were better places for us to be. Split couples headed in opposite directions. The fundraisers raised the money we needed but decided that they no longer wanted to give it all to the commune, so they gave each of us some money (not enough among us to make the balloon payment) and a pound of pot. My wife and I took ours and headed east on a harebrained whim. Some folks stayed and gave the old Oregonian rancher most of their share of the pot proceeds. They all were gone within a year. The cattle never left.

[*Guy Maynard is the author of* The Risk of Being Ridiculous: A Historical Novel of Love and Revolution.]

Love and Haight

LYNN PHILLIPS

When I graduated Radcliffe without having met a Harvard man who could support me in the style to which my mother, a lawyer, had always aspired, she took me shopping and made me try on mink coats. Obviously, I would need a disguise if I were to attract the right sort of victim. I put on a few to humor her and hated every one of them passionately. I wanted to look like I'd been dragged through a gutter by a herd of wild horses, not like I'd been insulated from the vicissitudes of life by a roster of ranch minks. It's important to remember that at this point in subcultural history it was hard to hate mink coats generically. No one was referring to fur coats as "dead animals" or spraying them with red paint. So if you didn't want a mink, you had to hate them one by one. As I did so, sneering at each one's hemline, color, and cut, my mother concluded that my attitude was too immature for real mink   so she bought me a *starter mink*.

It was the cheapest kind in stock—a black, dyed Japanese mink. It had a stand-up collar, raglan sleeves, and it tied at the waist with a thin leather belt, which was a good deal softer than the fur itself. I don't know what they feed minks in Japan, something perhaps grown in the ruins of Hiroshima, but whatever it is makes their hair quite strong. Almost wiry. The words mink coat evoke a luxuriant sensuality, but, I noted with a certain bemused fascination, my mink was more like a body-size beard. I resolved to wear it with irony. No sooner was I wrapped in its folds than I began to choreograph my escape from everything my mother hoped it would drag me into. My first move was to visit my friend Judy, who had dropped out of college to live with an artist on the Haight. It was 1967, and the Haight was what it called "happenin'." Judy's artist boyfriend had stopped painting and turned into a jeweler. Obediently, so had Judy.

They lived behind their little silver shop literally on Haight Street just a puff or two from Ashbury. I got to sleep on a foam rectangle on the floor in the back of their flat like a derelict—my lifelong dream. And sleeping, I soon realized, was all I wanted to do because to step outside onto Haight at that time was utterly and profoundly exhausting.

Mario Savio, the leader of the Free Speech rebellion that spawned the Love Generation, and the Diggers, who worked the Dumpsters and donors to feed it, were brilliant, industrious visionaries. They organized more positive human energy with less autocratic nonsense than any of us have seen before or since. The Haight was anarchists' last and best stand—a triumph of the human spirit, at least for the many who had some.

Inspired by the visible showmen who grabbed the media and ran— first away with it and then into its arms—a second tier of strong personalities flowed into whatever vacuums of responsibility arose. They certainly weren't in it for the money, and they weren't there to etch their names into history—the era is remembered for its marketable bell-bottoms, not for its remarkable success in refuting the need for top-down authority— but they came forward and did what needed doing for no reward other than the expression of their own generosity, hope, and style.

They wrangled with cops, overdoses, health problems, kids' animal needs, and questions of justice. They put out newspapers, organized clothing exchanges, ran a small subsidiary economy based on recycling and drugs. They worked, and worked hard.

Equally numerous, however, were the sheep. "Express yourself. Be an individual. Do your thing, man. Don't be conformist. I'm an Aquarian. Have another toke." These banal and ulterior words, or words so like them as to be dismally indistinguishable from them, gushed from the river of drug-crazed ersatz pirates, hobos, clowns, Edwardian decadents, and Peruvian peasants burbling down the pavement. A chick could not get to the corner to score a pack of cigarettes without a proposition of some kind. And she was obligated, style-bound, to look happy to get it, whether it was an offer for meth, or reds, or a toss on the mat with someone who would soon evolve into either Charlie Manson or a twelve-stepping bore.

Hey, Mamma: How about a groovy group grope in a purple-painted hovel? How about a chance to cook rice with some beautiful, blond, big-breasted beauties in tiny tie-dyed T-shirts while we guys drive up the coast to hammer nails into redwoods so we can fuck up the clear-cutters' band saws? Sounds ab-so-fucking-lutely like wow, but, uh, maybe later. Too many choices make me drowsy, man.

Judy and her boyfriend rapidly perceived that I had no desire to leave my foam, and he didn't like that. I was a bad influence, meaning, I think, that when I was napping in the cubicle next door, Judy felt constrained about making noises in bed. Because she loved me and didn't want to hurt my feelings by asking me to leave, they conspired to fix me up for the weekend to get me out of there.

The man with whom I was to journey was named Steve. He was from Connecticut, which Mother would have approved, but he drove a Norton, which, I was assured, was the coolest fucking motorcycle in the world. I crammed my starter mink into my little duffel bag, jumped on and behind him, and held on for the ride.

I don't remember where we went. Today, Judy said that she thinks it was Stinson Beach. Something like that. Anyway, Steve had a friend who was doing some construction work on a house sitting on stilts overlooking the Pacific, and we could stay there while construction was in progress. I don't remember seeing any construction, and I don't remember ever seeing the ocean. Either it was wrapped in mists, as often happens, or we were too stoned to distinguish ocean from sky.

What I do remember is that the pot was free, and plentiful, and that Steve and I did not have a very good time. I wanted him to find some reason to adore me. I didn't care what reason that was, nor could I think of any suggestions offhand, but that was all I wanted, and I was decidedly not getting it. I did my best to fake an orgasm, which was what one did back then to be adorable, but Steve, ahead of his time, wasn't buying it.

"I want to see your clit twitch," he explained patiently. "If it doesn't, it means that you aren't really coming." I considered this piece of intelligence with more credulity than I subsequently learned it deserved. I was still young enough to believe that there was something fun about my body left to learn. A little more dope, I figured, might help.

That set the pattern for the weekend. I desired; he refused; he demanded the implausible; I had another toke; and repeat. Eventually he wandered off down the hill to watch nature's clit twitch, leaving me on my cot with a copy of *Macbeth*.

I read it for what seemed like days. I was in the mood by then for the Shakespearean tool kit of storms and power and witches and murder. The words bounced around in my head, glowing, rolling down ravines of marijuana, and drifting up, burning off the page like fog rising up over the California hills. "Words to the heat of deeds too cold breath gives"? Puzzling and divine as California itself.

The next morning, still stoned, we headed back. A storm gathered up around us and the air turned cold. I put on my Japanese mink with a dirty olive poncho over it tied with electrical cord so that Steve wouldn't fixate on what a Bergdorf Goodman bohemian I was. It rained abruptly and dramatically (*The Tempest* came to mind), and then it was over. As the clouds swept away, a siren sounded.

Steve pulled over, and we got off the Norton, stoned and nervous. As if under orders from my mother, I removed my poncho to reveal my starter mink and my "good upbringing."

The cop swaggered over at a leisurely pace.

"We saw you throw that bottle away," said the cop to Steve, which was interesting because I hadn't noticed a thing.

The co-cop, who had gone snooping off to the side of the road, returned with an amber pill-bottle with crud in it. He opened it.

"It's full of roaches," he said.

"I guess we're going to have to take you in," the first cop gloated.

This was my chance to escape my fate. A jail term on a drug rap, even a trumped-up one, would take me out of the misfit class and catapult me all the way into instant hipness. I was envisioning myself in jail, strip-searched nightly by giant matrons, ripening slowly into a female Genet, when I noticed the two cops bundling Steve into their car and preparing to drive away.

"Hey," I actually said, "what about me?"

Cop Number One explained that I wasn't under arrest. He agreed to take me in so that I could get a ride back to Judy's from the station. But to do that we had to wait for a separate car and a matron. He waited with me.

On the way back, I asked the cop if he'd read any good books lately. He said that he was enjoying *Exodus*. Because he knew that I was from Jew York, as it was known in those parts, and that Steve's name was Levy, I understood that he was reassuring me that he, at least, was only interested in persecuting Steve for his taste in drugs, not his ethnic origin.

I encouraged him to deliver his synopsis of the plot, hating myself for feigning an interest in airport literature simply to flatter a tyrant. But I did strenuously recommend *Macbeth*.

Turned out that the place Steve had been arrested in was Redwood City. I didn't know at the time that it was one of the most conservative, hippie-hostile places on the West Coast, but as I sat in the molded plastic chair in the Redwood City Police Station, I started to worry about what would happen if Steve was actually jailed.

He could easily get five years for those joints. And I'd feel obligated to visit him in prison. I'd have to stay in California, learn to drive, and give up my entire life out of loyalty to this cool guy who didn't even like me, and who I wasn't all that crazy about, either.

At that point, just as my stomach was doubling its knot, a pair of cops entered from stage right with a German shepherd. They started giving it orders in German.

"*Alt!*" one exclaimed.

The dog sat.

"*Achtung!*" shouted the second new cop.

I clutched my rough mink to my cheek as if it was something Audrey Hepburn might want to be buried in, whipped out my trusty *Macbeth*, and tried to look both genteel and Gentile.

"Your dogs speak German," I observed graciously. "Is it because they were trained there?"

"We use German commands so that ordinary people can't order them around," lied the larger cop with the sort of smile a Nazi would use to lure you to the "showers."

After a very long time, during which I reread *Macbeth* with equally little comprehension and far less pleasure than before, the co-cop emerged from a "secure area" and asked if I was the girl who had been with Levy. I said I was and waited for the oppressor's ax.

"I hope your friend didn't pay money for that pot of his," said the cop dryly, "because according to the lab, if he did, he was had."

He took a kind of snickering pleasure, I felt, in eviscerating any delusions of hipness I might have had left. The upshot was they hit Steve up for a zillion parking tickets. Friends came to bail him out, and by nightfall I was back on my foam pallet at Judy's, dampening her love life.

Afterward, I imagined that my mink had saved Steve as well as me. I never really enjoyed reading Shakespeare before or since, so I knew our dope was good. Therefore, I surmised, it had to be pity for lovely, classy, minky me that had persuaded the Gestapo to let him off. It didn't occur to me until years later that he may have traded in his dealer for his freedom. I'll never know what exactly happened because I didn't see Steve again after that. I learned a few years later that he had drowned in shallow water while helping someone move a boat. He may have hit his head on a rock, Judy thought. The details were officially confusing.

Later I wondered if perhaps a dealer he'd ratted on had gotten out of jail and done him. I'll never know, like I said. But it was thanks to what happened that day with him that I finally understood the Great American Truth that my mother, the lawyer, was trying to impart to me personally, and it is this: The bad news is that, try as you might to move up or dive down, you will never escape your class. The weird news is that, no matter what your class is, no matter whose skin you're wearing or what you're smoking, there are fleeting moments in the vicissitudes of life when this bad news will save your hide.

Blind Munchies

Marijuana Meatballs

HARRY SHEARER

There was a time when I enjoyed marijuana (there goes the presidency) but disdained smoking it for health and esthetic reasons. Grass and brownies never seemed like a congenial combination, but I stumbled upon the idea of marijuana meatballs, and it struck me as perfect: The flavors didn't clash, as they did in brownies, but rather worked really well together. The only time I really enjoyed Disneyland was when I would take a break every couple of rides, sit on a bench, and munch on a bit of meatball before continuing. Nobody the wiser, except, maybe, me.

So one night, friends of my then-wife and me invited us to celebrate their anniversary. We went to a Chinese restaurant, had a bottle or two of Champagne, and enough food to fuel the retaking of Taiwan. We then came back home, and I passed around a plate of the magic meatballs.

We talked for a while, nobody got high, and we decided that something must be wrong with the batch. Good nights and hugs, and my wife and I went to bed around half past midnight. One AM, and *boom!* My head took off like an Atlas missile. I had forgotten the first rule of eating marijuana: The stomach is like a bakery; you take a number and wait your turn. The dope had sat there patiently until after the Chinese food had been digested, and then, in proper order, it was served. This was the Matterhorn of highs. There was only one problem: I had to get up early in the morning to do some actual work, and I didn't want to be high anymore. I wanted to sleep. But Mister Marijuana said, "No, sir."

The battle of wills was unequal and resulted in a serious anxiety attack. Actual shakes and tremors. Serious paranoia, the likes of which I'd never experienced before or since. "I can always go to UCLA emergency and get some Thorazine," somebody kept saying, either me or my wife. If my wife was saying it, why was she using the first person? She lit a fire, bade me to lie down, but I now had a case of the legs-that-wouldn't-stop-twitching and the mind-that-wouldn't-stop-going-*boom!*

About 2:30 in the morning, one of us turned on the TV. As usual in those days, old movies were on most of the channels, but nothing that spoke to me. Finally, though, we remote-hopped onto a rerun of *I Believe in Miracles*, evangelist Kathryn Kuhlman's weekly healfest. A lifelong stutterer off camera, she had a style of talking in her broadcasts that elongated almost every word, giving her time to pronounce it correctly. She had a taste for diaphanous gowns. I had made fun of her several times on my radio show. She always made me laugh.

And, miraculously, she did that night, too. Watching Kathryn Kuhlman got a message through the haze of paranoia and anxiety, a message that the melodrama was unnecessary, a reminder that I had a sense of humor. I lay down by the fire and got un-high. She brought me down. And I blessed her for it. But I didn't send her any money. I might have been super-high, but I wasn't crazy.

The Sign

HERBERT GOLD

My first year in college, at Columbia, I brought a joint home to share with my best high-school buddy—home from New York to Cleveland, Ohio, the Paris of the Midwest. My friend was terrified but brave.

"What'll happen to me?"

Sophisticated, a man of the larger world now, I said, "Nothing much. Oh, maybe you'll want something sweet, a piece of fruit, say."

He took a toke. His eyes went wild. He extended his arm, a sleepwalking, zombified victim of cosmopolitanism.

"A banana," he cried. "I gotta have a banana!"

Chocoholics

CHARLIE DAVIES

While living in a small college town, I was with some friends trying
out some "new" smoke on a Saturday night when one of them mentioned that a local drive-in was having a "special" on hot fudge brownie
delights!

This establishment offered free home delivery on orders over $5, and
that sounded too good to dismiss in our current state. When we finally
decided who was the most rational to place an order, one was phoned in
for four "specials" at $1.50 each.

After nearly an hour (this drive-in was at least two miles away), several
more tokes, and an ever-increasing desire for sweets, we made a confirm-
ing call. Yes, they did have our order but were very busy, and the delivery
boy should be back to pick it up shortly. We immediately fired up a couple
more joints in eager anticipation and put on some more great tunes.

About an hour later, it was noted that we still hadn't seen the goodies. We somehow found the phone and called again in case they had the
wrong address or were having trouble locating it.

They reconfirmed the order and restated that it was a really busy night,
but we were definitely on the list. Slight relief, but we were all starting
to get a little crazy with our craving. In order to mellow out, a few more
joints were started, and I think somebody changed the record.

After waiting three to four hours after the initial order, there were
four very uptight, very stoned, and very ravenous chocoholics climbing
the walls. We debated driving over to get the order, walking, or even
crawling. Before we could decide the proper course of action, there was
a knock on the door and it was the Delivery God! Money was shoved in
his hand, tip also, and before the door shut, warm fudge brownie delights
were being devoured!

Super Herb

POT STAR

Where I grew up in Texas, all that was available were varying degrees of shit-weed, just your basic run-of-the-mill Mexican commercial. Until I met K-Bone, that is.

K-Bone lived in an old house with a big extended family. Frankly, I was scared of the guy, but he had fresh Mexi buds as opposed to the usual dried-up and shaky schwag. It did sometimes get a little uncomfortable at his house, though, especially when tweakers lined up to pick up crank.

One day I went to score some buds from K-Bone, and I got a surprise. He had an elated look on his face, and he rushed me through the maze of corridors of screaming babies, kids at play, and aging elders melting on the couch.

"This shit's something special," he said, sticking a bright green bud under my nose.

It *was* special. I'd never seen a bud so bright green and skunky. I paid $35 a quarter and raced off to my friend JP's place to sample the wares.

We quickly smoked a joint and immediately headed over to Whataburger. Once inside, our bloodshot eyes glowed underneath the way-too-bright fluorescent lights. As we waited patiently in line to order our food, someone yelled out, "Stoners!" It was a group of cheerleaders with their jock boyfriends. JP and I flashed on what a bad situation this could turn into and how we might get our asses beat.

"Go Rebels!" cheered JP, erupting into a giant cartwheel. The act quickly came to a close, however, when a group of drunk cowboys walked through the door.

Although JP was scared of cowboys, I knew they liked stoners more than jocks. As long as we didn't piss off the shit-kickers, we should be able to grab our burgers and be safely on our way.

"What the hell are you people doing back there?" I yelled, banging my fist on the counter. "I've been waiting here for forty-five minutes and I want my fuckin' food!"

"Sir, may I see your receipt?" asked the middle-aged woman operating the register. "It says 12:53 and it's 12:56 right now. You've been here for three minutes."

The Brownie

This isn't the story of the atomic brownie, which was part of a batch made with butter that had been steeped for twenty-four hours with a pound of Mexican grass, which had been imported by a guy who ended up in a jail in Mexico and who I was always impressed with because he had rebuilt his motorcycle in his living room.

Could it really have been a pound? Now that I think about it, that seems like a lot, but what do I know, I wasn't a baker in those days. Now I love to bake, especially pizza, and sometimes I can even get people to pay me to do it, but that's another story and has nothing to do with the brownie in question, especially not the atomic brownie that is not the subject of this essay.

The brownie I want to tell you about is the one that my wife made for my dad when he was undergoing treatment for cancer. This all happened in those ancient times before voters approved medical marijuana. If I recall with any degree of precision, my dad was all in favor of trying medical pot even though my uncle thought it was a silly idea.

My uncle was actually a medical professional. He was some kind of special dentist who had developed an operation where he took part of a person's rib and used it to replace a diseased mandible in case that was needed. He had spent lot of time in England, and his recommendation was for us to get some heroin for my dad. Can we look for that? Medical heroin?

Of course, if dying people could use heroin, then the AMA would contrive ways to keep them alive longer, so that they could get addicted so that the DEA could arrest them and remove them from the hospital and throw them in prison where they belong. Maybe we should criminalize disease and thereby solve the health care crisis. Anyway, he was from a country where there was so much grass (and such good stuff, too) that in the land of his birth it was used as just another cooking herb.

The atomic brownie is not its actual name. I just made that up. I'm sort of an environmentalist and I would never equate grass, which is so obviously a gift from the gods or God or Mother Nature or whatever, with anything like nuclear energy. I mean, today I'm listening to the radio and I hear a story about cars being made out of recycled radioactive metal. Is that another reason to walk or what?

But the first thing that happened with the super brownie was that four of us ate one of them and then . . . and then . . . and then . . . all I remember is that my friends started giggling uncontrollably, canceled all their appointments, and went to bed. My wife (my second wife says she wasn't with me, so I'm assuming that I was with my first wife) and I couldn't drive home, so we called up some friends to rescue us, which they did, and in gratitude we gave them one of the brownies.

But back to my second wife, who once told me that if I didn't get her some grass, she would actually go out and get a job so she could buy some for herself. She says she uses it for artistic inspiration, but you know those addicts, they'll say anything to get their stuff. Me, I don't need it. I don't need any more anxiety and I certainly don't need to stimulate my appetite for Ding Dongs and Yoo-hoos. In the '60s, I ate my fill. God, I loved those Hostess CupCakes and Twinkies.

I heard Paul Krassner say that the shelf life of a Twinkie is longer than the jail sentence Dan White got for killing San Francisco Mayor George Moscone and Supervisor Harvey Milk. When I heard that, I used to wonder if the Twinkies I had eaten would eventually reconstitute themselves inside my body and eventually work their way out like a splinter that goes in real deep into one finger and comes out another one. It's never happened to me, but there is always a chance.

Now, my friends (the ones who gave us a ride, I can't remember where to) had a roommate who was a nurse, and after they put the brownie into their refrigerator, they went to bed. The nurse got up to go to work, and since she was a nurse, she ate a healthy breakfast of three cups of coffee and the brownie. I hesitate to even imagine. My wife would eat one of those brownies and probably go into her sewing room and make all the costumes for the *Star Wars* movies. Now that George Lucas has made the prequel, will he make the postquel?

So my wife had steeped the half ounce of pot with the butter, and this was organic butter from cows who weren't pumped full of BST antibiotics. But what am I saying, that maybe we should medicate our food? Wow, I am confused. We *do* medicate our food—I mean your food, unless you're like me and only eat stuff that purports to be pure. If this food is so good for you, how come I don't feel better? Well, after the butter was strained, there was this residue left in the pot. Oh my God, there's pot in the pot! At that point my uncle grabbed the pot and ate the pot.

The nurse with *the* brownie in her somehow negotiated the L.A. freeway system and ended up in a room with a patient who was lying very, very still. What could she do? Nothing. She just stood there staring for forty-five minutes. Maybe it was longer, maybe not. I wasn't there, thank God. Come to think of it, she wasn't all there either. After my uncle ate the pot that was in the pot, he wasn't all there either. Funny how that works.

Well, to make a couple of short stories just a bit longer, my uncle took to bed for three days. He always said that it was the butter that did him in. The nurse, nudged into action by one of those hospital volunteers in a strawberry-pink dress, took the patient's pulse. There was none, and she slowly made her way to the roof of the hospital where she spent the day sunbathing.

My dad didn't really like the brownies, so my wife ate them and made a series of chairs out of wooden clothespins that she sometimes sells at my pizza parties.

Laughing Fits

Identified Flying Objects

JOHN SINCLAIR

One of the greatest times I've ever had on weed—with my clothes on, to paraphrase the great Miles Davis—started one Saturday afternoon in Detroit in the summer of '65 or '66 when several of us got together to help Bo Taylor move some stuff to his sister's house in Highland Park, the little city surrounded by Detroit that was about two or three miles north of where we stayed in an old building called The Castle on the west side of the John C. Lodge Freeway service drive between Warren and Hancock, near the Wayne State University campus.

Bo Taylor was a young man of African descent who managed our building, worked at the Wayne County Jail, shot speed, and was related to the prominent Detroiter Hobart Taylor, who was at the time an advisor to President Lyndon B. Johnson. Assisting Bo were the urbane poet and jazz guitarist Ron English, a crazy little guy who lived in our building whose name was John Hornfield, and me. All of us were between twenty-one and twenty-six years of age and long cast adrift from the shores of everyday America.

Driving the car, a big old Detroit special of whatever make, was the painter, Joe Gruppuso, who had also brought a bag of bright green weed to help us through the afternoon. I had seen bright green weed before and had found it sadly wanting in mental elevation properties, so I was ill prepared for the incredible psychedelic buzz that quickly followed just a few small tokes. The whole carful of us was totally blasted, laughing and giggling as Joe poled us up the expressway toward Highland Park.

When we pulled up in front of Bo's sister's place, the guys got out and went into the spacious house while I remained in the car for a few minutes to try to pull myself together for the forthcoming series of physical tasks inside. I finally staggered out of the back seat of Joe's car, across the street, and up to the front door.

When I stepped inside, I was caught in the middle of a serious war of flying objects—pillows, seat cushions—anything soft and throwable was being pitched across the room by the stoned combatants hunched behind sofas and easy chairs. I found a protected spot and joined the fray, and for the longest time the five of us rolled with laughter and prolonged our play in the living room of Bo's sister's house.

Gradually, the high wore down a little and we looked around in a mild state of shock, assessing the minimal damage to the room with some relief and then breaking out in gales of laughter again. I've never been quite that blasted that way in all the years since.

Underground Paper

FRANK ATWOOD

The three of us decided to smoke a little of that infamous $10-a-lid weed. Since we had about a quarter pound of the commercial smoke, I decided it would be just wonderful to make a joint from a couple of ounces. Hey, what can I say? It was the days of those Cheech & Chong *Big Bambu* album rolling papers.

The immediate problem was no *Big Bambu* album rolling papers. Aha! I quickly determined that a newspaper would make far-out rolling paper. This wasn't just a bad idea; it was a *really* bad idea. We took the front page of the *Los Angeles Free Press* and put two or three ounces of pot on it.

The three of us were able to then roll this concoction into a joint . . . sorta. Mark wanted to fire up this bad motherfucker, so he grasped it with both hands and held it to his lips. Kevin fired up a Blue Diamond match and moved the flame toward the tip of the huge, homemade joint.

Hey, man, ever get one of those premonitions? You know, that feeling that something really fucked-up is about to happen? Well, as the match neared the joint, I got one. A strong one. I hollered, "Wait!" But it was too late. The flame hit the joint and, now trust me on this one, it wasn't just the tip that lit up. Man, the whole fuckin' thing went up in flames. Looked like Mark's head was engulfed in fire.

Of course, the joint blew apart and Mark's lap was covered with smoldering marijuana. Soot and ashes were floating around everywhere. Poor Mark, not only did the smoldering pot burn the shit outta the head of his dick (yep, burned right through his Levi's), but the ashes left black streaks all over his face.

Whew! Kevin and I simply burst into laughter. We rolled on the floor and made like hyenas. Mark somehow didn't find the situation so funny. He struggled to his feet, brushed some of the soot off—which for some reason sent Kevin and me into peals of laughter all over again—and headed for the bathroom to clean off his wounded pride.

Mark finally emerged from the bathroom, ego obviously still bruised. He simply had to restore his "presence" by showing us a gag. Well, he showed us, all right. Mark pulled out his Zippo and thumbed the flame to life. He then leaned back and spread his legs. You got it, the old light-a-fart-on-fire trick. I don't know what the fuck Mark had been eating, but this was no ordinary flame. The motherfucker shot out about a foot—and in three different directions.

Mark leaped up, grabbed his nuts, and started hopping around. Hell, the sight was just too much for us. Kevin and I rolled around on the floor makin' like hyenas again. Just about the time our roars of laughter started to die down, Mark quit hoppin' around and took his hands from his crotch. Lighting that fuckin' fart on fire blew a hole right through Mark's Levi's, and the fuckin' things were still smoldering. I thought I'd never stop laughing in my life.

Sans Screen

KEN MCINTOSH

The counterculture didn't really hit Toledo until late 1968. By that time, the term *hippie* had totally lost its cachet; dopers started calling themselves *heads*. The first head shop in Toledo was the Lunar Moth. My friend Bonnie had gotten a big chunk of Lebanese blond hash. Neither of us had ever smoked hash before.

In Vietnam, we had used corncob pipes and cut-slot toilet paper tubes with foil to smoke the evil weed, eventually learning how to roll joints. Bonnie and I decided to go to the Lunar Moth and buy a pipe worthy of her bounty. We bought an elaborate brass chamber pipe.

We went back my place and gingerly placed a three- or four-gram chunk of hash into the pipe. We puffed and puffed and started getting headaches, but no real smoke. The chunk was too large to ignite.

In frustration, I took the hash out of the pipe and ground it into powder. The buzz was slow in coming on, so we ended up smoking the whole bowl before we really felt anything. I got the last toke. Unfortunately for me, we knew nothing about screens in dope pipes. As I sucked, the last glowing dregs of the hash flew into the back of my mouth. Bonnie said she could see the little coals glowing as I screamed in pain.

After dousing the embers with a glass of water, she started laughing so hard that she peed her pants, which started me laughing. We laughed while she was in the bathroom, we laughed while we spent an eternity trying to find a bottle opener to use for a Pepsi, we laughed while we tried to remember how to use the telephone, and we laughed while trying to remember her address so the taxi driver could take her home.

After she left, I stumbled down to Frisch's and had a Big Boy dinner with a bowl of chili and a hot fudge sundae. When I got hone, I fixed myself a Chef Boyardee Hungarian Goulash dinner and read *Head Comics* until I fell asleep.

DEVO and the Sex Pistols

MARK MOTHERSBAUGH

It was 1978. DEVO had no record deal (although we all knew something was going to break soon). I had no money to speak of and no apartment. It was a hideously cold winter in Akron, Ohio, when, out of the blue, Richard Branson, the president of Virgin Records, called and asked me to fly down to Jamaica to discuss a deal. This was it!

Bob Casale and I arrived, shook hands all around, and watched Richard and the other Virgin execs roll up these huge joints—cigars, really. No one I knew rolled bombers like these and certainly no one had pot like this in Ohio.

We remained convivial, but in no time the ganja did us in. We were tripping, gone—incoherent. That's when Branson said, "The reason I brought you down here is the Sex Pistols have just broken up. Johnny Rotten is looking for a new band."

Bob and I looked at each other, stammered something, tried to hold on, but finally and unequivocally lost it, laughing harder and harder.

We tried to explain, through our spasms, that the Sex Pistols were great and everything, but we just couldn't get it out. *DEVO and the Sex Pistols*, it was all too much. All the execs were smiling uncomfortably, Johnny Rotten was in the next room waiting to become the new lead singer, and we were out of control.

Finally, we excused ourselves, went to our rooms, sat on the beds, and stared for a couple of hours, sure that we'd blown it.

Later that year, they signed us anyway.

Higher Education

Spacey and Spacier

My first college was a tough engineering school, and I joined a fraternity. It included a crazy-quilt collection of characters, most of whom did drugs to some extent or another, and a few, including the president and vice president of the fraternity, who did not.

There were some showdowns between the freaks and the straights, which resulted in the "discreet rule." Pot could be smoked in the fraternity house, but only if done discreetly. One day, Spacey came bouncing into the house, swinging a baggie full of herb. Larry, the president, saw him come in and, muttering something about "not discreet at all," grabbed the bag.

We followed him out to the back of the house and watched him pour out the bag and bury its contents. Meanwhile, inside the house, Spacey was on the floor laughing. He had just come back from the grocery store with a baggie full of oregano to use on the pizza he was making for dinner.

I finished up at a liberal arts school. Just about everyone smoked pot. One evening, as a group of us were sitting around toking and doing our usual *Marty* routine ("Whadda you wanna do tonight?" "I dunno, whadda *you* wanna do?"), I had a great idea. "Let's see Fellini's *Roma*. It's been in the theater a couple of weeks, and it looks really interesting." Everyone stared at me. "Really, let's see it. I heard it's one of the best movies of the year." I tried to convince them. Now they were looking at me like I was nuts.

My girlfriend finally said, "We saw it last week! With you!"

False Alarm

I had just left a party at the chairman of the Anthropology Department's house and returned home, where I reached into my pants pocket for the film can (which is always there) to light up and relax, when I discovered to my horror that it wasn't there. Where in hell could it be? My jacket pocket? No! Under the driver's seat in the car? No! I was wearing a pair of those foul pleated pants that inevitably deposit your change anyplace you sit, and, by golly, those pants had deposited my film can somewhere I had been seated during the day.

It might have happened at my office, where I had rolled one before I went to the chairman's house for the party. Had I left the can on my desk? I had to find out, so at 11:00 PM I got in my car and drove the half hour to the office to see. Nope, I hadn't left it at the office.

That meant only one thing. I had dropped it at my department chair's house. Damn, I could hardly go back to his house and say, "Hey, Dr. X, I dropped a can of dope in the house, did you find it?" By the same token, if Dr. X had found the can of dope, he would probably conclude that it was me who had dropped it, which would confirm in his mind all of his previous prejudices about me. Nor was he likely to return it, which, given the price of dope these days, meant a considerable monetary loss. What was I to do?

Nothing for the moment. I held my breath and went in to the office the following morning, when lo, a memo crossed my desk announcing a committee meeting from 10:00 AM to noon, which would keep the department chair busy for two hours. My window of opportunity.

I called his home when I knew he was just down the hall and talked to his gay roommate. I explained I had dropped something the evening before. Had he found it? No. Whew! Could I come by to look for it around 10 o'clock? "No problem," he said. So I drove over (knowing the chairman was otherwise occupied), was let in, did a quick survey of the chairs I had sat in the night before, and found the little can under a table on the patio.

I fessed up to my chair's roommate that it was dope and swore him to secrecy, a confidence that he appears to have honored. Narrow escape.

Disappointed

Back in the late '60s, I was a young faculty wife at the University of South Carolina. The department my husband was in had weekly seminars on Friday, with a party afterward. We were into alcohol, but nobody I knew did drugs (Valium didn't count).

One spring, there was an unusual new graduate student who had caught the interest of the faculty. He had a pickup with a camper on the back and was reported to have trekked across Afghanistan in it. He also lived two floors above one of our faculty members in a fancy new apartment building near campus. They said he came down and borrowed ice from them when he had a party.

But he seemed shy around us, so we didn't know for sure if the stories were true. After great effort, I finally got him to talk to me at one of the Friday parties. Once he got started, I couldn't get away from him. I never got him to talk about his travels or where he got all his money, but he went on endlessly about his work, which didn't interest me at all.

I wanted to change the topic, so when the group next to us started talking about the legalization of marijuana, I asked if he'd ever smoked pot. He had lots of pot stories. After a while, he asked, a little too eagerly, if I was interested in trying it. I was much too fearful to ever try anything illegal, but I didn't want to say so, so I waffled around.

"Maybe someday," I said, "but not now." I was relieved when a friend finally rescued me, and I avoided the graduate student for the rest of the evening.

The next Monday morning, I heard a car drive up to the front of my house and I went to the window. I was horrified to see his camper, but he just put something in my mailbox and drove off. It was a small velvet bag containing a matchbox full of pot. I was irrationally afraid of getting caught with it, but I didn't want to throw it away, so I finally hid it in the back of my kitchen junk drawer, behind the bulb baster and the package of chopsticks.

Several years later, tired and angry and ready to leave my husband, I searched the drawer in a fit of rebellion. I was going to roll that stuff and figure out how to smoke it, even if I had to do it by myself. I pulled out the bag and opened it up, only to find it empty except for the two fat (and, I presume, very happy) weevils in the bottom.

Watermelon Blues

When I was an undergraduate at Penn in the mid-'70s, a friend from high school was president of the student council. Well, one day he and his ministers decided to use some of the council's funds to purchase a pound of pot, and they set up a table right in front of Ben Franklin's statue to distribute it to the passing student body.

When I walked by with my wife, my friend invited me to have a few tokes. But they weren't just smoking joints. No, instead they had made a kind of fruit pipe out of a watermelon by cutting a small crater to hold the pot in one end and a slit in the other through which you could inhale the filtered smoke. Pretty ingenious.

So, there I was, sucking smoke through a watermelon, when who should walk by but the old conservative professor who I had been reading More's *Utopia* (in Latin, by the way) with once a week in his office for the last year. I didn't panic; I just set the watermelon on the table and introduced my wife to him.

We continued to read More for another year, and he never said anything about me sucking on a watermelon in the middle of the campus. My students (now, I teach English Renaissance literature) love this story.

First Time

Secret Clearance

I vividly remember the first time I got stoned. It was 1969 in San Jose, California. I had been trying for nearly six months, but I was so uptight and paranoid about it that my mind would not let it happen. My paranoia was not entirely unfounded. I worked in the engineering department as a mechanical designer on the M113 project, the armored personnel carrier used by the military in Vietnam, and had a secret clearance from the Department of Defense. If I got busted for smoking marijuana, I would lose my job and my secret clearance. I would have to try to start over in a new career at age forty. And I was not good at door-to-door sales.

I was at my girlfriend's house, and a mutual friend was visiting. We had smoked what they said was some very fine stuff. The two of them were sitting on the floor taking turns looking through a kaleidoscope and giggling a lot, and I was sitting on the sofa being as straight as a tournament-grade aluminum arrow.

After a while, my girlfriend handed the kaleidoscope to me. It was one of the kind—popular at that time—made of just mirrors, no colored glass pieces. It served to take my mind off my mind. I zeroed in on the ceiling-light fixture in the next room. The light fixture became a flying saucer flitting about, and before I knew it I was very stoned.

I left to go home about 2:00 AM, still very stoned. I drove to the end of the street, about half a block, turned left for about a hundred feet, and then right for a very short block to a T-intersection at a main street. I stopped at the stop sign, turned on the turn signal for a left turn, and waited for the only car in sight, coming from the left, to pass so I could turn left. As the car approached my street, he turned on his turn signal, indicating that he intended to turn down the street I was on.

As he turned, I saw it was a San Jose police car. I made my left turn and started up the street, keeping my eye on the rearview mirror. Sure enough, instead of completing his right turn, he made a U-turn and started up the street behind me. The dreaded red light came on, and I pulled off the street into the parking area for a small group of stores.

I was feeling really paranoid. Stoned for the first time and getting stopped by a cop. I had visions of being arrested, handcuffed, jailed, and fired from my job. I got out and walked back to the police car as the cop was getting out. This was a more mellow time when that was the thing to do. The cop explained that he had stopped me because my car was unfamiliar to him in that neighborhood, just apartment complexes, and I am Caucasian. He said he was going to fill out a report describing me and my car, and if I was ever again stopped for the same reason, to tell the cop that I was on file, he could check it in minutes, and I'd be on my way.

He stopped just in front of the driver's door with his clipboard on the hood of his car, and the searchlight aimed down at the clipboard as he filled out the form. I stood by his left side looking at the clipboard as he wrote. When he came to the description of the car, I told him it was a '60 Buick LeSabre, and he glanced up at it and said, "Two-tone, light blue with cream top." My car was a solid light blue, not a two-tone.

I turned to look at it. Beyond the car was a sodium vapor street lamp that was reflecting off the top of the car, which didn't really register on my stoned consciousness because all I saw, parked where I had left my rather plain old blue Buick, was a really sharp-looking '60 Buick LeSabre hardtop with a beautiful two-tone, light blue and cream paint job. What a rush!

I said, somewhat bewilderedly, "It's always been just light blue." He looked at me suspiciously—as if to say, "What's with this guy who doesn't know what color his car is?"—and my paranoia meter shot up another couple of decibels. Then he grabbed the spotlight and twisted it to shine on the car, and—*flash!*—it changed to solid blue before our eyes.

There was a pause. Then he said, also somewhat bewilderedly, "Uh, yeah. Uh, right. Uh, solid blue."

He continued looking at it for a moment or two, hand still on the spotlight. Then he twisted the light back down as he bent over to resume writing. He paused after two or three seconds and glanced up at the car again, once more a beautiful "two-tone, light blue with cream top." He shook his head and went on with the report.

When he finished, he thanked me for my cooperation and time, and we went our separate ways—he on his appointed rounds, me on my way home, thinking about repainting my car.

Jesus

JOHN MCCLEARY

It was my first time. Having just left the Pentecostal Church with which I was associated for much of my life, I hadn't had much opportunity to smoke marijuana. David was an acquaintance I met when I was hired to photograph his band. He rolled it in a filter cigarette after taking out the first half of the tobacco. We drove his Beetle along the freeway with the windows all rolled down to get rid of the smell. Paranoia was rampant then. For the first year I smoked, it was always in the bathroom so we could flush it if the cops broke in.

It was cold and windy and hard to keep the marijuana "cigarette" lit, tooling down the freeway in Dave's bug. At one point, sucking on the thing, I reached the real tobacco and got a lungful. I had almost as little experience with tobacco as with marijuana. I'm still not sure if I was stoned on the weed or sick on the tobacco.

It was the Fourth of July, so we went down to the beach to watch the fireworks. I was sitting in the cold sand, looking up at the stars with this unfamiliar taste in my mouth and a self-conscious feeling on my mind.

It was indistinguishable at first. Then it began to sink into my consciousness—singing. It had a strangely familiar sound. Yes, I knew that tune. Religious. They were coming toward me. A group of Christians working the beach. Walking and singing among the heathens. Hoping to save one lost soul. Coming toward me. The backslider. Getting closer. I was frozen in place. Should I get up and run? No, then they would see me and recognize a sinner. What should I do?

"Jesus loves me, this I know, for the Bible tells me so. Little ones to him belong." Oh my God, they were coming right toward me. Was it written in the fluorescent light across my forehead? FALLEN CHRISTIAN. What should I do if they come up to me? I know I'll break down in tears.

I'm doomed to be a Christian all my life. There they were. Young, fresh-faced, enthusiastic Christians my own age. "Yes, Jesus loves me. Yes, Jesus loves me . . . " Right in front of me. I'll look away, ignore them. Are they still there? What? They've gone? They walked on. They're off to terrorize someone else. I'm safe! I don't have to go back to church. I can smoke dope again.

Generations

When I first smoked marijuana in 1963, I was a student at Berkeley, and on my next trip home to Los Angeles, I told my parents about this fabulous discovery. They reacted with horror.

"We didn't work and save all those years so you could go to college and smoke dope!"

Four or five years later, marijuana had become an emblem of the youth culture, and much was written, filmed, and said about it, and my mother was now curious. My younger sister, who was going to UC San Diego, and I were home for the holidays, and our mother asked if we had some she could try.

We took on this "project " with glee, rolling a joint and showing her how to toke as we sat in the family room of the house we'd grown up in. Since it was her first time, we figured it would take quite a bit to get her buzzed, so after doing one joint, we lit another.

My sister and I were already ripped, but my mother was complaining that it had no effect; it wasn't working. So we smoked the second joint, my sister and I giggling and flopping about the couch, and my mother turned angry.

She started saying she'd prefer to do it with "my own peer group," that this was a mistake—it was probably just psychological, anyway— and then, virtually in midsentence, as she was ranting, with her finger jabbing the air for emphasis, she stopped.

"Oh my God," she said, pointing at the TV across the room, "everything's blurry. Girls, I'm stoned!"

Memory

Forgetting

ROBERT ANTON WILSON

The "funniest" experiences I've ever had with drugs all involved pot, and none of them seem comic when I try to write them down. Apparently, words, which cannot convey "mystical" experiences, also fail to communicate hilarious drug experiences.

For instance, a friend and I took a little too much hash one night and both got lost in stoned space. We knew who we were and where we were, but we couldn't remember the last thirty seconds. We spent what seemed like an hour saying things like:

"Jesus, I can't remember what we were talking about."

"What did you just say?"

(Interlude of spasmodic laughter by both of us.)

"I think I'm having a . . . what? What did you say?"

"I can't remember . . . what are we trying to remember?"

(More spasms of laughter.)

"We're trying to . . . what are we trying to do?"

As the effect modified with time, we understood what was happening, and one of us described it as "a visit to the islands of micro-amnesia."

Taking Inventory

JERRY OCHS

Once, while hitchhiking across the country, I was picked up by a very nice couple in a van filled with dried marijuana. When it came time for us to go our separate ways, they gave me three baggies to remember them by. I shared my good fortune with whomever gave me a ride, causing some of them to drive beyond their original destination.

Anyway, by the time I got to where I was going, I was down to two bags. I looked up my old friends Mike and Sue. They were happy to see me and the pot because they were dry, smoke-wise, although they did have ten hits of LSD. We smoked a little and decided to see a movie.

They lived in a "bad" neighborhood, and for some reason, once outside the house, while one of them was locking the front door, the other one, standing down on the sidewalk, shouted a question about what time we'd be back, and one of the bad neighbors must have overheard the answer because when we returned their house had been burglarized.

After recovering from the initial shock, they began to take inventory of what was missing. The TV, the stereo, Mike's camera, Sue's watch, the piggy bank, and two other items, adding up to seven. In addition, the dope was gone, both their stash of acid and my two baggies of pot.

For some reason, they called the police to report the crime, and when the policeman arrived, he asked, of course, what had been stolen. As he wrote each item down in his notebook, they described the TV, the stereo, etc. "Are you sure that's everything? Nothing else is gone?"

"Nope," Mike answered a bit too rapidly. "Definitely nothing else."

Sue, looking puzzled, said, "But, Michael, I'm sure we counted eight things."

Mike said, "No, you're wrong, Sue, just seven."

I hissed, "Nothing else, Sue. Nothing."

"I'm sure there was an eighth thing missing," she insisted, scratching her head as if to dig out the memory. The cop, pen paused in midair, looked slowly from face to face. Sue was still perplexed and refused to give up.

"If I could just remember the eighth thing," she said. "We were just standing right here, adding up our losses: the TV, the stereo, the . . . "

"Just seven things, Sue," Mike and I shouted in unison.

As soon as the cop left, we reminded Sue what else had been stolen.

She said, "See, I was right, there *was* an eighth thing."

Remembering

NOLA EVANGELISTA

I began smoking pot in college, when I was still a virgin and very shy around guys. Whenever a guy made a pass at me, I would freeze up in fear. I put this down to my repressive Catholic school upbringing and overall fear of the unknown. But as it continued to happen, I began to wonder if there was some other reason. One night after a date when the pattern repeated itself, I decided I needed to get to the root of my problem. I had just seen the movie *Harold and Maude* and was struck by the scene where Harold smoked pot with Maude and was finally able to express the source of his strange behavior.

I decided I should smoke some pot and think over my problem, hoping for a revelation. Smoking calmed me down, and as I was sitting, listening to music, not thinking about anything in particular, something suddenly popped into my head. I remembered a scene from my childhood when a neighbor boy had molested me. Apparently, I had buried the incident in my subconscious, unable to process it in my child's mind. With the knowledge of this incident, I was eventually able to overcome my inhibitions. If it wasn't for marijuana, I don't know if I would have ever remembered my past so that I could deal with it.

Over the years, smoking pot has helped me with the recurrent depression from which I suffer. It raises my spirits and changes my focus. But, importantly, marijuana doesn't put me into some dopey state where I avoid my problems; instead, it almost unfailingly helps me uncover the source of my sadness, so that I can address the underlying issues at hand.

Perhaps because I come from an emotionally reticent family, I've needed some help to tune into my emotions. Perhaps marijuana helps me reach a meditative state difficult to achieve in our fast-paced society. All I know is that marijuana has healed me emotionally and spiritually, and as an advocate for marijuana law reform, I am, as Al Green sings, "blessed in the service of my savior."

Radio Daze

Berkeley Boo

LORENZO MILAM

The best place to find your forgotten history is on the Internet. By typing your name into Yahoo! or Deja News, you will run across the many unlikely trails you've left behind as you wandered the ripe, green fields of injudicious youth. "See KBOO," said the computer.

"Oh, yes—KBOO," I said. "I remember them." At least I thought I did. Thirty years ago, under protest, I traveled to Portland, Oregon, to help a lady named Lloyd E. Livingstone found a broadcast station that was later to be named KBOO. And now, under the home page of that radio station, I found a reference to what we had done so long ago. It was interesting to see how the current KBOO handled their conception and gestation. It was most interesting to see that it had become a total fantasy.

"On Halloween day," they wrote, "Lorenzo Milam suggested several choices for call letters for the new station. The holiday spirit prevailed, and the letters KBOO were chosen. Milam helped several communities start their own stations. Some of KBOO's sister stations bear Milam's witty trademark: KCHU, WAIF, WORT, KDNA, KTAO, KUSP . . . "

Now, KBOO is a very politically correct station, they tell me—my baby is politically correct!—so they will always be in the pursuit of the absolute truth, right? Since the story of their naming was totally false, I wrote them, suggesting that they state only the correct facts of their genesis. This is what I wrote:

> Now that the end of October is upon us, I would suggest that you disabuse your listeners of the notion that KBOO was named for Halloween. That's about the silliest story that I have heard in my life, and I've heard a passel of them. KBOO was named for a very potent form of dope sold in the '60s in California

and the West called "Berkeley Boo." If you could advise your audience of this fact, I would be most appreciative.

And you should be appreciative of boo, too. If we weren't smoking dope at the time—or at least thinking about it—we never ever in a hundred years would have applied for that frequency in Portland back in those dark days of the late '60s. We certainly had better things to do at the time—what with FCC investigations, antiloyalty hearings, the FBI bugging us about our radical programming, none of us getting laid . . .

The thirtieth anniversary of the station will soon be upon you, and it behooves you to be generous with your past, even if it does involve a few disgusting scandals. Or, as Tolstoy said, "If we don't honor the past, we cannot honor ourselves—much less our future." Or something like that.

Flushing Toilets

In 1972, I was the chief engineer for a college radio station at a small liberal arts college in North Carolina. One Saturday night, I had the radio on in the background, as was my custom.

Suddenly, the music faded out, and a breathless voice shouted into the microphone: "It's a drug bust on campus, and the cops have a roadblock at the main entrance! Dump your stash quick, dudes!"

Since this was clearly not our regular newscast, I dressed hurriedly and started for the station. Through the dorm, I heard the scrambling of feet, shouts, ceiling panels falling, curses, and the frantic flushing of toilets. As I walked into the radio station, I asked the DJ about the source of the "news report."

"I got this call a few minutes ago," he said.

"From whom?"

"I didn't recognize the voice," he reported sheepishly.

"How do you know it's true?" I asked.

"Well . . . "

I drove out to the main entrance to the college and found that one of the students had a flat tire, and someone had stopped to help, and both vehicles' four-way flashers lit up the night. It took the better part of two days to get the plumbing back in order, a week in hiding for the midnight DJ, and about a year to get the radio station's credibility to the point where any of us would admit working there.

Waiting for Cookies

HANK ROSENFELD

I got a job as a news writer at the alternative radio station KSAN—the "Jive 95," they called it. "A San Francisco tradition since 1968," KSAN was a wonderful place. Even the building was shaped like a classic orange-and-red radio. Everyone there was hip and did drugs, and some DJs got blow jobs under the console as they did drugs.

Every year around Thanksgiving, a verbal memo spread through the station: "The cookies are coming." A shipment of cookies came each year from Oregon; with almonds in the middle, they were innocent-looking enough, like they could've come from Chinatown in a little pink bakery box, but these were soaked through with marijuana.

Someone called "The Rabbi" delivered them, and the legend was that the dope had been cooked "in the butter," thus keeping the entire KSAN staff flying through the holidays. The music got a little more intense, the on-air announcers a little more cryptic.

I'd chew a corner off a cookie and completely forget about my news duties—I couldn't remember how to "rip and read" anything. Then I'd duck into a production studio and just lock the door, turn off the over-heads, ratchet up the monitors, and dance, tight and alone in the tiny studio, to the music and the flicker of the pulsating console lights.

Once I went in there with a girlfriend who was an actual dancer who, in her far-out grooving moves, slammed her head down into one of the huge, solid-block Ampex tape machines, requiring seven stitches.

That was funny.

Concerts

Knee High

It was 1975. I was fifteen years old and attending one of my first rock concerts: Crosby, Stills, Nash & Young at the Cleveland Stadium. My boyfriend Carlo and I were sitting in the infield, watching the show and smoking dope—the first time for me.

We were sitting close and had our knees up, our arms wrapped around our knees. Suddenly, I realized I could not feel my legs—my knees were absolutely numb! First, I tapped them a bit to see if I could evoke any feeling. None! Then I hit them a little harder. Still nothing. Then I began digging my nails harder and harder into my poor numb knees, trying to get some feeling, any feeling at all.

As I sat there gouging my knee, Carlo yelped, "Ouch! Why are you gouging my knees like that?" Oops. Wrong knee. At least I felt better knowing I was not permanently numb in the knees.

Changed Attitude

PETER LIT

At the Inn of the Beginning in Cotati, California, a band from Mendo-cino—Cat Mother and the All Night Newsboys—had a gig.

During the break, they and some friends were in the back testing some homegrown herbs for psychoactive ingredients when in the circle there "magically" appeared a uniformed officer complete with radio, gun, and attitude.

What struck us the most, however, was that he was at least ten years younger (or so it seemed) than any of us. Other salient characteristics: He was about five feet two inches and alone.

The slow change was wondrous as the energy turned 180 degrees from an officer apprehending lawbreakers in the act to a group of people looking at some child interrupting their party.

He got nervous, started shuffling his feet, then walked away with the parting comment, "Well, it *is* illegal, you know."

Risk and Reward

DARRELL

One summer, while touring the country with an amazing band, my friends and I stopped in Indiana to see a show. The band would be playing for two nights at the Deer Creek Amphitheater.

I missed the first show, due to "lack of having a ticket," but was absolutely positive that I would get in the next night. And I did.

Anticipating a great show, I waited on the lawn with a friend. Knowing that we had some time to kill, my friend offered to pack a bowl with some beautiful blueberry buds from Eugene, Oregon. The only problem was that we had left all of our glass pieces in the van.

We looked over to our right, and sure enough there was a brother who welcomed our invitation, provided he could supply us with something to smoke out of. He smiled and pulled out one of the headiest chillums I'd ever seen—and I've seen my fair share.

This guy was a true old-school hippie, happy to be sharing what he referred to as "my baby." He had taken the bowl back and forth across the country at least a dozen times over the past four years. He smoked it at almost every show and had gotten compliments from smokers and even a cop who decided not to confiscate it. We were happy to pack it.

The bowl had made it around between the three of us only once when a polite-but-annoying security guard told us to put it away. No sooner had she spit out the words than another not-so-polite-but-very-annoying security guard took the bowl out of my hands. He proceeded to take the chillum and throw it over the amphitheater's back fence, which was close to where we were sitting.

Our kind friend looked at me with despair, almost in tears. I felt *so bad*, having been the last one with my hands on his baby. He was not very interested in my apology. The thought of never seeing his prized possession again was obviously on his mind. He asked me to get it for him, and I really didn't feel like I had a choice.

Here were the problems: First, the show was *just starting*. Second, the day was beginning to turn into night. Third, the fence surrounding the back of the amphitheater was at least twelve feet high. He offered to boost me over, but I sadly explained that there was no way for me to get back once I was over. He suggested trying to get back in through the front, but we both realized that once you're out, you're out. I had to come up with a plan.

I decided to take a walk to the corner of the venue, where the back fence met a chain-link fence at a ninety-degree angle. Looking at the point where they met, I realized that the slope of the venue left about a one-foot space between the ground and the fence. I thought that I might actually be able to slide through the opening and grab the piece. So I asked some stoned kid if he'd keep an eye on me and make sure no one saw me trying to squeeze through the opening. He curiously agreed.

So I got on my belly and stuck my head under. I couldn't see much, except that the venue had a huge slope on the other side (obviously, because the venue was a hill). It was getting darker, and the band was playing their second song. I decided to go for it and managed to squeeze my body through the hole. After standing up, I realized I was on the other side.

Now all I had to do was find the damn chillum. I started to look. And look and look. I continued to look until I spotted it. I started to walk over to it, almost ready to grab it. I was within two feet of it when I heard a voice: "Hey!" I had to think fast. I was pretty much planning on getting booted and spending the rest of the night in the parking lot.

"What the hell are you doing back here?"

"Some asshole grabbed my wallet and tossed it over the fence. I can't leave until I find it. I have to find it!"

"Okay, calm down," the guard said. "First off, how did you get here?"

"Uh, I crawled under a hole in the fence."

"Well, you have to go back in. I'll look for your wallet and meet you at the beer booth in twenty minutes. But you have to go back in now. If anyone sees you back here, you'll be kicked out."

I realized I had no choice. However, I was afraid he would look down about two feet behind him and see the chillum. So I gave him my estimated whereabouts of the wallet.

"I was sitting in between the beer booths, so it's probably over there somewhere."

"Okay, well, go back inside and meet me at the booth."

I crawled back under the fence and started to walk back to the owner of the chillum. I was getting ready to give up. It was practically dark, and I had just narrowly escaped being kicked out. But the sad look on this kid's face made me try it again. Not many people sneak out of a show, sneak back in, and decide to go out again.

So, crawl under again is what I did. Only, this time, I headed straight for where I knew the chillum was. I ran for it. I saw it. And I grabbed it. I ran for the hole, snuck back in before the second song ended, and handed over his baby to the kind brother. Not only did I get a big hug, but he was so happy that I found it he stuffed me a huge bowl of some greeny-green Humboldt weed.

Pranks

Smoking Bananas

PAUL KRASSNER

The office of the *East Village Other* was across the street from *The Realist* on Avenue A. I dropped by one afternoon when editors Walter Bowart, Allen Katzman, and Dean Latimer were discussing a book, *Morning of the Magicians*. They were intrigued to learn that LSD released serotonin in the brain and wondered if it could be found in nonchemical substances. And yes, *serotonin* could indeed be found in bananas. And so they decided to launch the great banana hoax. The *Berkeley Barb* picked up the story, and both the underground and mainstream wire services spread it around the country.

It quickly became public knowledge that you could get legally high from smoking dried banana skins. In San Francisco, there was a banana smoke-in, and one entrepreneur started a successful banana powder mail-order business, charging $5 an ounce. Agents from the Bureau of Narcotics and Dangerous Drugs headed for their own laboratory, faithfully cooking, scraping, and grinding thirty pounds of bananas according to the recipe in the underground presses. For three weeks, the Food and Drug Administration utilized apparatuses, which "smoked" the dried banana peels.

The *Los Angeles Free Press* in turn promoted yet another hallucinogen—pickled jalapeño peppers, anally inserted. All over Southern California, heads were sticking vegetables up their asses. And, at a benefit for the Diggers in San Francisco, I mentioned onstage that the next big drug would be FDA. Sure enough, *Time* magazine soon reported that there would be "a super-hallucinogen called FDA." Silly me, I thought I had made that up.

When *Time* decided to do a cover story on the hippies, a cable to their San Francisco bureau instructed researchers to "go at the description and delineation of the subculture as if you were studying the Samoans or the Trobriand Islanders." It was a proper approach. At the Summer Solstice Celebration in Golden Gate Park, the same hippies who ridiculed Lyndon Johnson's call for a national day of prayer were now imploring the sun to come out at 5:00 AM. They had given up trying to influence the administration, but now—perhaps under the influence of banana peels among other hallucinogens—they were still trying to influence the universe.

Banana Tripping

DAVID PEEL

The banana-smoking movement began around 1966–1967. It started in Berkeley. The inspiration was from Donovan's song, "Mellow Yellow." The first New York City Be-In featured banana grass being smoked along with marijuana. My first street band was called David Peel and the Banana Trippers. I saw articles about smoking banana skins in all kinds of news magazines, and I really believed that banana grass could get me high like marijuana.

I even went to the United Fruit Company's New York headquarters to see if they would sponsor my band to play banana grass songs. They said, sarcastically, that they sure would if only I would go to Quebec, Canada, and speak to the executives there.

Even the cops in Washington Square Park tried to bust me and some other fellow hippies for smoking banana grass. I wrote my very first song, "Banana Grass," in 1966 while I was working on Wall Street as a clerk for a small brokerage firm.

When I first sang the song in Washington Square, it caused an instant euphoria and the beginning of Peelmania. The crowd followed me like a Peeled Piper, singing along with my new anthem. I then knew that playing music was my new way of life and banana smoking was my new way of getting stoned.

The brokerage company fired me because I looked too much like a hippie in a suit, and I was focusing less on my work at the office. Ironically, it had been one of my supervisors who had brought the banana-smoking craze to my attention. I wasn't smoking marijuana or taking psychedelics in those days. Banana grass and a little alcohol was enough for me at that time.

I then went to Haight-Ashbury for a few months in the fall of 1967 and learned to become a professional radical hippie. When I came back to New York City in early 1968, I began to realize, along with my fellow hippies and straight-looking friends, that banana grass wasn't really happening; marijuana was the real thing. I learned that when I had my first joint before leaving for San Francisco.

I wrote my song "I Like Marijuana" for Elektra Records, which signed me as a recording artist. Elektra featured it as the main song on my album, *Have a Marijuana.* So before I became a total banana peel, my re-bong life turned me on to real sacred herb, marijuana grass, and turned me off to banana grass. But it was surely my first high fantasy, and marijuana music has been with me ever since.

Smoking Dog Poop

JAY LYNCH

In the early part of 1968, when satire magazines were few and far between, I edited and published a humorous journal called the *Chicago Mirror*. As editor, I wasn't above hawking the mag on Wells Street myself. This way, I got direct feedback from the readers as well as their twenty-five-cent pieces. There were reports in the mass media of hippies smoking banana peels, so I wrote an article for the second issue of the *Mirror* based on these reports. It was intended as satire. Here it is, reprinted word for word:

Groovy New High

Last December 15th, a hippie crash pad on North Larabee Street was raided by four members of the Chicago Police Department's Narcotics Squad. Narco officers were surprised to find twenty-five pounds of an unidentifiable substance in the hippies' kitchen. Eleven or twelve hippies of indeterminate sex were taken in for questioning, and the entire twenty-five pounds of the strange sepia substance were confiscated by the puzzled fuzz for analysis.

Police chemists were astounded to discover that the mass was composed of dog excrement. The arresting officers were even more amazed to learn from the hippies they interrogated that "doggie poop," as they referred to the contraband, was the newest psychedelic sensation among the local turned-on love children.

The busted hippies were released from custody soon after their account of "voyages to infinity" on a few snorts of poop were confirmed by police chemists. It will be a matter of months before Illinois passes a law against doggie poop. While poop is still legal, the *Mirror* would like to inform the unenlightened about the phenomenal consciousness-expanding qualities of the drug.

How to Do Poop

The most common variety of poop in the Old Town area is "Lincoln Park Brown." It can be found lying on the ground amongst the trees and bushes of Lincoln Park, distributed by loving doggies as a gesture of kindness. When poop turns white, it is virtually useless as a hallucinogen. Poop users, or "shitheads," warn that only fresh brown poop will do. To derive the full psychedelic benefit of doggie poop, it must be cured. Place a three-ounce "turd" (doggie poop is measured in turds rather than in kilos or micrograms) on a cookie sheet in a 300-degree oven. After baking for thirty minutes, the turd should be of brittle consistency. It can then be crumbled and rolled in cigarette papers into approximately six poop joints—a twelve-hour trip for two poop freaks.

Novice shitheads tend to inhale fresh uncured doggie poop from a plastic baggie. However, this method requires a longer period before the high is attained, and hallucinations are weaker than those produced by a poop joint. As a seventeen-year-old shithead told *Mirror* reporters, "The high is kind of like grooving on psilocybin, but more warm and human. To try to describe my poop high in earthy terminology would be a wasted effort. It's indescribable. All I could say while I was up there was 'Oh, wow!'"

Not a word of the above was true, of course. But while I was selling the *Mirror* on the street, I started to notice that the magazine's primarily hippie readership didn't understand that it was satire. Maybe I should have called it something less serious sounding than the *Chicago Mirror*. Maybe I should have called it the *Chicago Goofy Wacky Magazine*. I don't know. But the one event I remember that truly convinced me to give up on the *Mirror* and publish *Bijou Funnies* (one of the first underground comic books) instead, occurred while I was selling the issue of the *Mirror* with the dog poop article on Wells Street.

A young hippie boy enthusiastically approached me and said, "Hey, man! Thanks for that tip about the dog shit! It really works, man! And it's free!" The kid went on about how he and his friends had read the article and tried smoking dog shit. He claimed it was better than pot. He was serious. He wasn't kidding. Now that I think about it, dog shit might actually have enough nitrogen content to get a person high. Or maybe, like the banana-peel smoking craze, it was just the power of suggestion that got this kid stoned on dog poop. I took full responsibility, though. I tried to tell him it wasn't true. I tried to explain that it was humor. He wouldn't accept it. He had been in Dog Poop Nirvana. I could not convince him that it was meant to be satire.

That's the problem with satire, though. There's always going to be somebody out there who doesn't understand it. How many folks were duped into eating their children after reading Swift's *A Modest Proposal*? How many kids have adopted Beavis and Butthead as role models? How many seas must the white duck sail before he can sleep in the sand?

There was a time when people realized that if they jumped out of a tenth-floor window, they would ultimately fall to their deaths. Today, though, they'll metaphorically jump out of that same tenth-story window and then, on the way down, lobby for softer concrete.

The Great Yippie Valentine's Day Caper

ROZ PAYNE

The following Valentine appeared anonymously in the mailboxes of about thirty thousand strangers in New York City on February 14, 1969; it was printed on paper with hearts going around its sides, and each one contained a joint:

> Yippie! You are one of 30,000 lucky persons being sent this freshly rolled marijuana cigarette. We are doing this in order to clear the garbage from the air. Here are some facts:
>
> - Marijuana has been used for over 2,500 years throughout the world.
> - Scientific research at the University of Michigan and Boston University show marijuana to be as harmless as coffee.
> - Here is what an official study carried out by the British government had to say: "Marijuana is much less dangerous than amphetamines and barbiturates, and also less dangerous than alcohol."
> - Marijuana is not habit-forming any more than are the movies.
> - "There are no lasting ill effects from even the acute use of marijuana," say researchers Goodman and Gilman in *Pharmacological Basis of Therapeutics.*
> - The often-quoted fact that pot smoking leads to heroin addiction is just not true.
> - "Marijuana is not as dangerous as it was once thought to be," says J. Murphy of the U.S. Bureau of Drug Control.

It would be almost impossible to find more than a handful of researchers who would claim marijuana as harmful, yet the government and local authorities maintain the same attitude they have held for years. The penalty for doing just what you are doing right now runs up to life imprisonment in some states. Mayor Lindsay has just petitioned the governor of New York to raise the penalty from one to four years for possession. In 1968, over 60,000 people in California alone were arrested for smoking pot. Nationwide statistics to be released next month will show over 200,000 arrests last year. The law is very discriminatory with blacks, hippies, and other minority group members being the only ones prosecuted.

Anyway, we thought we would give you a chance to make up your own mind. It's very simple. Just get a match and light up! Plenty of people smoke pot who do not smoke regular cigarettes, and, besides, you can't get cancer from it. Just inhale deeply and hold the smoke down as long as you can. You've had enough when you feel kind of nice and mellow. If you already smoke, join us when we strike again on Mother's Day by sending out ten or more joints to persons selected from the phone book. Oh, yes, one more thing, don't call the cops, dig?

The story goes that Abbie and Anita Hoffman asked Jimi Hendrix for a $2,000 check to buy the marijuana. Jimi gave them $1,000 cash so that there would not be a record of the transaction. Six kilos of pot were bought for $800; the rest of the money was spent on stamps and envelopes. The marijuana was divided up among various groups whose job was to clean, roll, stuff and stamp the already addressed envelopes, and mail them in time for arrival on Valentine's Day. Anita, under the alias Ann Fettamen, wrote about this event in her book, *Trashing*. Because the acts were illegal, she changed names, places, and the date from Valentine's Day to Halloween.

Our group was responsible for rolling two of the six kilos. Anita said that each kilo produced seven hundred joints, or was it each pound? We had bamboo rollers, various types of rolling machines, and rolling papers. Rolling joints got tiresome, so you needed to change methods. We hung out forever, rolling, smoking, talking, listening to music, and rolling some more. In order to clean large amounts at a time, Anita and Abbie used a window screen while we used my mother's round metal sieve. None of us ever had that much marijuana before, so we lived in total ecstasy on one hand and in total paranoia of getting busted on the other.

Abbie showed up with envelopes that were addressed with a typewriter that had been destroyed, postage stamps, and thousands of leaflets. We stuffed the envelopes with the letter and one marijuana joint. The left-over joints were sent to people of our choice, some friends and some addresses taken randomly from the phone book. Some were mailed from mailboxes on Third Avenue in the Gramercy Park area, the same red and blue mailboxes that later were stenciled with a yellow star to turn the boxes into flags representing the National Liberation Front of North Vietnam. Anita and Abbie mailed some from uptown, and other groups mailed them throughout New York City.

Anita wrote, "There was no way of knowing how many people got high on Halloween [Valentine's Day], but we knew it was the busiest night in the history of the Narcotics Division." The story first broke in the afternoon papers and on the radio. The information was scanty, but there were shocked reports that thousands of city dwellers had received a marijuana cigarette with a strange letter. By evening, it was announced at regular intervals on all the late news programs.

One newscaster displayed the joint he had received, read the letter aloud, and, while on the air, he called the police, asked for the Narcotics Division, told them he had been sent marijuana, and then was told that the police were on their way to the TV station. While he was still on the air, the police arrived, took the joint, and announced to the American public: "If you have received marijuana in the mail, you must report it to your local police precinct. Marijuana is a dangerous drug that can drive people insane."

Other Species

The Raccoon

MR. HOWELL

Growing up in the subtropics of Florida, one of the things that can be done to defray the ever-rising cost of pot is to grow your own. So we did (and do) in every available place and way you can imagine. Since much of our lovely state is made up of mangrove swamps, estuaries, and barrier islands, our youthful efforts to produce clandestine crops of cannabis eventually moved to this final frontier of mosquitoes, mud, and the raccoon.

Accessing the chosen site was difficult, the shallow brackish waters surrounding these islands meant that only a canoe could be landed, and all supplies had to be hauled in by hand—building materials, dirt, water, fertilizer. The terrain underfoot was all knee-deep muck, black and thick. It would suck your toes right off your feet.

Mosquitoes were so thick that any bare skin would turn black with them in seconds. Massive amounts of repellant and full-length clothing were mandatory. Since full-length clothing is highly suspicious on anyone in Florida during the summer, we had to change in transit.

Despite these obstacles, the crop got planted and thrived through the summer under our meticulous and tender care. We weren't taking any unnecessary chances, and prior experience had taught us that wild animals also prized our lush, green stand of weed. The stand was made of chicken wire on all sides, so that only our hands, with their opposable thumbs, could access the secured barrier.

Or so we thought. Harvest time was fast approaching, and our anticipation swelled as harvest time drew near. The lush green of our lovingly tended plants was giving way to the purple, red, and yellow hues of maturity, and so we headed out for our last sortie into mosquito hell. This time there was no need for heavy water jugs or bags of dirt. Our labors would soon be repaid in full. Ready the bongs. This time we were coming back to party down.

Raccoons are clever and resourceful bandits, which is why I guess they have little masks on their faces. What makes them particularly successful are their front paws, which have opposable thumbs, enabling them to pry open shellfish, trash can lids, and chicken-wire cages.

That is exactly what we found when we arrived at our clandestine pot farm: one very stoned raccoon, stuffed to the gills and sound asleep on his back, lying inside the chicken-wire cage and surrounded by the stumps and scattered leaves of our former dope plants. While we were quite upset, it was obvious we'd been had. The blissful look on that raccoon's face said it all: "It was good dope and I enjoyed it quite a bit. Thank you."

The Duck

FRANK ATWOOD

We stopped at a store in Big Bear for some drinks. Things were just fine at first. One friend went into the store for drinks, the other was rummaging around in the van, and I was tripping on the outasight blue sky and toking on some hash. Suddenly my friend whispered, "The Man is coming."

I kept toking on the bowl of hash and whispered back to him, "But I ain't done yet." He freaked and went around the van to head off the cop when this duck walked between him and the cop. I got the distinct feeling that this cop believed he had to save this duck from the long-hairs. Don't think the duck felt the same way. My other friend came out of the store with our drinks, so I glanced over at him. When I turned my attention back to the cop saving the duck from the freaks, I simply fell over laughing.

Fuckin' duck was chasing the pig down the road! Yes, really. The cop would run a few steps, the duck would sort of cock its head to snap at the cop's foot, the cop would jump in the air to click his heels together like Dorothy in *The Wizard of Oz*, and then land and run a few more steps. Of course, we were cheering the duck wholeheartedly. I don't think I ever saw a funnier sight. Needless to say, the whole store was watching, so we got the fuck out of there. Still, every once in a while, as we journeyed down the mountain, we'd simultaneously burst out laughing, one of us making quacking noises, as our collective conscious envisioned the cop running down the road clicking his heels.

The Finches

In 1988, my husband and I moved to the canyon lands in Central California. Our closest neighbor was a retired fisherman who owned ten acres of scrub brush on which sat a nice old farmhouse and a commercial greenhouse. Richard was his name and he had lived a colorful life with fascinating stories about the movie studios in Hollywood, leaving there to fish the sea in Northern California, a stint in prison (we didn't ask), and the usual macho talk about kicking people's butts.

Richard had a German temper and more of a grimace than a smile. He loved to get on the subject of the Holocaust, and his eyes would bulge while he told us that the Germans would never, ever have exterminated anyone and that the story was a myth.

He really believed this. He would inevitably fire himself up so badly he'd start running around his property, kicking the cars in his old rotten collection on the rear ends. He had about fifty cars, trucks, and tractors that didn't run and had large dents or broken windows.

Richard also loved to smoke pot. We considered how he would act if he *didn't* smoke it. Luckily, he had given up alcohol years before. After we'd known him a few months, he took us out back to his greenhouse. He had five hundred marijuana plants neatly placed in rows. It was April and the plants were about two feet high. He was telling us that he'd been really busy knocking down all the bird nests near the ceiling of the greenhouse. The little finches got in through the gap between the walls and the ceiling. We admired his plants and then walked home discussing the risk of growing so much pot.

The next day we saw Richard jumping around his yard like an ape in heat. He was yelling and literally flipping out. We thought maybe he'd had another conversation about the Holocaust, but it turned out to be much worse.

Apparently, the little finches were panic-stricken when they had discovered their nests destroyed, and they had worked overtime pulling out all of Richard's seedlings to rebuild their homes. They had even used some of the threads on his blue flannel shirt that he had left hanging on a hook in the greenhouse.

Richard was livid. He was beyond livid. He was freaking. We approached him as he was about to destroy the bird nests again with a long pole. We talked him out of knocking down the new nests. The birds were done building, so why not leave them alone and let them hatch their eggs? They wouldn't bother any more seedlings.

So, Richard replanted his crop, and both he and the finches lived happily ever after. When the season was over, Richard gave us one of the nests made of pot and a blue flannel shirt. We still have the nest and it's quite a conversation piece.

Gerbil Power

KEN MCINTOSH

One late fall Michigan weekend in 1973, on our way to Saginaw, Pam and I stopped in to visit some friends of mine in Ann Arbor. I had met them at a Free John Sinclair rally and kept up the contact. They had been members of the White Panther Party, which, on its way to oblivion, had changed its name to the Rainbow People's Party.

Darby and Lee had a huge apartment in one of those rundown Victorian houses that seemed to be endemic to midwestern college towns. Their place was as messy as most places rented by career undergraduate stoners are wont to be. Most of the furniture was second- and thirdhand, except, of course, the stereo, which was state of the art. The décor consisted of lots of books, dope paraphernalia, burned-out candles, incense residue, and dead or dying plants. Dirty clothes were scattered everywhere, and posters and graffiti covered the walls.

The kitchen walls, though, were slick with grease. The refrigerator held a couple of beers, a couple of shriveled-up carrots, and some other stuff covered with a blue mold patina. The sink contained every eating, drinking, or cooking implement or vessel they owned, plus a colony of cockroaches, thriving on the food residue and dripping faucet. The bathroom was so fetid that both Pam and I decided to hold it until we stopped for gas later. Every room was badly painted a different color. The living room was black. This black room was where the stereo and albums were and, surprise, the black lights and Day-Glo posters of Jimi Hendrix, the Grateful Dead, and the recommended astrological sexual positions. Pillows were festooned about the room, which was dominated by a corded oval area rug and the biggest circular Naugahyde ottoman I have ever seen. The room was lit (it's hard to think of black lights as being illumination) by candles and gerbil power.

Darby, it seems, had once been an electrical engineering major, way back in the mists of time when his academic career first began. The day after his strobe light broke, he had turned a rodent wheel into a small dynamo and hooked up a light bulb. Then he went out and bought a gerbil, which he ensconced in a large, cracked-glass aquarium. The gerbil was quickly named Lemmeoutahere because that's all he kept trying to do the first few days in his new domicile. We called him Lem.

Darby would put the dynamo wheel in with Lem to entertain visitors. He did so for Pam and me. The twenty-five-watt bulb was soon flickering away. After a couple of minutes of this, Pam asked to pet the cute little fella. Darby retrieved Lem and placed him in Pam's palm. Pam sniffed while she cooed at him. When she tried to pet his cute little head with a free finger, he bit her. Pam screamed. Lem hopped off her hand onto the floor and disappeared. We examined the damaged digit and found no blood, just a tiny red spot. Darby again assured her that Lem was really no threat and that Lem had just been sampling the salt on her skin. Pam was relieved and a little embarrassed at her reaction to the nip. Lee told us he had the perfect balm for her injury. He had just scored some Nepalese temple balls.

We huddled around the ottoman for a Himalayan high. Pam, crossing her legs, reminded me pointedly about our need to stop for gas. I must confess that I was more concerned about trying the gooey hash than Pam's bladder. Lee was twisting off a goodly portion of a ball and placing it in a hookah. Lee sat the diminished temple ball down on a serving tray beside the pipe. We each grabbed a hose and started sucking.

After a couple of tokes, Pam's bladder signals lost intensity as she settled into a comfortable buzz. She didn't like pot, but she absolutely loved hash, for some reason a fairly common trait among distaff mid-western heads. We three guys started talking about our shared political past while we all drank some fresh cider from Dixie cups and filled Pam in on the things that I had failed to mention during the drive up U.S. 23 from Ohio.

While we rapped, listened to Pink Floyd, and sipped the pressed apple nectar, we would occasionally catch brief glimpses of Lem as he hopped around the room. Suddenly, Lem jumped up onto the ottoman to every-one's delight. He hopped around the periphery, sniffing at each of us in turn. It was quite charming. He then stopped by a burning candle set in some driftwood and sniffed the air, standing high on his rear legs, resting one forepaw on the wood to steady himself. Obviously catching a whiff of something specific, he hunkered down, rotated about forty-five degrees, and made a beeline for the hash. He grabbed the ball in his forepaws, turning it like corn on the cob, and nibbled away for a few seconds.

Lee retrieved the hash and we all waited for Lem's reaction. Lem was masticating earnestly as he moved away from the serving tray. He hopped very slowly to the edge of the ottoman in front of Darby and just lay down. Darby scooped Lem up, petted him tenderly, and placed him gently into his litter material. Darby assured us that Lem would be fine. It seems Lem had done things like this before, and, if his past behavior was any indication, he would quickly sleep it off. Pam and I got up and went over to check Lem out. He seemed to be peacefully sleeping.

We sat back down and took a few more tokes. I talked Lee into selling me some of the hash. We were all famished at this point, but there was no food in the house, so I offered to pop for dinner. We all rose to leave, putting our coats on. While Lee and I completed our transaction, Darby and Pam chatted. Pam was giving me a strained smile and crossing and uncrossing her legs. Just as we were about to depart, the twenty-five-watt bulb started flickering again in the black room.

We all rushed over to the aquarium. Lem appeared in fine fettle. The flicker became a steady glow. I imagined Lem fleeing the THC snake pursuing him with all his strength. We all clucked at Lem. Lee gave him a little power salute and whispered, "Right on."

Pam and I left with plans to meet up with Darby and Lee at a restaurant after getting a motel room for the night. About a block from the boys' house, Pam made me stop by a small stand of trees. She ran into the woods to relieve herself. That supper was the last time I saw Darby.

I ran into Lee a year or so later in a commune. It was called Rainbow's End, named for a Doors' song, and run by deflated former radicals. When

I asked after Lem, Lee told me that Lem had been mauled to death by a stray cat that had gotten into the house the summer after Pam's and my visit. Darby had then gotten another gerbil he named Rommel, the Desert Rat. Lee assured me that Darby had reformed in regard to his treatment of rodents and that, as far as Lee knew, Darby had kept Rommel straight.

Unfolding the Quantum Butterfly

RAY TESLA

So my brain unfolded in April of 2001 and I went into a higher dimension. Mystic experiences are often discussed as if they're the soul province of mountain-sitting Tibetan monks and the delusional, but the world's not so exclusive sometimes. The agony and the ecstasy can hit you anywhere, anytime, and leave you just as fast.

I thought I was locked out of the club myself until a gigantic quantum butterfly opened its wings in my parietal lobe and, for a few hours, I lived in a limitless reality where there was no such thing as time. That tends to change how you look at daily existence. It remains one of the happiest experiences of my life.

Just like everyone thinks before this kind of thing happens to them, I didn't believe in visions.

I was in the dorms in college; I'd been having one of the best weeks ever, studying journalism and Tae Kwon Do and lying in the sun with my friends and just dopily grinning all day long. It seemed to be leading up to something.

I'd smoked with some of my friends early in the day; it's been my experience that pot tends to both sensitize the self and to exaggerate the emotions, for better or worse, but marijuana does *not* spontaneously create sensations like the following one. This was not a drug experience. This was something else.

I was alone in my room, typing at the computer, and something hit me. I was suddenly overflowing with ecstasy and euphoria. I could barely contain all of it; I was sitting in my chair and I could suddenly *see* the sense of linear time in my brain as a physical thing.

It was like I could see the clusters of neurons where I stored my associations with the idea of "time." It was an aggregate of associations and beliefs, all of the images I associated with linear time—ventilation shafts, rivers, roads, metal corridors—and they all added up to an image that appeared in the shape of a snake or a worm. I also perceived that either it wasn't meant to be there, almost as if it was a parasite—put there by somebody or something—or that it was something that I had outgrown.

I decided to approach it shamanically, to work with it, to see what it wanted. Could it be a caterpillar, I wondered, just waiting to become something higher, more evolved? With a bit of coaxing, will, and imagination, this proved true.

I hatched it in my imagination and suddenly I could see it like a huge, shimmering cross between a butterfly and a quantum cloud. It fluttered slowly, and I was suddenly struck by the depth, the texture of the world: the infinite possibilities of interaction between myself and everything around me.

Imagine being a character in a two-dimensional TV show that suddenly remembers that he's an actor in the three-dimensional world. I remembered, I think, a higher dimension. I was suddenly able to see the moment, the infinite possibilities around me, that I really could do anything once I had sloughed off the chains of narrative and linear time.

I saw my friends in the hall, and when I embraced and talked to them, it was like light dancing into itself—infinite love with no suspicion or hesitance. I was operating as a full human being, not imposing limits. It was love light, love light.

I went out into the sun. It's a blur from there. Love light.

After a day or so, it faded, slowly at first, and then altogether, as I slipped back into the old patterns, still radically altered but without that catastrophic bliss overload, leaving me trying to piece together what had happened so that I could get back to that state.

The psychic trigger was the growing realization, extrapolated from my martial arts work, that both the past, and even more so the future, are fictions that we use to limit ourselves. The problem isn't how we interpret the past, it's that we think we can see the future and predict future events, which amounts to locking ourselves in chains. We labor in our minds over what we can and can't do, which is laziness. It's not up to us to determine the results of our actions; it's up to the world. Otherwise, we're fastening our ankles to stones and not living human lives. I wanted to eradicate the idea of the future in my mind. Then the situation would really become clear and action that much freer and truer.

I remain altered. It was this experience that really awakened the feeling that I had an energy field, for lack of a better term. I also began to walk around with a constant, low-grade feeling of physical euphoria, which, although nowhere near as overwhelming as the original experience, remains present. It also awakened basic psychic abilities; that is, I soon realized that in conversation with other people, the most important thing wasn't what was being said, but the intent in each person's mind, that what each person was thinking was just as important to good communication as what was being said—if not more important. Several other revelations followed; it was one of several experiences I had that year in which I could step back and say, "I've grown up."

Also, it suddenly dawned on me why so many postadolescent girls get butterfly tattoos.

Months later, I startlingly found references to the experience I'd had in literature. In the 1910 story "The Surgeon" by the Hungarian writer, doctor, and opiate addict Géza Csáth, translated into English in 1980, a neurosurgeon talks to an acquaintance in an absinthe café:

> I have found time in the brain. It doesn't differ externally from an ordinary brain cell. Yet it's the nucleus of misery, sickness, the senseless sorrow of passing on. It can be quantitatively greater in one man than another. It elaborates its appendages, it branches and forks like a polyp into the fresh and healthy brain—hence into every aspect of our thoughts.
>
> Of course, this is a great task for the surgeon, but it's absolutely simple. All we have to know is what to cut. I know it. And I'll offer my discovery to the man who wishes above all to be rid of time, who is borne down by the idea of passing

on . . . I just spoon out this evil hornet's nest of human grief. In a few minutes the whole thing's finished. I hand the time cells round in a dish . . .

I waken the fellow . . . This is the man of the future, the really new man who's able to solve today's secrets and tomorrow's truth with his fresh clean brain. He has total recall because facts don't pass away for him—they line themselves up as equal powers in his consciousness . . . Time has exhausted itself! All of the psychic energy stolen from us by the silent madness of mortality is left over for us in the form of tremendous life-energy.

Csáth also suggests this would lead to immortality! But my view was that time wasn't so hardwired, more of a new arrival on the scene, a fictional concept created by society and only enforced on Western perceptions shortly before the Industrial Revolution. As the anarchist writer John Zerzan has said, "Cause-and-effect exists, time doesn't."

Then, from the notorious and brilliant Aleister Crowley, in *Liber LXV* *(Liber Cordis Cincti Serpente)*:

I am the Heart; and the Snake is entwined
About the invisible core of the mind.
Rise, O my snake! It is now the hour
Of the hooded and holy ineffable flower.
Rise, O my snake, into brilliance of bloom . . .

Much of Crowley's writings, like a lot of more recent psychology, philosophy, and social movements, spoke to the idea that man is an unrealized being and that there are concrete techniques to evolve to a higher level. *Liber LXV* is a poetic account of that process of evolution, and what is described above—the opening of the snake into the flower—is the very first passage.

Robert Anton Wilson, the novelist and consciousness theorist, had this to say about one of Crowley's drawings from *The Book of Thoth*: "The serpent is the rising of the Kundalini serpent, a Hindu metaphor for imprinting this Circuit V neurosomatic bliss-control . . . Temporary neurosomatic consciousness can be acquired by (a) the yoga practice of pranayama breathing and (b) for those who can handle it, by ingestion of cannabis drugs, such as hashish and marijuana, which trigger neurotransmitters that activate this circuit."

I didn't find these texts until several months after my experience. It was a stunning early introduction to the strange world of inner space. And it certainly encouraged me to continue to peel the lid off that inner space and keep looking, for years to come.

Political Protest

Blessing in Disguise

JACK HERER

I was thirty years old when I first started smoking pot. That was the summer of 1969, and my life would never be the same. Everything was immeasurably enhanced—eating food, making love, listening to music—so it was completely understandable that I started dealing pot in the spring of 1970. Four years later, "Captain" Ed Adair, my ally in the marketing of counterculture posters, tie-dyed clothes, and general head gear, insisted that we take a joint oath: "We swear by our life and our love for it that we will work every day of our lives, all day, all night, to legalize pot—until we're dead, or it's legal, or we can quit when we've turned eighty-four."

The more I learned about marijuana and the suppressed history of hemp, the angrier I became that I had never heard any of it during my entire formal and informal education. In May 1980, I began a series of protests on the front lawn of the Los Angeles Federal Building in Westwood that would last for as many as one hundred days at a time. The demonstrators fed, clothed, and provided portable bathrooms for petitioners who were attempting to get legalization initiatives on the local and state ballots.

On the flagpole, we hung a huge marijuana-leaf flag underneath the American flag. The local and federal police were friendly and trusting. Often, instead of busting drunks, they would drop them off to sober up with the pot protesters.

One morning in January 1981, President-Elect Ronald Reagan came to Westwood. It was five days before his inauguration, and he needed a haircut from his favorite barber. With his entourage of Secret Service agents, Reagan visited the Federal Building.

"You're doing a fine job," he told the manager, "and I want you to know that you can bring any of your problems to us. Incidentally, why are those Canadians down on the lawn?"

Reagan had mistaken the five-pointed hemp leaf for the maple leaf that is featured on the Canadian flag.

"They're not Canadians," said the building manager. "Those are the marijuana protesters, and they live down there twenty-four hours a day."

"Well," said Reagan, "I'll be on the job in a few days, and I'll see what I can do for you."

That dialogue was reported by one of the secretaries in the manager's office who happened to support the initiative. In the evenings after work, she got high with the demonstrators and let them take showers at her home.

A week later, after only two days in office, amid celebrating the return of the State Department hostages from Iran, Reagan reissued a World War II anti-sabotage act that had originally been passed in 1943 as a wartime measure to prohibit anyone, such as saboteurs, from being on federal property after regular business hours. So six of us were arrested for registering voters on federal property after dark.

Arrested, that is, for patriotism above and beyond the call of duty.

Unlike the five others, I refused to accept a year of unsupervised probation and pay the maximum fine of $5. (That was the original amount specified; the law was reenacted so hastily that federal authorities had neglected to adjust the fine for inflation.)

In court, Federal Judge Malcolm Lucas—a Richard Nixon appointee, later named chief justice of the California Supreme Court by his former law partner, then-Governor George Deukmejian—asked the supervising officer, "Now, what were these people doing there all night long?"

"Registering voters and listening to music."

"Oh? What kind of music?"

"Things like the Grateful Dead."

Whereupon the judge suddenly stood up and roared, "I threw my own son out of the house in 1975 for listening to them. As far as I'm concerned, the Grateful Dead would be better off appreciably deceased!"

He then sentenced me to fourteen days in jail.

In my defense, I told Judge Lucas, "I can't think of a higher honor that I could ever have in my life than going to jail for registering voters after dark on federal property at the busiest intersection in the country. If I'm not willing to do that, how can I call myself an American?"

I appealed my conviction all the way to the U.S. Supreme Court, but they wouldn't hear the case. In July 1983, I did my time in Terminal Island Federal Prison. It was the best thing that ever happened to me. I had never been given the opportunity to write so clearly and without interruption.

In that dreary cell, I composed an outline for a comprehensive book about hemp, which I called *The Emperor Wears No Clothes* after the Hans Christian Anderson fable in which the emperor gives his gold to swindling tailors to be made into fabric for his imperial robes, but it is stolen. I saw a metaphor there for the U.S. government. It struck me as the perfect analogy for creating laws against hemp/marijuana. The most useful plant would become the most criminal.

And, to extend the metaphor, "only those with pure eyes could see that the clothes were not made of gold."

I scribbled notes in my jail cell based on treatises I had written and published about hemp entitled *Everything You Should've Learned About Marijuana, But Weren't Taught in School.* That outline turned into the first edition of *Emperor,* which I published in 1985.

Without major distributors, wholesalers, advertising, or reviews, the book became an underground best seller: four hundrde thousand copies were promptly sold in the United States, mostly on college campuses during my hemp tours in the late '80s and early '90s; two hundred fifty thousand copies of translated editions were sold in Germany (one hundred fifty thousand), France, England, Italy, Japan, and Australia, with more translations scheduled for Spain, Poland, and Greece.

My partner in hemp, Captain Ed Adair, died in 1991.

Three years later, when I was presented with an award for activism at the annual conference of the Drug Policy Foundation—a respectable drug-reform organization based in Washington, D.C., which had previously given awards to former presidential candidate George McGovern and economist Milton Friedman—I delivered my acceptance speech in a green 100 percent hemp suit, a hemp shirt and tie, hemp hat and sneakers, and underneath was the same hemp T-shirt that I wear every day (one of an identical dozen), proclaiming, HEMP: HELP ELIMINATE MARIJUANA PROHIBITION and on the flip side, HEMP FOR THE OVERALL MAJORITY FOR EARTH'S PAPER, FIBER, FUEL.

I said that I was accepting my award for Captain Ed, too. However, I neglected to thank Ronald Reagan.

Postscript: At the annual Cannabis Cup in Amsterdam, a new strain of marijuana, four years in development, was christened "Jack Herer." He mused, "Long after I've died, people will be smoking Jack Herer." He died in April 2010 at age seventy. On the first anniversary of his death, *High Times* asked its readers: "Should 4/20 be renamed Jack Herer Day?"

For and Against

RUTH STRASSBERG

My memory's a little (a lot) fuzzy on the details, but I know it happened in the early '70s (possibly late '60s) since it was a combination smoke-in and Vietnam protest in New York City. Who knows, you may have been there, and I wouldn't be surprised if other people send you this story.

I can't remember if it started from Washington Square or Central Park, up Fifth Avenue, smoking pot, to protest in front of Attorney General John Mitchell's apartment on Fifth Avenue and a street in the eighties. I believe it was probably from Washington Square because I remember a very long walk and all of us being very stoned.

I believe Abbie Hoffman was our leader, but even that detail has faded with the years and billows of pot smoke. We were so stoned, in fact, that we went several blocks too far and had to backtrack to the Mitchell's apartment. And, no, John Mitchell didn't make an appearance, but Martha stuck her head out the window.

Students for a Democratic Society

JOHN JOHNSON

Great, now I have to relive those times. In 1966 or so, we had an SDS office on Hyperion in Silver Lake. I was rooming with Mike Klonsky a couple of blocks away. People would come in from around the country and crash there. Other locals would hang out a lot.

One guy decided to store four kilos of grass under the house. Mike found out about it (the house was in his name) and told the guy he was an idiot and to get the dope out of there. I did not know about this.

That night Mike and I are at home, and a bottle full of liquid crashes through our window (we were on the second floor of a house). We had been getting right-wing threats and a lot of police and FBI harassment at the time. So I thought we were under attack.

Mike and I stayed up the rest of the night with a shotgun. Around 5:00 AM, I hear a car slowly coming up our hill. Couldn't see it. As it gets to our house, I ready the shotgun. Something comes flying out of the car. It was the *Los Angeles Times* being delivered. Obviously, the guy Mike told off was the person who threw the Coke bottle through our window. He heard about this shotgun incident and fled the city.

Barry and the Burning Question

MICHAEL SIMMONS

White House Drug Czar General Barry McCaffrey announced the Institute of Medicine's report on medical marijuana at the Community Coalition Center in South-Central Los Angeles on March 17, 1999. The two-year, million-bucks IOM study has something for everybody, from red-eyed legalizers to grim-faced antidrug warriors. The drug czar gave an overview of the study and opened up the floor for questions from the press.

Yours truly, though tired of debating what ought to be a nonissue but has continued to report on it because *medical marijuana is about sick people*, leapt to his feet and breathlessly reiterated the study's conclusions:

"Two and a half years ago you said there's no evidence that shows that smoked marijuana is either useful or needed. According to the science in this report, more patients found that oral THC, or Marinol, which was once heralded, is more disorienting than smoked marijuana, which we've been told by advocates for years . . . that smoked marijuana does supply relief for certain patients . . . that there are benefits for easing anxiety, i.e., getting stoned . . . for some patients, such as the terminally ill, long-term risks are not of great concern . . . the adverse effects of marijuana are within the range of effects tolerated for other medicines . . . that there's no proof of immunosuppressive . . . no conclusive evidence that marijuana is carcinogenic . . . "

As I sputtered on, the vein in the generalissimo's temple began to protrude and he cut me off.

"I can read the report. If you will, please ask the question."

I laughed, apologized, and continued. "What I'm saying is that the report seems to support everything that medical marijuana advocates have been saying for the last two and a half years and yet at the very end there's this obtuse statement: 'Until a nonsmoked, rapid-onset cannabinoid drug delivery system becomes available, we acknowledge that there's no clear alternative for people suffering from chronic conditions that might be relieved by smoking marijuana, such as pain or AIDS wasting . . . '"

"Please, if you will, get to the question," repeated the czar, gently but firmly.

I resumed, undaunted. "Until a rapid-onset nonsmokeable delivery system is developed—of course, there are vaporizers that exist—but until a system is developed that makes everyone happy, what happens to the patients who are sick, dying, are in jail or awaiting trial, who say that smokeable marijuana is the only thing between them and pain or suffering and life or death?"

I'd never seen a general dance until McCaffrey waltzed around my question. "What I need to do is stand firmly behind the report. Go read the report and take from it what the authors' conclusions are—we support them." He went on to call for more cannabinoid study and to deny that marijuana is medicine. He also generously emphasized that the smoking of marijuana for any reason is "a legitimate discussion in and of itself. I think democratic societies ought to be able to talk about whether they want to have smoked marijuana available. But it's a separate issue."

I actually agreed with him on the last point, but I was frustrated. "You didn't answer my question. What about patients who say that smoked marijuana is the only thing that works for them and saves their lives?"

He deferred to Dr. Don Vereen from his own Office of National Drug Control Policy. Dr. Vereen basically said that anecdotal testimony is not science. After answering a few more queries from reporters, McCaffrey headed to the exit.

I chased after him and once again repeated my mantra: "The patients and doctors who say that smokeable marijuana . . . "

He was clearly not going to respond. "I've already answered that question. NIH, FDA, American Medical Association will examine this report, and it opens the line to scientific inquiry."

In a proverbial puff he was gone, my question remained unanswered, and in spite of the enormity of the IOM report, sick people are still subject to handcuffs, prison time—and even death—for using the oldest rapid-onset cannabinoid delivery system known to humankind.

[*Originally published in* High Times *in 1999.*]

Police and Politicians Foil Proposition 215

LANNY SWERDLOW, RN

How has California descended into such depraved lawlessness that the feds have come in to restore order? This is not like Alabama where the feds intervened to end desegregation—it is more like the 1894 Pullman Strike when the U.S. government sent marshals and troops to break the strike and destroy the unions.

The lack of objection by state officials to the federal government acting like a raging bull in a china shop with its heavy-handed efforts to close medical marijuana collectives is a disgrace. Considering that little effort has been expended by the Obama administration on the fraud and multiple violations of federal laws by Wall Street bankers, the intense focus on wiping California's legal medical marijuana collectives off the face of the earth is puzzling at best.

Until you understand who is behind this and how it got started.

In November 1996, California voters passed Proposition 215, which allowed the use of marijuana medicinally. The police did not like this law. At a meeting in December 1996, organized by then-Attorney General Dan Lungren, law enforcement met, not to work to implement the law passed by the voters, but to *undo* it.

They didn't do much for the first eight years other than arrest a few patients and shut down some large grow operations. Their actions keep marijuana pretty much underground just like it was before 1996.

In 2004 came Senate Bill 420, which allows patients to associate collectively and cooperatively to cultivate marijuana. Although there is much disagreement as to just what it actually means, it did give patients some kind of a legal way to obtain their medicine.

Collectives formed with many choosing to operate a store as their method of distributing the medicine to their members. This makes sense, as stores are how this country gets the vast bulk of goods distributed. When the police saw stores opening up, they were mortified and sprang into action.

The California Chiefs of Police Association issued a white paper in 2009 falsely maligning collectives as agents of crime and degradation. It came complete with a sample ordinance with the novel idea that cities could locally repeal a state law, such as allowing patients to form collectives, by banning its implementation under their zoning ordinances.

Throughout the state, police went to city councils and county boards, and, using the white paper as proof of the problem, inundated them with false stories of crime, youth degradation, and neighborhood deterioration.

Not used to having their police lie to them, elected officials, out of concern for their communities, enacted the bans on medical marijuana collectives that the police wanted.

Collective operators and patients fought back. State law allows patient collectives, and many believed a state law cannot be undone by banning it. With no regulations in place and patients needing a legal source of medicine, collectives began opening up all over the place.

Police were now totally mortified, as their worst nightmare was happening right under their noses. A thousand or more marijuana collectives using stores as their distribution system had opened throughout the state. As far as the cops were concerned, it was marijuana legalization with a doctor's recommendation.

Cities, cops, and patients took their disagreements to court with mixed results for all of them. Cops are not used to losing or even compromising. They got tired of waiting and, with having lost more court cases than they won, called in their biggest gun—the federal cops. *Yes, they called them in.* The *Los Angeles Times* reported the following in an October 2011 story about the feds intervention: "[U.S. Attorney Andre] Birotte said the new strategy was not triggered by any specific event but was inspired by a stream of complaints from California law enforcement officials."

People are upset by giant corporations and billionaires controlling our government. Frankly, cops controlling government is even scarier. For police to work to overturn a law enacted by the voters, especially on the taxpayers' dime, is disingenuous and dangerous.

The residents of California have seen the extreme measures the police will go to to get their way as they witness the invasion by the *federal* government to arrest, prosecute, and jail the state into submission.

Along with medical marijuana patients throughout the nation, I believed Barack Obama during the 2008 campaign when he said, "What I'm *not* going to be doing is using Justice Department resources to try to circumvent state [medical marijuana] laws."

It was his statements that led many to campaign and work for his election. It was his statements that led medical-marijuana advocates to believe that if he was elected, he would allow the states that have enacted medical marijuana laws to go ahead with their programs—the kind of the social experimental laboratory that states are supposed to be. Along with thousands of others, I took Obama at his word and to the best of my ability went about the convoluted process of providing patients with legal marijuana. I invested my savings, and, even though I knew it endangered my freedom, I trusted him.

If he had not made these promises during the campaign, I doubt if many of the people who opened collectives would have done so. I know I wouldn't have. Because I believed in the "change" candidate Obama promised to implement, I now find my life upside down, unbearably stressful and threatening to my physical, mental, and financial health.

I had pinned great hopes on President Obama and was emboldened by Attorney General Eric Holder's memo issued in 2009 stating that the feds would steer clear of states that had passed medical marijuana laws. We took the memo as a partial fulfillment of Obama's campaign pledge that he was not going to be "using Justice Department resources to try to circumvent state [medical marijuana] laws."

I was now confident enough to help form a medical-marijuana collective that utilized a unique farmers' market model of medicinal-marijuana distribution capable of providing over six thousand medical-marijuana patients with marijuana safely, reliably, locally, and more affordably. Now I, like other operators, am under attack by the feds. I'm facing a five-year mandatory minimum sentence for distributing marijuana to qualified California patients as well as bankruptcy since the IRS does not allow any business expenses to be deducted on our taxes.

I just don't understand why President Obama has decided to be an all-out drug warrior by sending the feds in. He didn't have to—and I don't buy that the invasion was beyond his control. If he can end the war in Iraq, he can end the war in California.

Sixteen states and the District of Columbia have legalized medicinal marijuana, and that represents close to a third of the population of the United States. Obama has cast himself as a problem solver—as a president who brings people together to iron out differences so there is no need for fear or violence. He will send emissaries or even go himself all over the world to promote self-determination and to try to prevent conflict.

Here in California, it is President Obama who is causing the fear and the violence, or at the very least not ending it when it is within his ability to do so.

Whatever problems we are having in California with our medical-marijuana laws, we are perfectly capable of solving them ourselves. We do not need any federal help and we certainly don't need it in the form of federal law enforcement coming into our state threatening landlords with seizure of their property and state and local employees with arrest, prosecution, and imprisonment for implementing their state's medical-marijuana laws.

The big question is why did he authorize the federal invasion, and if he didn't, why is he not ending it? Why is he breaking his campaign promises?

I have heard a lot of theories. The pharmaceutical and alcohol beverages industries stand to lose billions if marijuana is legalized, which would result in millions of lost campaign contributions. Even more important is the theory surrounding law enforcement. Petrified at the thought of

losing the $20-billion-a-year, taxpayer-funded, full-employment mari-
juana prohibition program, they are promising their re-election support,
or at least not supporting his Republican opposition.

The local cops calling in the feds is trickle-up. Obama allowing it to
happen is trickle-down. The federal invasion would not have happened
if local police had not requested federal assistance. The federal invasion
would not have happened if Obama had told Attorney General Holder
to stop it.

Whatever the reason, it really doesn't matter. What does matter is
that he broke a campaign promise that many believed and acted on, and
his failure to follow through on his campaign statements has ruined
their lives and made miserable the hundreds of thousands of California
medical-marijuana patients who depend on people like me to provide
them with marijuana as permitted under California state law.

The change Barack Obama promised never came, and in the case
of medical-marijuana patients, his broken promise has ruined my life
and the lives of thousands of medical-marijuana providers, and brought
dismay and fear to the medical-marijuana community.

Warning: Trusting cops and politicians can be hazardous to your
health.

Sentimental Journeys

The Undoing of Matilda

ROY TUCKMAN

The felonious smoke drifted brazenly into the skies of downtown Los Angeles. I, the imbiber of the holy weed, drifted lightly into the confused interior of myself. The feeling of smoking freely, and privately, in the middle of a workday, in direct line of sight of tens of thousands of people, was a strange mixture of self-congratulatory respect for my courage, fear of the criminal act I was performing in "the belly of the beast," and profound gratitude for the beauty of the sunlight reflecting off the skyscrapers and the wonder of existence.

It was my lunch hour, a rigidly defined period of time in this civil service environment. Yes, I was into the whole thing with house, tie, freeway commute, and, of course, a comfortable salary and future. Financial future, that is. The other part was bleak. The so-called '60s, for me and others, was not a celebration of peace and love with hearts and flowers. Added to the mix was Vietnam and so many political assassinations. In the mix was the realization that all our major political leaders considered us the enemy. We were threatening *"their America."* But of course it was forgotten that they were destroying us.

Pot is a gateway herb of sorts. It is a gateway into the land where you see for yourself, in your own experience, that your society is a liar. We were already being told that "war is peace" and "black is white." And so, many sought to supplant this fallen leadership. And there were choices to make that our parents would not have dreamed of. And now, after two and a half years of psychiatric drugs and a radical squarization process, I was contacting the memory of the acid-inspired insights of the past to ask for a judgment on my life. Matilda helped me with the answer.

Matilda was the bane of the office. She was an attractive woman who strove to live up to the stereotype of the "hot Latina." Before you start

salivating, let me add that there was no sexual component to her tempera-
ture. But she was professional in her ability to stop the office cold with
her shrieks and cries, brought on by the least perceived slight or criticism
or any of the other slings and arrows that jobs are prey to. And with this
emotionalism, Matilda ruled the office from her secretary's desk, rattling
at will even the second-in-command of the entire department. I don't
recall what it was about me that motivated Matilda to aim at me; I must
have been a quiet and pleasant, if slightly depressed, type.

And I was square, absolutely square. And there was certainly no racial
component in this relationship. My graduate years in anthropology had
specialized in the study of the astounding cultures of Mexico and Central
America and had only the greatest respect for her ancestry. I had climbed
El Castillo in Yucatan (before Raquel Welch) and passed my graduate
Spanish exam at UCLA. I never insulted her, but I never bowed to her
either. I was living with a real woman and considered Matilda's childish
games to be, well, childish games. She probably found that approximately unforgivable. Fortunately, most of my job was out of the office,
so relief was just a few steps away.

I looked at my watch—my schizophrenic watch, that is. I often told
people that the two shimmering spider turquoise stones ornamenting
the band were a second watch, telling the real time, which is always Now.
But my chronometer dictated that it was time for me to go back to work.
So I disposed of the rest of the joint—in those days it was by eating the
rest of the marijuana but not (usually) the paper—and left the roof of
my downtown office building, descended the stairs, washed my hands,
combed my short hair, straightened my tie, and sat down in my shared
office cubicle with my papers and adding machine.

Matilda came prancing down the office aisle, carrying a load of three-
by-five cards. She would soon walk past the three-foot-wide entrance to
my cubicle. I sat at my desk in absolute calm, glowing from the rooftop
experiment, and enthusiastically planned the rest of my day and my life.
Then she screamed: "Ohhhhh!"

Matilda had tripped or otherwise slanted her office-supply burden, and a stream of dozens of three-by-five cards slipped out of her hands and all over the floor around my desk and chair. The shrill woman whose pride would have done credit to an Aztec headdress was forced to crawl and grovel all around my office for several minutes.

The victory was too obvious for me to feel any sense of revenge, accomplishment, or satisfaction. I felt compassion for her plight, although, in my memory, my compassion did not extend to actually helping her to pick up the cards. But I was a beginner, as I am now. And there were other cards being dealt, cards foretelling my future and my relationship with marijuana and the meaning of my psychedelic years. In one second, while I was busy in relaxed and joyful contemplation, the number one office problem had been solved for me. Matilda would never again try to goad me. We both knew that the war was over and we had witnessed the final battle. I knew, although she didn't, that I credited the Spirit of the Herb, whatever that was, with this little adventure as a sign that the herb was an ally, not an enemy, and our separation would end.

The Midwife

DEW U. CARE

Oh, I suppose it was a miracle. An act of love that began with a line of poetry, climaxed in the back seat of an economy-size car, and culminated in the birthing of a babe.

The midwife and husband stood at the ready, humbled by the complicated simplicity of the event. Unlike examples of women who'd paused in their daily labor, squatted in a field, commenced with a more personal type of labor, then bit the cord that binds, and, with babe on back, went back to the other labor, Madelaine's had been going on for twenty-three hours.

Perhaps it was because it was her first child. Maybe it was her narrow pelvis. Or perchance the months of abstinence, having given up cigarettes, wine, coffee, pot, dying her hair, and all her favorite clothes, made her unable to give up one more thing. But we can state for a fact that the mother-to-be was not gently glowing and sweetly gasping as in the movies; she was sweating pools and cussing in three different languages. "Fuck! *Mon Dieu*! *Mon Dieu*! Oh, *pinche tu madre*! Help! Oh, I told you that you shouldn't have cut off the end of the condom because it was too long!"

"Breathe," said her life partner gently.

"If you're so damned hot on breathing, *you* breathe!"

"Now, darling, you were great during the Lamaze classes."

"Dr. Lamaze was a man. I want drugs!"

"Now, sugarplum, you were the one who wanted a natural birthing experience."

The friend operating the video camera nodded his head in agreement.

"Why don't you all just die?" the lady was heard to ask (all present gave the lady the benefit of the doubt and assumed the question was rhetorical). The midwife counseled, cajoled, massaged in ointments, wiped the woman's brow with linen dipped in aromatic herbs. She related stories of easier births, then she told of more difficult ones. She recited haiku and Bible verse and African birthing stories. To no avail. The uterus dilated, the contractions increased, as did everyone's frustration. Yet the babe refused to come until, it seemed, conditions known only to it were met.

The midwife consulted with the husband. An ambulance would take the woman to the hospital if the birth was not started soon. This was not the unthinkable alternative it had been just twenty-four hours earlier.

Midwifery is as much an art as a science, and the midwife whispered, promised, cajoled, sang, and massaged some more, for she wanted to be the one to bring the babe into the world. She whispered in the woman's ear, "Let go of the gift and I will roll you a joint the likes of which you've never seen. Not just any joint, but a spliff rolled from the tips of buds grown in *campo sancto* by monks, blessed by a rabbi, and wrapped in organic rice paper by the delicate fingers of an aged Tibetan sage. It's six inches long and as fat as . . . " Here she cast a flirtatious look at the flushed life partner, who, if possible, looked even more bedraggled than his lady love.

"Give it to me now," gasped the poor mother-to-be.

"No, my sweet. No substance shall pass your lips until you deliver what you've brought me here to deliver."

"Don't make me get off this table," yelled the lady.

"No. Only afterward. That is the deal. I don't negotiate. If you have to go to the hospital, you'll be in a cold, sterile environment where the sacred smoke is not welcome, and they serve bad coffee to boot."

And we, gentle reader, will never know if it was the babe's own sweet time, the deity's will, or the promise of some truly righteous weed, but it did come to pass . . . literally, and the mother delivered a beautiful bouncing baby girl.

The midwife made good on her promise and delivered the sacred spliff.

And then the third miracle occurred (the first being the conception, the second the birth)—no one told the mother to pass the joint. And yet she shared the sacred six inches of her own volition.

And what of the babe, hallowed by the halo of sacred smoke? She grew into a wise, brilliant, beautiful, kind, very patient, and calm woman— who likes her wine, her cigarettes, her coffee, and her herb.

The Blind Mime

DEW U. CARE

It was a blind boy who brought me to pot, and I never had the foresight to thank him.

It was my junior year in college and I was floundering about, looking for a major that would carry me through life. As if. But one is young and impressionable, and in my trying out of various guises, I worked with Handicapped Student Services. Part of my job entailed reading to visually impaired students.

My favorite was a boy named Bob. Bob had a "photographic" memory and incredible audio retention. He could hold hundreds of bits of information in his mind at once (i.e., retain a fifty-question multiple-choice quiz, each with five possible selections). A psychology major, Bob also had the ability to generate amazingly original ideas. Add to that a wry sense of humor, a kind heart, and the sweet, good-natured, broad-shouldered "gee, ma'am, are my boots under your bed?" charm the South is known for, and you have Bob.

Sitting on the grass, Bob pulled out a joint. I stared. Then I quickly got over it. Bob could always seem to tell when I was staring.

"But that's illegal," I gasped.

"No, it's okay, really. I use it for medicinal purposes. It keeps me from going blind."

"Ah . . . Bob . . . "

"Yes?"

" . . . um . . . um . . . you *are* blind."

"You're right." Pause. He screams. Other people turn around. Bob continues. "I can't see! I can't see! I'm blind!" People continue to stare. Bob puts his hands in front of him. "No! No! Anything but this!"

It's his Mime in a Box because, in a misguided moment of compassion, I had encouraged him to distract himself from his Humphrey

Bogart and Bob Marley and Bette Davis impressions. How was I to know he'd keep at it? Then he sat down.

"Look," he said, "I've enjoyed pot for five years. I'm getting into grad school. Science, the scientific method, is my forte. Pot has never been proven, after decades and decades of research, to have detrimental attributes. On the contrary. Most scientific and anecdotal evidence leads to the opposite conclusion. The most harmful thing for your body is stress and depression.

"Smoking pot enhances my perceptions and appreciation for the world around me. Okay, maybe I shouldn't pilot an airplane, go through a pregnancy, or perform neurosurgery under it, but you've got my word of honor that I wouldn't dream of doing any of those three things under the influence of THC. Scout's honor."

"Uh, Bob, are you a scout?"

"While I did say 'scout's honor,' I never, by word or deed, only the assumptions you brought, said I was the scout in question."

"But if marijuana was okay, it'd be legal now."

"Segregation was legal in this country until the '50s. Gay legal rights are still iffy. And an amendment that said women were equal was struck down. We do funny things. But I do believe that we're evolving as a species. Continually maturing. By my reckoning, we're in our adolescence. Some day future generations will look back at pot prohibition with the same proper horror with which we view bloodletting."

"But I'm afraid it will interfere with my ambition," I said.

"I've been meaning to tell you, you're a type-A personality. You bite your nails. I can hear you, you know. Shouldn't nibble on the cuticle like that."

I pulled my finger out of my mouth.

"You mean, I'm type-A because I bite my nails?"

"No, you bite your nails because you're type-A." Here he broke off into his Groucho Marx imitation, complete with ashing an imaginary cigar. "And I don't mean a blood type. I mean a tenseness. Let me put it another way. Are you usually the first person on and off an elevator?"

"Yes, why?"

"Even though you know it's not going to move until the last person's on, you'll push and pull and weave and elbow and stand stubbornly in the front?"

"Yes, what's your point?"

"Do you understand how oxymoronic the phrases 'trying to relax,' 'military intelligence,' and 'right-to-work-state' are? Are you the same religion, political affiliation, and economic status as your family?"

Silence reigned as I pulled on the loose hem of my Sears shorts in a charming pastel color.

"Here," he said, "try a hit. Hold it for a bit, exhale gently. Ready, set, go!" And with that he handed me The Torpedo.

First it was the scent that intoxicated me, fresh and vital, musky and straw-like, yet with sweet overtones. Then it was the way the ember flared as I pulled the warm spring air and the smoke into my lungs. The sound of wind blowing through the leaves and grass. I closed my eyes.

I experienced the world through my other senses. I tried to experience the world as Bob did.

Through the years our lives took different roads, and the paths we'd chosen seldom crossed. Bob never did work with the differently abled, as he'd planned then, except as a volunteer. He worked as a lawyer for various progressive causes, his family growing—the last time we met he had a seeing-eye dog in the lead and his youngest taking up the rear in a royal red papoose pack.

"During my act, I tell people I'm their worst fear in a packed airplane—the guy with the kid and the dog."

"You do stand-up?"

"Yeah, I added it to my mime routine. Mime in a Box!"

"How do you find the energy?"

For an answer, he pulled The Torpedo out of his coat pocket.

I looked at him fondly. We'd known each other many moons. I took the spliff and the smoke and the shared memories and held them deep. I closed my eyes. I felt his arm around my shoulders. I sighed with satisfaction. Then I handed him the joint.

"My little pothead," I said. "I think I'll keep him."

The Funeral

DEW U. CARE

As funerals go, I suppose it went well enough. No one threw themselves at the casket, the religious leader I'd rented for the occasion mouthed the words I'd fed him with a passable sincerity, no one barfed at the wake—at least not in the hall itself—and the check I'd written for the whole shebang cleared. All in all, a success—as such things go.

Now, where there's a will, there's a way. Usually your way, my way, Yahweh's, or the highway. Which brings us to the subject of my story, my beloved sister. The good Lord has a sense of humor, no one can take that away from Him, but there has to be a rhyme and reason for the madness around us, and my madness has included going through life as a clone—an identical twin.

I've grown up with a pair of eyes that mirror my own staring back at me, a gallery of similar gestures, a certain stride that marks us—and that's it. My Republican, "free the magic of the marketplace," MBA, lawyer sister is to me like the cream in my coffee (i.e., the scum that rises to the surface). In her patented manner, she lost herself in grief until I'd taken care of the funeral, only to find herself in time for the division of the estate.

I've never minded my sibling's single-minded self-interest. All right, I have, but there's a difference between ideological differences and being dicked over in the particular. We all can't cuddle orphans, pen sonnets, bake bread, comfort the dying. Some of us were made for other things—mergers, acquisitions, takeovers, and litigation, for example. Some of us frolic with the dolphins, and others swim with the sharks. And that's okay—or at least it was until she stole from me. Even then I didn't take it personally. You can only steal what you have access to. And what she had access to was me.

During the probate period, money, stocks, bonds, certificates of deposit, and just about anything worthy of a serial number disappeared as quietly and efficiently as a Central American dissident.

But then the bitch absconded with our parents' wedding bands. Feigning ignorance, she prevaricated, stalled, stonewalled, and flat-out lied. My first impulse was to . . . well, it's pretty much unprintable, and it may be, in fact, a physical impossibility to bend an appendage to an orifice in quite the manner I'd contemplated, so I went for my second impulse. I got stoned.

Then I got her stoned. Now at this stoning, stamina came into play. You just can't compete with a hard-core ounce of red-haired bud a month. I was hitting my stride as she slid under the table. I was wetting my lips with an innocent pink tongue while her parched lips went through contortions. And in exchange for a package of Hostess products and some pizza-flavored potato chips, she caved. It was Jacob and Esau updated. Only, instead of the pot of thick porridge for the birthright, I got her stoned and let her walk away with her integrity—and her life.

"I took the wedding rings," she sobbed, chocolate rimming the corner of her lips, nacho crumbs in the lapels of her Armani.

"Honey, I knew you did."

We hugged. We kissed. In the morning she woke up with a fresh conscience. I had helped her to do the right thing. Sure, I had to weed her up to do it, but as Voltaire said, "Cultivate your garden."

Happily, my garden grows a righteous weed.

The Bostonians: A Pot Family Saga

JOMO RASKIN

When I remember the hordes of marijuana growers I've known in California, I can't help but be reminded of the Bostonians, as I've always called them, because they came from Boston. They were an Irish, working-class, Catholic family, though by the time I met them they had long since stopped going to church or taking communion. I don't mean to say that there was a direct relationship between their ethnicity, family background, and pot. There was none at all. Other growers were Jewish, Protestant, Buddhist, and more. Still, the Bostonians worshipped pot like no one else; pot was their religion, their creed, and their calling. They grew it, harvested it, transported it, sold it, smoked it, talked about it almost all the time, and taught me the ABC's of the industry.

Every spring, they invited all the growers in the vicinity—seventy-five or so—to an outdoor "pagan ritual," as they called it, and urged everyone to bring an ounce or so from the previous year's harvest and burn it on the bonfire that raged all night. The idea behind the ceremonial burning was not to become attached to the herb, but rather to let it go up in smoke. Just sitting around the fire and breathing, we all were stoned. Couples would go off on their own, have sex, come back, smoke weed, and then wander off again for more sex.

All summer long, the Bostonians gave tours of their pot garden; they insisted they had nothing to hide. They talked about cannabis history, cannabis culture, and cannabis botany and smoked dope from dawn to dusk. Of course, they grew their plants outdoors in direct sunlight in a large garden surrounded by sunflowers, corn, fruit trees, and vegetables—all organic. At harvest in the fall, they invited everyone on the mountain to a potluck with mounds of pot as well as a variety of casseroles that were set out on the dining room table.

There was no official competition, and no trophy, just hours and hours of smoking and talking about weed, as wine lovers talk about Pinot Noir or Zinfandel. There was cocaine, too. Without cocaine almost everyone would have gone to sleep or faded away early. No one really cared about the coke; the growers snorted it so that they could keep on smoking pot and comparing notes with one another.

In the story of the Bostonians, there was no happy ending, though they were never arrested, not over the course of several decades. But Mr. Boston turned to meth and had a heart attack—"speed kills." Mrs. Boston's health declined rapidly. She died a slow, painful death.

They were both intelligent and did no harm to the environment, to animals in the forests, or any human beings, except to themselves, and they harbored no evil thoughts either. They built their own home, repaired their own vehicles, kept them running, and read books—everything by Stephen King. Despite their burning rituals, they became attached to the savage god of marijuana. They loved marijuana too much, and more than they loved themselves or their children, who were raised in the cannabis culture and never attended school or received a real education. The Bostonian kids lived isolated lives in the woods, wandered into town and found jobs at McDonald's, or turned to petty crime. After their parents died, they squabbled over the thousands of acres that they inherited—the property their parents bought with hard work and marijuana dollars.

Their family trajectory might have made for a convincing argument about the agony of addiction. They smoked cigarettes, too. I loved them dearly and learned mountains from them about rural living, and so it was sad to see their bodies fall apart, the family implode, and the surrounding community of growers disintegrate. One day, when the drug war is over, I plan to build a monument in their memory. Yes, they did themselves in, but they were also victims of the drug war; I like to think that if there was no pot prohibition and no war on pot farmers, they'd still be alive, still planting, cultivating, harvesting, and leading healthy lives. Hey, Bostonians, may you rest in peace.

[*Excerpted from* Marijuanaland: Dispatches from an American War.]

Disneyland

Peer Pressure

BOB WIEDER

In 1972, I went with a bunch of friends from a Berkeley anarchist collective to Disneyland, where we all got stoned.

There was one slow pseudo-ride called the PeopleMover that was more of an elevated tour of Tomorrowland than an actual attraction. It made two leisurely passes through (and overhead) the spacious Tomorrowland gift shop.

On our first pass, we all started calling out at the shoppers: "Buy! Consume! Spend!"

A few minutes later, we made our second pass and repeated our cheers. Only, this time, all the people shopping in the store joined in, evidently with no sense of sheepishness or irony, yelling: "Buy! Consume! Spend!"

Fickle Finger of Fate

WALDO STEVE AND THE WALDOS

In the early '70s, the young Waldos—a group of friends from Marin County, California—were planning a stoner's trip to Los Angeles and Disneyland. We were planning it for weeks. The day before the trip, two of the Waldos phoned me in the afternoon and said they could not go because they did not have the cash. No money, no trip. A big letdown. About nine that same evening, I got a surprise phone call from the two cashless Waldos. They said, "We can go now! We have lots of money. Wait at your house and we will come right over to explain." When they arrived, they got out of the car holding brown-paper shopping bags.

Because my parents were having a party in the front of the house, we went around the side gate, through a back door, and into my room, unnoticed. As soon as the door was closed and locked, they opened the shopping bags and started pulling out and throwing cash in the air. I joined in, reaching into the bags, grabbing fistfuls of money, and throwing it into the air. It was raining money, and the floor was completely covered with green bills. The previously cashless and now rich Waldo explained that he had suffered for a long time while working for an ex-boss, who was an extremely abusive asshole. And this money was a revenge-related windfall.

The next morning, we packed up my 1966 four-door Chevy Impala (with a killer Craig eight-track stereo system) to head for Southern California. The cargo consisted of four guys and a girl with long brown hair, named Laura, who needed a lift to L.A. The cargo also consisted of six lids of fresh, green smoke. Driving south on Highway 101, we were in a hurry because I was extremely determined to make it to Burbank (to be an audience member) for an afternoon taping of *The Tonight Show Starring Johnny Carson*.

Unfortunately, I had to slow down. Around San Luis Obispo, a police car got onto the highway directly behind us. I warned my passengers to put out their joints. However, my passengers thought it was sufficient to just keep the joints down low. A second police car got onto the highway in front of us. Now there was one cop in front and one in back of us. Besides the police cars, ours was the only car on the freeway. We put out the joints and watched the speedometer.

Within minutes, more cop cars got onto the highway. Now there were two behind us and two in front of us. Then, there were three squad cars behind us and three in front of us. We put the lids down our pants and continued to drive the speed limit. Then the cop car directly behind us lit up his bright, flashing, colorful lights.

We pulled over to the side of the road and so did all six squad cars. The officers jumped out and pulled their guns but did not approach our car. Stoned, we sat and waited for ten minutes while the officers walked around at a distance. Would we be busted?

An officer approached the car and asked for all of our licenses. He took the IDs back his car and we waited. We waited for a full half hour in total suspense inside our rocking automobile. Would we be busted?

The officer came back to our car, handed me our drivers' licenses, and said we could go free. I questioned him about our detainment. He said the cops thought that the girl in our car was Patty Hearst and that we were the SLA (Symbionese Liberation Army) headed south.

Very stoned and very miffed about the delay, I then reprimanded the police officer saying, "You goof, now we're going to miss Johnny Carson."

We got to Los Angeles in the early evening and went to a motel to try to get a room. They had no vacancies. The second, third, fourth, fifth, sixth, and seventh motels we tried also had no vacancies.

With no other options, we filled up the gas tank. Gasoline was only about forty cents a gallon and we had six lids of grass. We cruised the freeways of L.A. nonstop, continuously smoking weed until the sun came up. Cheaper than a motel.

Later that morning, the Waldos arrived at Disneyland, determined to smoke out everywhere in the park. And we did. At one point, we hopped a fence, ran up a little hill, and down into a phony Disney-created desert scene. Consisting of a few acres, it was made to look like Arizona or Utah. We smoked all over the phony little Southwest.

A train whistle blew. There was a train tunnel leading to our Southwest desert mock-up. Happy Disney customers were all aboard and quickly coming our way. We ran up a hill and hid behind a giant, phony red rock. Crouching tightly behind the boulder, we lit up a new joint. The train stopped in the middle of the desert.

The tour guide on the train pointed directly at us as he exclaimed to the passengers, "Oh, my!" All eyes on the train looked right at us. We froze still. The tour guide then continued, "Oh, my! It's Old Faithful!"

Suddenly, about two feet from my right foot, a water geyser shot up. First two feet high, then six feet high, and finally fifteen feet high. The Waldos took a good soaking. The train drove away. We were soaked, but we didn't spoil the vacation for the Disneyland customers.

The Disneyland Memorial Orgy

PAUL KRASSNER

When Walt Disney died in December 1966, I remembered a couple of his statements with peculiar affection. "I love Mickey Mouse," he had once said, "more than any woman I've ever known." In 1945, Aldous Huxley went to work for him as a consultant on the filming of *Alice in Wonderland.* There was gossip that Huxley had turned him on with magic mushrooms. "If people would think more of fairies," Disney said a year later, "they would forget the atom bomb."

There were rumors that Disney's body had been frozen, although it was actually cremated. Somehow I had expected Mickey and Donald Duck and all the rest of the gang to attend the funeral, with Goofy delivering a eulogy and the Seven Dwarves serving as pallbearers. After his death, as a personal pilgrimage, I thought it would be appropriate to visit Disneyland. I went with three friends, one a lawyer whose dog jumped into the car as we were leaving his home. We ate marijuana brownies for the occasion.

Dogs were not allowed in Disneyland. In fact, male humans with long hair or beards or other stereotypical hippie accouterments were not allowed in. The Beatles, who were more popular than Christ, would not have been permitted to enter Disneyland—unless they were performing there. Indeed, Jesus himself would not have been permitted to enter Disneyland—unless *he* was performing there. We bluffed our way into Disneyland by convincing a ticket-taker that the manager had given us permission earlier on the telephone inasmuch as the dog was needed to guide my friend with the impaired eyesight. Inside, we continued to fake it, explaining that the dog had already been cleared by the ticket-taker.

After lunch, a large man with a small walkie-talkie approached us with the choice of putting the dog in the Disneyland kennel or leaving the place altogether. My friend explained how this exception to their rule had been arranged two weeks ago, and he asked to speak to "the chief of security."

"I *am* the chief of security."

"Ah, just the man I want to see."

Incidentally, I should mention that the canine in question was *not* a Seeing Eye dog (which would now be called an assisted-living dog). It wasn't even a German shepherd. There was no metal brace for the owner to hold on to, just a rotten, knotted leather leash. Moreover, the dog was a bloodshot-eyed basset hound that kept stumbling all over the ground because it had to pee and was searching for a spot where a dog had previously peed, any dog, but no dog had ever peed in Disneyland. Especially not Pluto.

Okay, then, if we had to leave, were we not entitled to a full refund? Yes, we were. So, while the others waited at the gate, I was escorted to a building called City Hall. There, a woman was requesting that her lost child be paged over the loudspeaker, but she was refused because it wasn't considered an emergency.

I didn't wish people to think that I wanted them only for their money, so I asked if there had been any special ceremony when Walt Disney died.

"No, we kept the park open. We felt that Mr. Disney would have wanted it that way."

"Well, wasn't there *any* official recognition of his passing?"

"We did fly the flag at half-mast for the rest of the month."

Disney stock rose one point the day after his death and continued to ascend. The company earned $100 million the next year, and even though Disney was dead, Mickey Mouse would continue to bask in his own immortality. Disney's death occurred a few years after *Time* magazine's famous "God Is Dead" cover, and it struck me that Disney had indeed served as the Creator of Mickey, Donald Duck, Goofy—that whole stable of imaginary characters who were now mourning in a state of suspended animation.

Disney had been *their* Intelligent Designer, and he had repressed all their baser instincts, but since he had departed, they could finally shed their cumulative inhibitions and participate together in an unspeakable Roman binge, to signify the crumbling of an empire. I assigned *Mad* magazine artist Wally Wood to create—as a black-and-white center-spread for *The Realist*, which then became a popular poster—the infamous Disneyland Memorial Orgy. (A digitally colored edition of the original poster is available at paulkrassner.com.)

Pluto is pissing on a portrait of Mickey Mouse while the real, bedraggled Mickey is shooting up heroin with a hypodermic needle. His nephews are jerking off as they watch a combination bed and cash register where Minnie Mouse is fucking Goofy. The beams shining out from Cinderella Castle are actually dollar signs. Dumbo is simultaneously flying and shitting on an infuriated Donald Duck. Huey, Dewey, and Louie are ogling Daisy Duck's asshole as she watches the Seven Dwarves groping Snow White. The Prince is snatching a peek at Cinderella's snatch while trying a glass slipper on her foot. The Three Little Pigs are humping each other in a daisy chain. Jiminy Cricket is leering as Tinker Bell does a striptease and Pinocchio's nose gets longer and longer.

Anyway, still thoroughly stoned, we left Disneyland to fend for itself.

Amsterdam

Space Cake

I smoked a lot of dope in college. I had my reasons. I went to an engineering school. In Cleveland. At the outset of the Reagan years. Women were outnumbered on campus by more than three to one. Almost all of my potential male friends played Dungeons & Dragons.

This was even more depressing than it sounds. So my roommate and I kept the bong lit and the Firesign Theatre records playing, and we prayed for graduation or death. This was the entire extent of my drug use in school. Once I got out and around some actual women, my interest in marijuana ended.

Fast-forward ten years. By 1994, I was living in a beach house in Santa Monica with a beautiful, sweet, funny woman named Mindy. We intended to marry someday, and we filled the interim by inventing new sexual practices and naming them after states where we thought they would be illegal.

This was great for public flirting. We would stand in line at a drugstore checkout, and I would lean over and whisper the word *Mississippi*, and we would both be titillated for an hour until we got home and actually committed that crime. This was true love.

At least until Christmas Eve, when Mindy told me (and I swear this is true) that she had been sleeping with another guy, didn't know why, and she was therefore going to sort things out by moving to Ecuador.

I started smoking dope again.

Fast-forward six more months. In summer 1995, I was killing time by riding trains around Europe. I had stopped smoking weed again. Instead, I spent most of my free time hanging around historic churches and cathedrals. Not because I'm religious—but because they're remarkably good places to pick up women, who are often so awestruck and reverent that they don't realize you have a plan.

I once spent a whole week cruising the Vatican, trying to score chicks from every member of the Warsaw Pact. None of this made me forget the thing Mindy could do with her teeth that we called "Louisiana."

One day, I was in Paris, paying my respects to Jim Morrison and wondering if it would be nice to be buried in Père Lachaise. My travel agent, who had once been *our* travel agent, told me that Mindy was visiting Amsterdam. The next day, so was I.

Mindy and I hooked up in a place called the Boatel, a stationary love boat docked near the Centraal train station. Our window was at water level, and the seagulls ate bread from our hands.

Except for the fact that we had nothing to say to each other, it was romantic as hell. So, then. What to do? See the sights, we decided. Specifically, there were three places Mindy wanted to visit: a flower market where she could buy some souvenir tulips; the Anne Frank House; and the Oude Kerk, a big, old church Mindy was interested in.

This pleased me greatly. If my lucky streak in cathedrals held, we'd reach "Alabama" by nightfall. To our surprise, however, the first sight we saw was just as carnal—the Red Light District, where in addition to Surinamese women and bestiality magazines, cafés and bistros openly sell marijuana. Ever the eager travelers, we decided to sample the local cuisine. Ducking into a smoky little brown place, we found a menu of dope like a wine list. And since neither of us spoke Dutch, we ordered the only item listed in English: "Space Cake," also known as hash brownies.

We ate our first pieces in silence. Elapsed time: thirty minutes. I had completely forgotten that hash brownies take an hour to kick in. Since we didn't feel particularly stoned, we decided the stuff probably wasn't very potent. After all, how could it be? They sell it to tourists, for Pete's sake. If it was pungent, some idiots might accidentally eat too much, right?

Determined to get our money's worth, we ordered a second piece. Soon we were talking like we hadn't in years, as if we were a couple again. I mentioned "the Carolinas," and Mindy kissed me in a way that let me know she remembered that particular crime.

I had completely forgotten that when hash brownies kick in, they do so really hard. We started feeling pretty happy after our second piece.

Elapsed time: one hour. And so we decided, what the hell, let's have a third. I don't recall much after that.

I remember noticing that when you're stoned, Dutch sounds a lot like English spoken by people from Wisconsin. And after that, there's a blank spot in my memory, a gap where the time is simply missing. And then I remember . . . suddenly noticing . . . that I was wiping my ass.

I wasn't sure how long I had been wiping my ass. But definitely I was wiping my ass. Probably for a long time. I noticed sitar music. Still I was wiping my ass. Evidently this was some sort of toilet place. How long I had been there, I did not know. I was relieved to learn I was wiping my ass in a toilet and not somewhere else. The sitar didn't seem to be in the toilet with me. My ass seemed pretty sore. Possibly from all the wiping. The sitar music was nice, though.

And then: Where's Mindy?!

Panic-stricken and clinging to one frayed thread of awareness, I searched frantically for my pants. After several minutes, I found they had been conveniently placed around my ankles. I ventured out of the toilet, unsure of what I might find. I was in a restaurant. It was an Indian restaurant. With really nice sitar music. I wasn't sure where the music was coming from. I didn't see a sitar anywhere. I also wasn't sure what I was looking for. The sitar music couldn't be coming from the toilet. That much was for sure. Mindy didn't even like Indian food. Surprising, then, that we would be in an Indian restaurant. Perhaps Mindy would know what I was looking . . . for . . . Mindy?!

Panic-stricken again, and still struggling for that one frayed thread of awareness, I desperately searched the room for Mindy. After an exhausting struggle, I discovered her approximately two and a half feet to my left, giggling facedown in a pile of garlic naan. There was a tulip in her hair. Two down, I thought. And as a bonus, I was no longer wiping my ass.

There's another blank spot here. And then I remember: Mindy and I were suddenly sitting under a tree next to a canal with our arms around each other. We were scared. The high was getting more and more intense. Apparently we had decided to sit down and ride it out for as long as it lasted. We quietly rocked back and forth and murmured, "It's gonna be okay, it's gonna be okay . . . "

I looked up and realized we were sitting almost directly in front of the Anne Frank House. Tourists were watching us and pointing. Three for three, I thought. Mindy and I held each other tightly and looked into each other's eyes, knowing that, at least for a while, we needed each other desperately. It wasn't love, but it was certainly real.

A church bell struck noon. "It's gonna be okay, it's gonna be okay . . ." Before long, it was getting dark. My ass was way beyond numb from sitting on the pavement. The high was still peaking. We were still almost directly in front of the Anne Frank House.

I was convinced that by now everyone in Amsterdam knew we were stoned. Surely every tourist in Europe had heard about the fucked-up couple rocking and moaning in front of the Anne Frank House. Fodor's was rewriting their guidebook for Holland. Animals stared at us in dismay.

"It's gonna be okay, it's gonna be okay . . . "

There's another blank spot here, a long one. And then I remember: I awoke . . . as our train (huh?) rolled into a station. It was morning. We were in Berlin. Vividly I recall thinking, Whoa!

I took inventory. Finally, I was sober, at least as far as I could tell. Mindy was sound asleep in the next bunk. All of our things were packed and nearby. And we were in a sleeping compartment on a train. Entering Berlin.

Mindy didn't know why we were there either. The prevailing theory is that we felt so guilty in our delirium for having disgraced the Anne Frank House that we sought the Nazi stronghold as penance. That's pure conjecture. If you can make up a better explanation, I'm all ears.

So Mindy and I wandered around Checkpoint Charlie (which was becoming a shopping mall) and the Brandenburg Gate (which is now an open-air market) and the weird giant onion-dome radio tower the Communists built (which now has a T.G.I. Friday's across the street).

We tried all day to feel connected again, but Berlin is no damn place for young lovers. The romance was over. She got on a train for London that night. I never saw her again.

Thanks to Mindy, I'll never think of Ecuador or spend another Christmas Eve without feeling sad, and I'll never think of the states of the deep South without wistfully recalling a satisfied soreness in various obscure muscle groups.

I still have no idea what was in the Space Cake, and I know that the same neural overload that gave Mindy and me one last day of closeness also caused me to wipe my ass for perhaps an entire hour. But somehow it makes me happy to think of the whole ordeal this way: If Bogart and Bergman can always have Paris, then Mindy and I will always have Amsterdam.

Borderline Paranoia

CAT SIMRIL ISHIKAWA

I was driving through Europe with my friend Jack in the summer of an earlier year. Jack was from a country that set new standards in straightness, and I was just in from the land that Paul McCartney thought had legal weed. Fly, jailbird, fly. Neither of us had been stoned in ages. Then we got to the Netherlands. Rivers of hash. We ended up using it as a mosquito tranquilizer and eventually had to leave.

Jack wanted to see Belgium. The guidebook said it was what you'd expect from a country with a national symbol of a boy pissing, but Jack insisted. He'd heard (quite rightfully) that it had the best beer in the world. But, of course, it was not the smoke-utopia Netherlands, and we grew more and more worried as we neared the unknown land.

We sure tried to get rid of all our hash back in Amsterdam, but we still had a couple of orca-size joints under the seat. Jack was sure the border guards would find them. To smoke them would make us legally blind. What to do? I suspected Jack's worst nightmares weren't likely, but paranoia has a contagious quality, and it's better to be safe, insisted our jail-loathing consciences.

We spied a waste orb by the side of the road. Adieu, dear doobies, we said, and hurled them into the orb. Thanks for the Dutch treatment. Back in the car. We drove another few kilometers through fields of small green things, and then we came to a store offering to change our money.

Change it into what, we wondered, and went inside. And discovered that we were already ten kilometers inside Belgium. There is no border. Between anything, after a while.

My Cannabis Cup Runneth Over

PAUL KRASSNER

When Steve Hager, creative director of *High Times*, invited me to emcee the awards night at the Tenth Annual Cannabis Cup, I had to decline, regretfully, because I was committed to be in Detroit that week to cover the trial of Peter McWilliams, who had AIDS and cancer. He had been there for a family reunion and got arrested at the airport for possession of seven joints. Judge Tina Green said she would allow a medical-marijuana defense, but one week later, she changed her mind.

That decision would be appealed, of course, and the trial was postponed, so I could fly to Amsterdam after all.

The Quentin Hotel, a friendly, funky place, was now filled entirely with Cannabis Cup attendees. In the lobby, folks were sitting around, drinking hot chocolate, talking, laughing, and openly rolling, smoking, and passing around huge doobies. I savored the culture shock.

In my tiny room, just around the corner from the lobby, there was a view of the canal and, right outside my window, a plain brick wall where someone had spray-painted the word SHIT in letters two feet high. Was this an omen or what?

Hager greeted me with a bud the size of a cucumber. Since all strains of marijuana at the Cannabis Cup have their own brand names—Purple Sage, White Shark, Stonehenge—I asked, "What's this one called?" He replied, "Dr. Kevorkian." I figured it would be killer weed. Actually, it cured my jet lag immediately. Yes, Dr. Kevorkian brought me back to life. It wasn't even entered in the competition, but it was already a winner.

In the lobby, a pot purist was pointing out that judges should avoid using a lighter when trying out a new brand because the butane would taint the test. Rather, they should use a long wooden match, but wait until the sulfur was burned before lighting a joint. What about the glue on the rolling papers, I wondered. Someone offered me a cannabis cough drop. What a perfect concept. I sucked on it without missing a toke. And it worked; I didn't cough.

Over a period of five days, the judges tried out various kinds of pot grown by Amsterdam's top marijuana seed companies. They also traipsed around to a score of coffee shops whose own brand names were in a separate competition. And, unlike at a wine-tasting event, these judges were not spitting out each new sample.

At 4:20 each afternoon, I went to the Council at Hemp Hall. There are different beliefs about the origin of 4/20 as a countercultural iconic symbol. One theory is that 4/20 is the police code for a pot bust. Another is that there are 4/20 substances in marijuana. I thought that maybe it came from the old nursery rhyme about "four and twenty blackbirds."

Actually, in 1971, a group of students—who named themselves "the Waldos" because they hung out at a certain wall outside their high school—chose 4:20 in the afternoon as the time they would meet at the Louis Pasteur statue to go hunting for an abandoned cannabis crop. The code word for this ritual was "4:20 Louis," which shrank to just plain "4:20" and it became a popular synonym for pot-smoking time. Personally, though, I always light up promptly at 2:15, just to honor California's Proposition 215.

I hadn't expected that the ritual would also be celebrated in the lobby of the Quentin at 4:20 every *morning*. Drumming, singing, chanting, dancing, raucous conversation, loud giggles, and wild guffaws woke me up in the middle of the night. Naturally, I interpreted that as a sign to select something from my stash and seized the opportunity to roll still another joint on *The New Testament*—printed in English and Hebrew, which surprised me. I thought that the Jewish people are still waiting for a messiah to appear for the first time. Jesus Christ, I was wrong again.

Ah, my ever-increasing stash. The seed companies and coffeehouses were giving out little baggies of their product and rolled joints to all the judges, so it was a case of equal-opportunity bribery—oops, I mean free samples. But, no matter how tempting, I was afraid to bring any of it back to the States. Simply not worth the risk. At a *High Times* dinner, I sat next to Rita Marley and asked if she would be able to bring back any marijuana to Kingston.

"No," she responded with a queenly air, adding, "isn't it a pity?"

Joints were being passed around the table, but when I gestured to pass her one, she shook her head no. She was busy smoking a bomber of her own, which she didn't pass. I learned later that this is the practice in Jamaica. Apparently, there is no Rastafarian word for *bogart*.

My old Prankster friend Mountain Girl told me she was entertaining the notion of buying a shovel and burying her gigantic stash. Next she thought of befriending a Dutch citizen and keeping it in his home. Or maybe she could obtain a safe-deposit box at the local bank—except that she'd have to open an account there first, and there wouldn't be time for a check to clear. She even considered renting a small apartment in Amsterdam and living there for a couple of months until she had literally smoked herself out.

In my capacity as a stand-up satirist, I refrain from doing the comedy club circuit, which David Letterman calls "babysitting for drunks." Instead, I perform at alternative venues—from a Neo-Pagan Festival to a Swingers Convention—but I have never been at an event as joyful as the Cannabis Cup. I remain horror-struck by the severe contrast between the drug laws of my own country and the rational approach I found in Amsterdam.

Before leaving, I climbed out the window of my hotel room and spray-painted on the brick wall so that the graffito would now read GOOD SHIT. At the airport back in America, I experienced a moment of paranoia when I thought the narco-dog was about to sniff out *The New Testament* that I had borrowed from the hotel, but he passed by my luggage. *Whew!* The tension was almost worth the relief.

Now I was ready to cover Peter McWilliams' trial. The prosecutor in Detroit had legally changed his name to Luke Skywalker in 1977, when he was in his twenties and got inspired by *Star Wars*. Luke Skywalker battles medical marijuana. In court he would have perceived McWilliams as Darth Vader. If this is justice, may the farce be with you.

Customs

Car Sale

NANCY CAIN

During the mid-'70s, I'm working with a company called Media Bus. We are funded through the New York State Council on the Arts and travel the state, teaching people how to make their own television shows and taking them over to the local cable company to gain access.

One time, Media Bus is hired to stir things up a bit at the public access channel in Ann Arbor, Michigan. I make the trip with David, Carol, and Skip. Carol is a little distracted because this is the first time she has left her daughter Sarah since she was born two years ago.

We're going to take the Canadian route instead of the Pennsylvania Turnpike. We'll drive up New York State and across Ontario to Detroit. Then we can stay with my mom and dad, and drive out to Ann Arbor in the morning. Relaxed, no-traffic country roads all the way. Idyllic day, at least for me, just riding along incommunicado, as if free.

Canada has a different vibe. A slower beat. After a while I relax and stop thinking that we're going to get pulled over by the cops at any moment— like I do when we're on the New York Thruway, for example. A sunny, happy day away. That is, until U.S. Customs. That's the price you pay for taking the scenic route. You have to go through U.S. Customs.

Always a complex and dangerous game.

Sometimes it's not paranoia. Sometimes it's intuition. Sometimes you just know when your number is up. That's the way I feel when I see that the Customs inspector moving toward me is a woman. She escorts me alone through a door into a small anteroom.

The officers have already ripped our car apart and taken our video reels out of the boxes and held the tape up to the light. They have already taken out the back seat, and they say, "Found a seed." Jesus. A seed. Maybe they did. Shit.

Oh, they would have stopped us anyway because we fit a profile. Skip with his thick blond hair flowing way down his back, and David with his black beard out to there—Carol and I are not exactly in business suits either—and, well, I guess we do seem like a suspicious bunch.

The Customs inspector is closing the door behind her. She stares at me. Dry mouth. Heart palpitations. Mine, not hers. The little leather pouch of pot is burning a hole in my shirt pocket. I am a guilty murderer.

"You'd better give it to me because if I find it, it's gonna be way worse."

I hear the squish-squish of my blood pumping past my eardrums. *Poomb! Poomb!* My heart. I examine my options and hand over the pot. And I keep my mouth shut. Now she wants me to strip and squat to make sure I don't have anything else stashed up inside me. Gee, this is happening to me and I'm not dying. Hey, it's just a little dignity. Take it.

Turns out they searched Skip and David and Carol, too, but they were clean. Now the four of us are sitting on a hard bench, waiting for the Customs inspectors to come up with the next scenario. Here they come. The deal is that we are guilty of bringing a controlled substance across an international border in a vehicle, and the U.S. government consequently is going to take ownership of our vehicle.

"Wait a minute," Skip says incredulously. "You mean that the government now owns our car?"

Yes, it's true. That's the bad news. The good news is that we can buy it back from them for only $100. Wow! Really? Because this is a brand-new 1973 Dodge Dart four-door. Same color green as the phone company's cars. A hundred dollars is a bargain. We buy it (leaving us with maybe $30 between us) and are kicked unceremoniously out onto Jefferson Avenue, Detroit, Michigan, USA.

It's nighttime. We arrive at my mom and dad's late, and we're all excited about our border experience, which we relate breathlessly, leaving out the part where they find my pot.

Producing our live video-chaos television show in Ann Arbor is as bizarre and controversial as ever, but nothing tops U.S. Customs for a thrill.

[*Excerpted from the memoir* Video Days.]

Lobsters

DAN DENOV

It was sometime in the winter of 1971–72, and we were in the homestretch of a jaunt to New York and Boston, a mere couple of hours away from Lansing, Michigan. To save time we cut across Canada from Niagara Falls toward Windsor and Detroit. Somewhere in that stretch, we pulled off the highway to get a cup of coffee, take a leak, and stretch.

While searching in this small town for the way back to the highway, we picked up a cop who threw the lights on and pulled us over. He said it looked like we were lost—white VW bus, Illinois plates, and three somewhat unkempt guys at nine o'clock that night. We said yes, and he showed us the way out of town. Nice country, that Canada. Anyway, our stash of an ounce or so wasn't even close to an issue at this point. Onward to the border.

In due time, we made it out of Canada at Windsor, over the bridge, and on to Customs in the U.S. It was so easy to get in to and out of Canada we anticipated an easy reentry to the good old USA, but just for safekeeping, we stashed the pot down one of our pants. It was now around two in the morning.

A youngish guy in a uniform came over, asked me details of where, when, and why, and then proceeded to look at the two pretending to be asleep in the back with that haze of road buzz about them. He asked us to step out and into the Customs house. We, at that point, were starting to worry a bit, and that worry quickly expanded when the young guy came in and said he'd "found some seeds" in the car and that everything needed to be searched.

We had all the usual paraphernalia for a road trip—sleeping bags, fast food containers, eight-track wired into the dome light in the back, and a supply of Firesign Theatre, Doors, and Jimi Hendrix tapes—but we had also picked up, at one of our compatriot's request, some live lobsters in Boston to bring home. Among all our bags and boxes of crap now in the Customs house, the guards proceeded to empty the cooler box, at which point the two lobsters started crawling around on the stainless steel countertop.

The officer must have figured that there were "bigger fish to fry" and corralled the clawed creatures back into their temporary home. Not finding much of anything in all the stuff they hauled out of the bus, they proceeded to strip-search us one at a time in the bathroom. I forget the order in which we went, but I do remember the oldest of the officers said to me, as owner of the vehicle where they had found the stashed stash, "Son, you're in a lot of trouble."

It came down to this—I had an hour to come up with $150 or, in their words, they'd tear my bus apart. At first I thought it was a bribe, but I figured out later, after looking at the official receipt I have to this day, that the only federal law concerning marijuana was an importation tax of $100 an ounce! I was busted for trying to smuggle the stuff in without paying the tax.

Of course, this revelation didn't help in terms of finding the money at 4:30 AM. A good college buddy of mine was living in Detroit at his folks' house, so I gave him a call. His mother answered the phone and, although she mainly spoke Ukrainian, she understood what I was saying and put Head on the line. I quickly reeled off the scenario and he said he'd be right down.

Now this guy is about six feet five inches and around 250 pounds and at the time was selling phone systems for AT&T in the Detroit area. When he walked into the Customs house clean-shaven and in his three-piece suit, put his attaché case on the counter and clicked it open, the officers weren't quite sure what was happening.

When he said, with a glance toward us, "What kind of trouble my boys in?" their jaws seemed to come down a little slack. I told the Head to give them $150, which he peeled off of a small wad of bills. They wrote a receipt, and we were out the door to a doughnut shop (sans the dope). Those guards must have figured they had run into some connected freaks when we got that kind of response with one call at four thirty in the morning.

Got One!

KATHLEEN EDWARDS

As two carefree people taking a casual tour of the northern United States, we opted for a detour into Canada. Never been there. Wanted to see what it was like. We thought it might be a good rehearsal for our impending yearlong trip through Europe. The Border Patrol on the U.S. side of the Canadian border at Sault Ste. Marie took one look at the 1968 Volkswagen van with bicycles on top, California plates, and a long-haired, bearded driver, and their eyes lit up. You could see them mentally rubbing their hands together. "Boy, this is gonna be fun."

"Get out of the van and step inside." Since we had finished off the last of the half-pint of whiskey the previous evening and we were sure the van was "clean," we faced this challenge casually. We were escorted into a dreary room with a handful of potbellied, ruddy-faced career cops. "Wait right here." We watched as a pair of these cops ambled toward the van.

A few minutes passed, then the "searchers" returned. In their stubby hands, they held what appeared to be a short, fat roach. We looked at each other's eyes and the look that silently passed between us said, "Where did that come from?" Although we are admittedly partakers of the herb, this roach didn't resemble anything we'd ever seen.

They then explained that this roach was to be dropped into a solution and, if it turned purple, that would prove it was cannabis. They stood around like Einstein-wannabes and indeed the solution did change to a purple haze. One cop rushed to a telephone, pushed a couple of buttons, and proudly shouted, "Got one!" We surmised that they kept a supply of these roaches around as an excuse to search any "suspicious persons."

Since they were going to search the van, they would, of course, find it necessary to search our persons. While waiting for a female officer to arrive (forty-five minutes later), these protectors of our borders methodically went through every corner of the van. They were itching to get us on something. They even went so far as to count our traveler's checks because, as was explained to us later, it is illegal to carry more then $5,000 across the Canadian border. Imagine their disappointment when they found only $3,800.

As for the strip search, that has to be pretty high up there on the humiliation scale. The female officer was curt but judgmental. "You must have had something for them to call on me to search you."

Through this entire scene, my partner and I never spoke to one another, but merely nodded knowingly. Surprisingly, since they found nothing in the van, they unceremoniously handed us the keys without a word of acknowledgment or apology and went back to their doughnuts.

The lesson here is simple. We were about to embark on a journey through foreign countries, yet we endured an experience within our own borders that evoked visions of *Midnight Express*. The story itself is really the middle of a longer story that has a beginning story and end story to it.

The beginning of the story involved being turned away from the Canadian border by the authorities because my partner and I answered their questionnaire with complete honesty, and he said that he had been arrested as a teenager for marijuana possession. They refused our entry and turned us back to the United States, which initially explains the actions of the U.S. Border Patrol. We suspect they received a phone call.

The end of this story involves the same VW van and two hits of LSD. All I can say about this is, if you want to put something somewhere no one will find it, try the inside of a Tampax box. I'm willing to bet that there's no male officer out there who'd put his hand inside such a box, even though the contents are clearly wrapped and unused.

Pleasant Surprise!

Back in the late 1960s and early 1970s, hitchhiking was part of the culture for hippies. I learned to hitchhike when I visited my sister in San Francisco for two weeks. Hitching was more than a means of transportation; it was an expression of communalism—those who had transportation would share with those who didn't.

I was living in Chicago, and I soon made it a practice to hitch a ride down Halsted Street to get to school rather than taking the bus.

It was sometime around 1971 when my friend Steve and I decided to hitch to Toronto to visit a friend who was dodging the draft. Someone with more hitching experience than us had advised us not to accept a ride to Gary, Indiana. He said you could get a ride very easily with someone going to work at the steel mill there, but it would be hard to get another ride from that point. It was far better to turn down ten rides to Gary and wait for a car that was traveling further.

We started out early in the morning, and within five minutes a car stopped and the driver offered us a ride to Gary. We shrugged out shoulders and got in. Boy, that was easy! By late afternoon, we were still in Gary. We had progressed from the west side of Gary to the east side. But we were still a whole lot closer to Chicago than we were to Toronto. The sun was beating down on us. We were tired and sweaty and talking about giving up and hitching a ride back home to Chicago. Hitchhiking was supposed to be fun, but this was discouraging.

Finally, a van full of hippies stopped to pick us up. They said they were going as far as London, Ontario. It was a stroke of luck. Better yet, they had a bag full of dope. After a couple of joints, all of the day's earlier frustrations were forgotten. The music was good, we were having a good conversation with some good people, and everything was mellow.

We got to Detroit and we were about to cross over into Canada when we realized our dilemma. We couldn't cross the border with a bag of dope. The Customs agents might search the vehicle and arrest us. But it would be an awful shame to waste a bag of good weed. What should we do?

Someone got the idea that we should drive around and look for a hippie to give it to, so it wouldn't be wasted (better that the hippie should be wasted than the dope). We drove around for ten minutes, knowing nothing about the neighborhood. We saw Tiger Stadium, we saw some policemen, but we didn't see any hippies. Okay, let's go into a restaurant, get a snack, and maybe we'll find a hippie in there. There were a couple of tables occupied by cops, but no hippies.

We got back in the van. We were determined to give this weed away to someone who would appreciate it before we crossed the border. We drove around some more, but we had no luck. Finally, we stopped beside a parked car with an open window, dropped the bag of dope onto the seat, and took our chances. We laughed at the possibility that some totally straight person would discover it. We hoped some happy freak would discover it and that we would make his day.

As it turned out, the Customs agent didn't search the van. He just asked the driver a few questions and waved us on through. We could have kept the bag in the van and smoked a few more joints. But then I wouldn't be able to contribute this story to Paul Krassner's book. Of course, we have no idea how the story ended. I've often wondered about it in the ensuing years. I can hope for the best, but I can also think of some rather unpleasant scenarios:

1. A mother and her teenage son return to the car, and she screams, "Junior! What in the world are you doing with this?"

2. A couple on their first date return to the car, and she says, "Philip, you said you didn't do drugs."

3. A paranoid freak discovers it. He wants to smoke it, but he thinks it has been planted by the cops.

4. An undercover cop returns to his car and plants the bag of weed at an apartment he wants to bust.

I guess we'll never know. We were just trying to give someone a pleasant surprise. I hope we did.

Spanish Lie

BOB WIEDER

In 1970, I was returning to Spain from Morocco. Spain was notorious then for its draconian attitude toward drugs. I had everything I owned stuffed in a massive duffel bag. "Everything" included some *kif* that was really too valuable and salubrious to leave behind and a bunch of long wooden pipe stems and clay and sandstone pipe bowls, which to this day I find the optimal vehicles for pot-smoking.

The people I was traveling with had all left their illicit goods behind, but I put my remaining *kif* at the very bottom of my duffel bag and all the pipe stuff right on the top. The general opinion was that I would wind up learning a lot of Spanish over the next ten to fifteen years.

At Spanish Customs (off the ferry from Tangiers), an inspector opened my bags, saw the pipes, and did a whopping double take.

"What is this?" he asked.

"Those are pipes," I said.

"For what?" he asked.

"For smoking."

"For smoking what?" he inquired knowingly.

"For smoking marijuana back in the USA," I said.

He gave me his *aha!* look. "You have the marijuana in the bag, too, right?"

I gave him my don't-be-ridiculous look. "Are you kidding? I'd go to jail! Everybody knows that Spanish Customs is the toughest in the world. I want the pipes to use back home, but I knew I'd never be able to sneak them past you. That's why I put them right on top to just get it out of the way. But, come on, I'd be nuts to put hash pipes where a Spanish Customs officer could see them if I was carrying drugs. Nobody fools you guys!"

He gave me an eminently pleased smile and waved me in.

Divine Intervention

CELINA HERRERO

I was on the second leg of a three-day trans-Mexico odyssey—a forty-eight-hour bus ride from Tijuana to Mexico City. Two friends had driven me across the border and, as carrying drugs into Mexico from the States is rarely an issue, I had a quarter ounce of fragrant, potent skunk bud in a clear plastic sandwich bag, ever-so-carelessly tossed into an upper side pocket of my camping backpack, together with several pairs of rolled-up socks. Not cleverly tucked inside a pair of socks, mind you, nothing that prudent, rather just sitting where it would be immediately visible to anyone who happened to unzip that particular pocket.

I was sleeping soundly, as we veteran travelers tend to do on long, tedious bus journeys, snoring away as our "luxury coach" sped through the star-infested nightscape of the endless desert, a nothingness broken only by scattered stumpy cacti and a few frolicking nocturnal jackrabbits. Suddenly, heart-stoppingly, the bus came to an abrupt halt outside an ominously official-looking building in the middle of nowhere, a hideous squat concrete hut crouching malevolently in the night.

Several uniformed officers invaded the bus and immediately began pulling luggage off the overhead racks, shouting in Spanish: "Customs! Everybody off the bus! Let's go, baggage, suitcases, everything, let's go, keep it moving." They swaggered up and down the aisle—half a dozen of them, at least—banging suitcases about and roughly shaking people awake in that endearing, people-person manner in which law-enforcement officers the world over seem to have been specially trained.

One minute I'd been dreaming of my upcoming month in a hammock under a palm tree in a Caribbean utopia, the next I was facing cops, all kinds of unpleasantness (or am I being redundant?), and, barring divine intervention, some serious time in jail. Mexican jail.

They were everywhere all at once, leaving no window of opportunity in which to surreptitiously dump the bag of weed onto the floor of the bus or take any other ass-saving measures whatsoever. Under the watchful eye of a veritable army of Customs officers, every last passenger, blinking and groggy, dragging along pieces of baggage, was prodded and shoved into the Customs dungeon.

The place was enormous, with some twenty different stations, each consisting of a long concrete table on which to have a proper snoop through our belongings, and staffed by a series of weary-eyed, heavy-set older women. As we waited in a single line for the next available life-wrecker, I, with a knot in my gut the size of Jalisco, sent out a fervent prayer to the universe: "Please, God, the young guy. Please, God, the young guy." I chanted this silently over and over, a heartfelt, desperate, I-don't-want-to-go-to-jail-in-Mexico mantra.

Happily, my prayers were answered. To my great relief, when my turn came, I was spared the fate of dealing with the grouchy grandmas and was sent instead to the lone young guy for my baggage check. I relaxed slightly at this point, taking it as a sign that, for the moment anyway, God, or someone with considerable cosmic pull, was on my side. If only my luck would hold.

The young man, predictably enough, was friendly and curious and made casual flirty small talk with me as he (gulp!) began to very thoroughly inspect the contents of my bag. He opened every lipstick, leafed through every magazine, took every cassette out of its box, felt up the padded collar of my winter jacket, and poked a finger into the coin pocket of my jeans (destroying any hope I had that they might be looking for guns).

By this point, I was kicking myself for actually requesting this earnest, out-to-prove-something, takes-his-job-way-too-seriously young go-getter. Maybe I would have been better off after all with one of the bad-humored old ladies, who probably just wanted to get it over with and go back to her siesta. Maybe he was prolonging the search in order to continue flirting with me a little longer. In any case, I was stuck with

him, and I played the eyelash-batting, flattering gringo senorita role for
all it was worth.

He was full of questions. "Your Spanish is so good, senorita. Where
did you learn to speak it so well?" "How long will you be staying in
Mexico?" "What is your final destination?" I chatted his ear off, prat-
tling nervously away about my previous trips to the Yucatan, how much
I loved the southern part of the country, how open and friendly I found
the Mexican people.

The young cop was conducting a painfully thorough counter clockwise tour of every nook, cranny, and crevice of my huge, overstuffed
rucksack, and behind my bright-eyed, beaming flirtatiousness, I was
hopeless. No one searching that thoroughly could possibly miss a big,
stinky clump of sticky, hairy buds in a clear plastic bag.

After all, no attempt had been made to camouflage or hide it in any
way; it just nestled in among the rolled-up socks in plain view inside what
would be the last pocket to be searched, silently screaming, "Bust me!"
In my imagination, I had already fast-forwarded to my years in prison.
Would it be as bad as I thought? How much time would they give me?
Would I finally get that novel written?

Cop-boy had by this time gotten to the toiletries and cosmetics pouch,
which would be the second-to-last pocket to be inspected on his counter-
clockwise search of my belongings. Last (but by no means least) would
be, of course, the "socks and controlled substances" compartment. He
began rummaging through my most personal items, pulling out sham-
poo, vitamins, a toothbrush—and condoms. Lots of them.

Before embarking on this journey, I had found myself enduring a
flurry of last-minute get-togethers with friends and family members.
Though I was only planning to be gone for a month, girlfriends, my sister, and my mother all insisted, "Let's meet for a drink before you leave.
I have a little going-away present for you."

By some hilarious "coincidence," the going-away gift was in each case
the same: condoms. Boxes of condoms, loose condoms, ribbed, extra-
sheer, flavored condoms (chocolate, grape, jalapeño, molé), industrial

strength condoms, lubricated condoms, condoms in a variety of colors (red, blue, green, purple) and a variety of sizes (small, medium, and *ay caramba*).

I had thought it so funny that so many different people had seen fit to give me condoms for my south-of-the border adventure that at the last minute I tossed every last one of them into a gallon-size plastic freezer bag and brought them along. There must have been eighty or ninety condoms altogether.

I was sweating by this point, as the sole remaining pocket to be searched contained my one-way ticket to Sonora State Prison. I trembled and breathed deeply and tried to savor my last few seconds of sweet freedom. I had forgotten about the condoms—at least, forgotten how many there were, how varied and colorful and downright impressive they looked in the huge clear bag. The young officer's eyes grew wide and he stammered slightly as, incredulous, he repeated one of his earlier questions to me.

"Uh, how long did you say you were planning to stay in Mexico again?"

"About three weeks," I replied, smiling sweetly.

He blanched visibly. Holding the bag gingerly between thumb and forefinger as if afraid that mere contact with that many condoms might somehow infect him with some life-threatening disease, he carefully replaced the bag and toiletries case in the pocket, zipped it closed, and pushed the backpack over to me with a grin and a leer.

"Have a wonderful time in our country, senorita."

Varieties of Paranoia

Lapse in Judgment

HUNTER S. THOMPSON

I have always loved marijuana. It has been a source of joy and comfort to me for many years. And I still think of it as a basic staple of life, along with beer and ice and grapefruit—and millions of Americans agree with me.

I've always been quite moderate with my use of marijuana except for eating it, which has caused a lot of trouble—overindulging on brownies, eating hash. Those are some of the worst physical reactions I've ever had. Being in someone else's car in some strange neighborhood. Not being able to get a cigarette out of your pocket, horrible cold sweats, unable to talk, thinking you're yelling for help and just whispering—praying for death, really.

I was in Zaire during the Ali-Foreman fight and everyone was smoking this black, grainy East African weed. It was utterly paralyzing, terrifying weed, not necessarily hallucinogenic. It was more like running into a closed door. You think it's open, you start walking through, and bash your head into an oaken slab. It could put a room full of people into a coma one by one. I smoked it all the time—huge spliffs—went a little psychotic, overtones of everything.

I became convinced I should eat all my malaria pills, which were supposed to be eaten once a week on Tuesday. Very powerful orange things. The doctor assured me he didn't mean Wednesday or Monday, that it was important to follow the prescribed dosage.

I had this conversation with a guy named Big Black, a conga drummer. We got to know each other pretty well. Big Black knew a lot more about malaria pills than I did. He had white ones that he took once a day. So, I said, what the hell, and began eating my pills just like Big Black. I didn't have that many, but I had enough to give myself malaria—a real psychotic episode. I went absolutely crazy. I lost about three or four days wandering around Zaire.

Hide and Seek

GERRI WILLINGER

I walked in the door and crashed on the couch after a three-hour night class at the University of Wisconsin in Milwaukee. I always kept my stash on the coffee table. I was lying on the couch and heard a knock on the door. Mom opened it. I heard, "FBI, ma'am, can we use your phone?" I could hear my mom laughing as she walked past me. As though it was a natural thing to do, she tossed a blanket over me (my head and torso mostly) as she led them to the phone. She just said, "She had a hard day at school."

I had a wolfhound that was not pleased with my lying stiff as a board with only two legs showing. She had the personality of Catherine the Great (or any other empress) and decided to jump on me with her five-foot-tall body and act as though I was a trampoline. That was her way of letting me know she was displeased. She did this the entire time the FBI agents were there. There I was, being used as a trampoline by an imperial dog while the FBI was calling in to headquarters because they had lost the address of the house they were supposed to bust, and they did not want any bad publicity.

I was under the cover with my eyes opened wide enough to roll out of my head, pretending to sleep, as these very polite men apologized for bothering us. As I was about to have a heart attack, I wondered what they were thinking of my mom's giggling.

When they left, I immediately went for my stash and rolled a big one.

Vega

MR. HOWELL

Do you remember the Chevrolet Vega? It came in a number of versions and was the Big Three's response to rising gasoline prices in the early '70s. I owned the station-wagon version. Compared to the true station wagons of the era like Ford's monolithic Country Squire, it was a true miniature and intended, I suppose, to confuse anyone thinking about buying something foreign-made. You could still pack a lot of stuff in a Vega wagon. Everything I owned could fit in it and still leave room in the front passenger seat for my dog. Her name, of course, was Vega.

Vega is an okay name for a dog, and it gave me one less thing to remember. I was doing a very short tour of duty in the Army at the time and living in the enlisted barracks at a fort in Georgia. We were all young and very glad we were not going to Vietnam. The U.S. Army was in a state of shock: Tricky Dick had been canned, our current [Gerald Ford] commander in chief apparently couldn't climb stairs without injuring himself, and we were left to do pretty much as we pleased.

We partied a lot. Even right in the barracks. Guys were rotating back from Asia who had actually been shot at, and—when the Army felt they had decompressed enough—began joining us in the regular barracks. These guys were so glad to be alive—reprieved from death at the hands of an enemy most of them never even saw—that no amount of debauchery or intoxication was too much. But, God, we tried.

Pretty soon we ran out of dope. In fact, the whole base went dry, and it was time for a logistical resupply mission of some magnitude. This would turn out to be the only mission of any merit that I would ever be sent on, so I took two weeks' leave and headed south. My orders: Score four pounds of the best pot I could find.

With Vega next to me in the passenger seat, it was nice to be on the road. The two weeks went by, and I was headed back to station with the shopping list filled and a case of real Mexican-made Kahlua to boot. I was on U.S. Highway 1 north, and just passing through many small rural communities that populate its roadside, when the blue and red lights of a municipal police car slashed across my rearview mirror.

Bummer, adrenaline, life flashes. Can you say *Midnight Express*, y'all? The Georgia correctional system was not perceived as a positive life experience, judging from the ever-present roadside gangs. I didn't look good in stripes, couldn't eat fifty eggs in one sitting, and people with mirror sunglasses and shotguns made me uncomfortable.

I pulled to the side of the road and looked at Vega. Dogs can sense when you are scared shitless. My ears were ringing with fear when I heard a voice say, "Let me see your license and registration, son. You were doin' thirty-seven in a twenty-five zone back there." I pulled my wallet and fished the other papers out of the glove compartment. I had everything in my right hand and was reaching across my chest to hand over the papers when Vega struck.

In an instant, she had hold of the constable's blue jacket sleeve, and there was considerable growling and cursing. As I pulled her away from the window, the jacket sleeve gave way with a loud—really loud—ripping noise. With my right hand on top of Vega, I reached out in vain to hand over my papers. All I could see of the policeman's face was my own reflection in the mirror aviator frames and a frown that looked extremely pissed off.

"All right, boy, follow me to the station."

I did as he asked, of course. We pulled into the gravel and red-clay parking area with the lights of the police car still flashing. He didn't even look at me, just waved his hand as he trudged into the building. I followed him into the building, and he was already seated with the offended jacket lying on the desk in front of him. I was shaking like a leaf while he stared at my driver's license, and we waited for a call back on whether I had any outstanding warrants.

Everything came back clear.

"You ready to pay the fine now, son, an' you can go. You're a service-man, so that's all I'm gonna do. That'll be thirty-seven dollars—cash."

I about pissed myself walking out of that building. Vega seemed pleased to see me as well.

Bank Job

Pam and I were on our way to the desert when we realized neither of us had any pot. We called around, and the only person we could get was the man who sold "tea." You ordered it by code, and I even had my own pin number.

We were on our way out of town, so it was decided we would meet Jack on the off-ramp of Lincoln Boulevard at the gas station. When he arrived, he told us that the pot was still wet, so we should spread it out and let it dry.

We were in too much of a hurry to wait, so we took our first hit immediately, and we were off to the bank to replenish our funds. When we arrived at the bank, Pam decided to stay in the car and let the motor run so she could use the heater to dry the stuff.

I went into the bank and immediately felt there was something wrong, but I was very stoned, so at first I thought it was my imagination. I got into line and noticed that everyone seemed to be standing still.

I waited a few moments and still no one moved, so finally I got up my courage and turned around and called to the manager, "What's wrong— is this a holdup?"

As I said this, it unfroze everyone, and the robber ran right by me out into the street. I realized that Pam was in danger with the car motor running, parked right in front of the bank, and all that pot in her lap. Paradise for anyone.

As I ran out toward Pam, the police and guards gave chase after the robber. I jumped into my car with the motor still running, hoping the police would not mistake me for the thief. They didn't and we were off onto another adventure . . .

Stems and Seeds

A poor little rich boy I worked with named "Joe College" asked me to score a quarter pound of pot for him to take back to school. As usual, the late summer dry spell was upon us and pot was scarce. I had heard that this guy across the street had been busted a couple of years before for coke, so I thought maybe he still had some connections.

We sat on my front steps shooting the shit for a while, and then he told me to stop over later and he'd have the pot for me. When he let me into his apartment, there were a half dozen or so guys sitting around. I was probably stoned and didn't pay much attention to them, but I was taken aback a bit when he handed me the quarter pound out in the middle of the room in front of everybody.

But I thought he was cool, so I assumed the rest of the guys were, too, or he wouldn't be conducting business in front of them. I took the pot home and after a while Joe College came over to check it out. Like I said, we were in a dry spell, but Joe was picky and didn't want the pot. Too many stems and seeds.

Oh, well, it was fronted to me, so I'd just take it back. As I was getting ready to walk out the door a while later to do just that, someone knocked on the door. I didn't know the guy but I recognized him. He hung out at the same bar my friends and I went to every weekend. It was a dive bar that we sat around in, smoking joints. It was paradise, soon to be a parking lot.

He said he was from "John's" across the street and was wondering what was up with the quarter pound. I told him I was just on my way back over with the pot because my friend wasn't satisfied with the quality and we hadn't smoked any. I gave it back to him and he left.

Some weeks later, after Joe College had gone back to school and paradise had been razed, I was telling a girl at work, who also knew John, about the whole incident. "After John got busted," she told me, "he turned narc to stay out of prison." What?

It all became clear then. The crowd in John's apartment, the guy popping in with the excuse that he was concerned about the pot when he was really trying to see who I was getting it for, and the bar where no one hassled us about smoking joints. Hell, Big Brother was probably watching us the whole time! I was sure glad then that Joe College hadn't wanted the pot. He would've been looking through books, and I would have been looking through bars.

Radical Luck

TOM CRAIG

It was early spring 1971. My wife, young child, and I shared a house with two fellow students in a working-class suburb of Washington, D.C. We had all moved in together after leaving/being asked to leave the major radical commune of our university because of a perceived lack of proper revolutionary spirit. It was the wild and woolly times of the revolution.

Even our staid, old, preppy college, Georgetown University, had risen up the previous spring after the invasion of Cambodia, Kent State, and "Shut It Down," and even that fall there had been a local version of the "Days of Rage" protest in the streets of trendy old Georgetown, which required a massive mobilization of D.C. cops to restore order.

Our two roommates, Steve and Ray, were wildly wacky anarchistic dope dealers who, about every two weeks, had a well-dressed visitor from California fly in and deliver a large suitcase full of Acapulco Gold and other goodies for local distribution. Needless to say, our house was unique on our little side street, where office workers and tradespeople left early in the morning, lunches packed, to pursue their version of the American dream.

We even had a Virginia state trooper living about five doors down, who parked his patrol car out in front of the house. It was a living reminder that we were, if not in the belly, at least in the gullet of the beast. For the most part, we were fairly discreet, but after one large shipment from the Golden State, we planned our first big party. The May Day demonstrations of that year were winding down, and there was major steam that needed to be released.

Ray, the trickster of the dynamic duo, organized a gathering of our fellow art class students, assorted radicals, and hippies, and even some of the Vietnam Vets Against the War from around the country who had trekked to Washington and whom we had brought out from their encampment down on the Mall.

Steve, not to be outdone, invited his band down from Long Island to provide musical accompaniment for the spectacle. So, here we were in a small two-story house in sleepy little Falls Church, Virginia, with a loud band wailing in the basement and about forty stoned people sipping Boone's Farm. Soon the sickly sweet smell of righteous herb seemed to be wafting from the very heating ducts themselves.

I had always been the "father figure" of the household. Everything was in my name, and I fixed the clogged sinks, etc., so naturally I was feeling a little paranoid and responsible. I remember even going out in the front yard to check the noise and hilarity level, which much to my surprise was relatively under control. Finally, I decided to abandon myself to the revelry and proceeded to compete in the shotgun and bong events with great relish. After my consciousness had been significantly altered, I drifted into a relaxed state and began having a marvelous time.

I thought our little house had been successfully launched into an orbit around Jupiter and was far beyond the clutches of the sad, violent, gray world it had once stood in. Somewhere along that time, I heard someone calling my name loudly from a distance. I swam down through the haze and wandered toward the front door where I saw Ray, grinning widely to someone outside and motioning me to come and deal with these new guests, who were just hidden from my sight behind the opened door.

All right, Ray, I thought, what is waiting for me: a face-painted ghoul, a naked lady, a pie in the face? Ray, still beaming, stepped back to get a better look at my facial reaction as I came around the door. There on our doorstep stood two fresh-faced, red-cheeked Virginia troopers, grinning almost as beneficently as Ray. I swallowed hard, smiled weakly, and tried to ignore the wafting ganja smoke escaping from the upper doorway.

"Can I help you?" I managed to ask. Still grinning, one of the troopers addressed me in a broad cracker drawl: "We were just passing by and we noticed that one of the doors on that red van was open, and it being after midnight and all, we wanted to make sure everything was okay." I jumped at the chance to go inspect and lead them away from the smoking house, thanking them profusely.

The next day as I was leaving for town, I saw a state police car rounding the bend in front of our house. The driver wore the same grin he'd had last night as he waved cheerfully to me, happy to greet his new neighbor. Was he a nice guy, just doing his job? A curious but benign straight hoping to catch some orgy scene? Or a good ole boy just a-messin' with our minds? Damned if I know. I'm just glad I kept my underwear clean that night.

Foolish Question

JERRY OCHS

In the early '70s, I shared a house with seven other people—some college students, some married working couples. We liked to smoke pot, and there was always some around, except for one horrible day when we realized that we all had run dry at the same time.

Everyone being conscientious communalists, each person made an extra effort that day to score, and at dinnertime the results spoke for themselves: a kilo here and a half kilo there and minimountains of pot in front of each person.

In order to judge the quality of this cornucopia of Mary Jane, we each rolled a joint, and we smoked them one at a time. At about the time we were toking on contestant number five, which had reached the status of roach, there was an abrupt and violent knocking at the front door.

Bob, the nervous type, holding the roach and sitting at a table piled high with pot, eyes wide with fear, squeaked, "Should I swallow it?"

Not Busted

These Untidy Guys

MICHELLE PHILLIPS

Our rented car with almost all our worldly possessions had been stolen from the underground car park on Franklin. We reported it to the police and, in the pace of events, forgot about it.

After moving to Flores, we had a visit without warning from a member of the FBI. The car had been found and had been stolen by someone they were interested in. I invited him in, and he began to spell out his story while I, horrified, froze.

All across the coffee table was an array of marijuana in various stages of preparation and cleaning: a hundred joints, all neatly rolled, separated and stacked by Denny. Buds still clinging together from the fields, some cleaned, some twigs, a lot of seeds. A whole mess of pot.

While the FBI agent told his tale of sleuthing rewarded, I decided that the only way to deal with this awful sideshow of cannabis was to busy myself like a housewife. I took a big paper bag from the market and started shoving all the marijuana into it, all the while playing the scene as if to say: "These untidy guys around here—always leaving things around."

If the FBI man knew or suspected anything, he never indicated it to me. His eyes didn't stray to the table. He just kept to the subject at hand—the stolen car—while I showed suitable interest: "Really? How amazing! Well, now. Gee!"

The Hole-in-the-Floor Gang

A whole bunch of us jumped into my friend's van to go to Starved Rock, Illinois. For the fourteen of us, we took three ounces of high-grade weed. After spending several hours there and getting very stoned, we started back. For some reason that made perfect sense then, we decided to travel down one of the main streets of town.

Suddenly, the driver said that the cops were right behind us and wanted to pull us over. Underneath the carpeting on the floor was a big hole that had once been part of the frame but was now surrounded with rust. Out that hole went pipes, papers, roach clips, and, in three different baggies, an ounce and a half of smoke.

The cops stopped and searched each of us, the males much more thoroughly than the females, but we were all lucky that we had dumped our stashes. We had to follow the squad car to the cop shop where they gave the driver a bogus ticket—why didn't they do that on the spot?—and told us to get out of town. They were not amused when we pointed out to them that we already would be if they hadn't made us go to the station.

We went back to see if we could find any of our stash, as most of us figured that we needed a smoke. We were able to find two pipes, one roach clip, one pack of papers, and about half an ounce of weed. After going over the drop zone twice, we left town fast.

About a month after the incident, I was helping the van owner replace the muffler. Stuck in the frame just "downwind" of the hole, we found a bag of dope. We figured that we should forget the muffler and, in honor of our trip to Starved Rock, we should smoke the dope.

We started to and his brother and a friend arrived home to help us. When they heard the story, we turned it into a religious ceremony and got totally stoned.

The Grateful Living

WOODY

On a typical Saturday evening around 11:00 PM, some friends and I decided to go to the cemetery just to smoke and be with the dead. (Don't worry, we're not vampires or anything.) We hopped over the fence surrounding the burial ground and lit up a huge joint. We went to the back to lay down on the hill. We had brought along some more weed 'cause we do smoke too much.

This cemetery being close to the highway, somebody must have seen us and called the cops. Flashlights were seen coming from afar, but we thought nothing of it, assuming more friends were on their way. Hell, no! The cops said that if we wanted to smoke, to do it in a safe place, not in public like that.

As we were exiting the place, we had to walk alongside the highway to return to our homes, and they passed by us with their sirens on, yelling over the intercom, "Yabba dabba doo" over and over again as they vanished in the fog.

Nickel Bag

Back in 1964, on a hot summer day in New York, my friend Mitch and I (both seventeen years old) were in his '52 DeSoto going the wrong way down a one-way street under the old West Side Highway. We were stopped by cops who found the joint that Mitch couldn't ditch in time, but they didn't find the one I tossed under the parked car.

We had discovered a method of grinding up peyote buttons and putting them in gelatin caps to get them down painlessly. I don't know what the cop thought as he opened the vast trunk to Mitch's car, which was stuffed with thousands of empty caps contained within a deflated inflatable life raft. After an hour of telling various cops that I didn't know any kingpins of the dope world to set up for them on King's Highway in Brooklyn, they turned us loose after confiscating our nickel bag.

I had just reached the car and scooped my joint (our one remaining) up off the street from under the car when the cop came back again. Oh, shit, I thought. Changed his mind. He leaned into the window and said in a gruff cop voice, "Have you got any papers?" I gave him my pack of Bambu, which he confiscated with a big grin, and he was actually rolling a joint as he strolled back to join his fellow fuzz.

Dementia

BOB WIEDER

In 1969, I was in a political satire performance group truly worthy of amnesia, called Dementia, and one night after a gig in San Francisco, we were heading home in Berkeley on Telegraph Avenue and got pulled over by two Berkeley cops for God knows what in front of the Forum Café, whose backyard was People's Park.

They kept asking us what we were up to, and where we'd been, and I'd had a few beers at the gig and had to piss terribly, so I finally asked them to let me pop around back of the café (it was the wee hours) and take a leak. One cop said okay, but he had to pat me down first.

In my shirt pocket he found a matchbox with a lump of hash in it, that being my drug of inspiration at the time. He asked me where I got it. I said some fan had slipped it to me at the gig, I didn't know anything about it, blah, blah, lie.

He said okay, go pee and come back. I ducked around back, peed, and, God knows just why, I came back. When I reappeared around the corner, both cops gaped at me in shock. My return was clearly quite unexpected. They didn't seem to know what to do.

After a brief consultation, they said something like, "Well, it's late, so we'll let you go this time. But we'll just keep this." Meaning the hash, of course, which they did. I suspect they were trolling for stash, and once they'd landed mine, hey, this shift's over. The last thing they wanted was an actual bust to complicate their evening.

Rare Moment

I returned home after my freshman year of college to a small town in Westchester County, New York, with no job, no money, and a girlfriend in tow. Under the circumstances, I was prepared to take whatever job I could find for the summer and eventually ended up as a maintenance worker at the local dump. I will spare you the details, since you might have eaten recently, but suffice to say that if this is not the worst way to make a minimum wage, it is definitely in the bottom five.

One result of this situation was that I spent a great deal of my time fighting depression by smoking considerable quantities of marijuana, along with several of my friends who were in similarly difficult circumstances. Much of our commiserating took place at Nick's house as he lived in his own apartment downstairs from his father and thus enjoyed more freedom of action than the rest of us.

So there we would sit, miserable and stoned, but at least in company, for many hours at a time. Nick had an excellent music collection, and the quality of the dope was very good, as I had maintained my college connections and was supplying the local scene, such as it was. Excitement was rare, to say the least.

This particular evening, I had just picked up an ounce or two of lush green buds and had brought them to Nick's for a test drive. Now, Nick lived seven miles from anywhere in the woods on top of a mountain. It wasn't exactly isolated, but I will point out that I once spent the better part of an hour (under the influence of some designer drug) lying in the center of the road outside the house, howling at the moon, and was not disturbed. So we were not expecting visitors as we shared the bong around and listened to early Pink Floyd that night.

At once, Nick announces, "I thought I heard something," and he leaves the room. Returning from the entrance hall a moment later, he pokes his head into the cloud of smoke with a look of pure terror on his face and says, "Dave, there's an officer here to see you."

I am holding the steaming bong at the moment he says this. I am very high. I do not immediately understand what he is saying to me, but my girlfriend Karin does, and begins to hide bags of dope under pillows and sofa cushions with remarkable efficiency. At some point she removes the bong from my hand, and I stumble out of the room and into the presence of two Westchester County police officers who are standing just outside the front door and shining flashlights around the perimeter of the house. I have decided that they are here to tell me that someone in my family has died after being hit by a bus, and I am wondering who it is. Or they are here to arrest me, having tracked my drug deal from Manhattan to this house. I brace for the impact of the announcement.

"Is that your car parked out there on the street?" says the lead cop, who is shorter than me and wears a bushy mustache.

"Yes," I reply, curious about what this has to do with my tragically departed family member or impending bust.

"Well, you are parked illegally. I could give you a citation, but instead I'll just ask you to move the car so that . . . "

I do not hear what he says next as wave after wave of relief rolls over me. No one is dead, and I am not in any real trouble. His voice continues, and the effect soothes me further. I am nodding gratefully, promising to move the car directly, when suddenly his voice stops. He stiffens and reaches toward me. I look down where he is reaching and notice a bag of dope sticking out of my left breast pocket.

I have just enough time to think, "Oh, shit," which I understand are the most commonly used last words, before his hand reaches my pocket. This is it: I'm going to prison at nineteen.

He grabs the bag, pushes it down into my pocket, and says, "Put that away where I can't see it."

It is not clear what I did in response to this, although I do recall feeling like my legs were about to buckle. Most likely, I simply grinned like a fool as an enormous love for Westchester County police officers welled up in my chest. I wanted to bow before these men. Had I a son, I would have wished him to become one of them. I'm sure that I once again promised, with great sincerity, to move my car to a proper and highly legal parking space. And after they left, I'm sure I did.

Paradigm Shift

JONATHAN PEKAR

My brother Jefferson and his friend Steve are hanging out in a Volkswagen bus—they had searched the whole car for roaches—when the cops come up.

"What are you all doing?"

"We're just sitting here getting ready to drink beer. We haven't started yet."

"You guys don't have any pot in here, do you?"

"No, sir, there ain't no pot in this car."

"Lemme look in the back, too."

And he opens it up and closes it up real quick.

"That's cool," the cop says. "I like your van. Now, don't be drinking and driving—you guys should be smoking instead of drinking."

That's weird. The cops drive off. My brother and his friend sit there for a minute, and then they drive home. My brother goes in the car, opens up the back, and fuckin' lying there is a film can the cop left there with a half ounce of Chronic marijuana.

"Well, dude," my brother says, "we searched the car for an hour. It's an empty van. There were no roaches, nothing in the whole car, then I open up the back and it's lying there. You gonna tell me two guys looking for an hour can't find it? A film canister? There's no way. Dude, look at this Chronic!"

It was purple, I mean purple, and the cops put it there. It was a gift— "You guys should be smoking instead of drinking"—and they left. I'll never forget my brother coming in: "Dude, you'll never believe this, ever." I grilled him for hours. I said, "This didn't happen." He says, "No, come look, it was an empty van." Those cops must have had a good laugh, can you imagine? Perverse, but good perverse.

It almost seems like the cops have lightened up. They don't care if you're smoking it, they just don't want you selling. It's all about "don't be a drug dealer." But when it gets to the point where cops are *giving* you pot, is that just not the fuckin' weirdest thing you ever heard? I could not get over how wacky that was.

Almost Busted

Romantic Interlude

WAVY GRAVY

It all began lifetimes ago at the Living Theatre in New York when I was doing *The Phantom Cabaret* every Saturday at midnight with Tiny Tim and Moondog.

One night, Tiny Tim comes off the stage after fifty minutes of Rudy Vallee, and he says, "Mr. Vallee came inside and he wouldn't leave—I've lost my Crosby power."

And Moondog says, "When I went blind, it was like suffocating."

And, oh, my head is pounding, and I wander outside after the show, and I got this big headache, and there's a burning mattress and a dead cat and broken glass and a guy screaming, "I'm an American, and I killed forty-three Japanese in Iwo Jima," and I stagger into the Fat Black Pussycat, looking for an aspirin, anything.

There's a table of folks sitting around, and they had a big bottle of Excedrin in the middle of the table, and I kicked back six without water to keep my innards crisp. Well, they turned out to be bennies (Benzedrine).

So, three days later, I tried to sneak home before my tongue woke up, and I get in the alley, and this woman says, "Do you wanna get high?"

And I says, "Sure."

She whipped out one of these skinny little cigarettes you didn't see advertised in any magazine, and I lit it up, and we started passing this joint back and forth, and suddenly I'm on the other end of an Eveready flashlight—gotta be the Man behind the light, do not pass Go, do not collect $200—so I swallow the roach and start kissing this strange chick.

Now, I got this roach burning in the back of my tongue, and I got no spit—the bennies have stolen all my spit—so what I have to do is reach my tongue into this strange girl's mouth and scoop out some of *her* spit to extinguish the roach, which I finally do as the cop says, "All right, you lovers, let's break it up."

State Line

WALDO STEVE AND THE WALDOS

A couple of the Waldos were driving from San Francisco to Lake Tahoe in 1972 for some summer fun. The glove box of my 1966 four-door Impala contained a fresh new lid of grass, and in the trunk in our suitcases were two additional lids. As I drove, I expressed my fears about being busted.

One of the Waldos in our car was the son of a cop. In fact, his father was a narcotics officer. Familiar with many of the details of his father's profession, he tried to calm me down by educating me on search-and-seizure laws. We drove for hours, memorizing every detail of California law on search and seizure. I became an expert. Effective knowledge and strategies—nobody was going to bust us. Above all, I remembered that a police officer could not make you open a locked glove box.

We arrived at Lake Tahoe and pulled into the parking lot. The other Waldos got out and went across the street to look for a bathroom. I moved to the passenger side of the front seat and began rolling joints on the lowered glove-box lid. All of a sudden, a car door slammed behind me. A cop had pulled in behind and was walking toward the car. I moved fast, rolling up the bag of weed into the box, closing the glove-box lid, inserting the key, and locking it. I breathed a huge sigh of relief; I was safe, armed with my new knowledge of search-and-seizure laws.

The officer knocked on the window. I rolled it down and he asked for license and registration. I complied. He returned them and asked, "What's in the glove box?"

"Maps," I answered.

The cop said, "Let me see those maps."

"No," I said.

He said, "Open up the glove box."

"I don't have to," I said.

He said, "Yes, you do."

I said, "California Law 66294 (or whatever the number was at the time) says that I do not have to open a locked glove box."

And he said, "You're in Nevada, boy!"

I looked over my right shoulder. The state line was about twenty yards away. I looked over my other shoulder to see that two more cop cars had arrived, including an unmarked narc car. I opened the glove box and handed over the lid. The officer handed the lid to the cop from the unmarked car who started examining it closely.

The narc remarked, "Doesn't look too good. Too many seeds and stems."

One of the cops then said to me, "I'm going to give you a choice. If you have any more weed in this automobile, you can hand it all over to us right now, and we may or we may not bust you. Or, we can search your car, and if we should find anything, we will definitely bust you." He added, "It's your Nevada gamble."

I opened up the trunk and handed over the two lids.

The narc officer asked me, "Do you want a receipt for this?"

And I responded, "Do you give trading stamps, too?"

He chuckled.

The three officers had a little meeting while I waited patiently. Then one of them walked over and showed me a children's school–style notebook with a list of names and numbers written in it. He started writing my name at the bottom of the list.

He said, "I'm going to give you exactly one minute to get across the border. You are number 324 in the state of Nevada and you cannot come back to Nevada for as long as you live."

I said, "What about my friends? How will they find me?"

Holding up his watch, he said, "You have one minute to get out of Nevada, starting now."

I raced to the state line border marker located on the sidewalk next to the casinos at Lake Tahoe's South Shore and waited. About a half hour later my friends walked up.

We really wanted to go to Nevada because Nevada had the best beaches. We spent the entire following day trying to find a lawyer. Nearly every attorney we contacted would not talk to us. A few said they would talk with us; however, they quoted astronomical rates we could not afford. We were frustrated but determined to get an answer as to whether or not I could enter Nevada for the rest of eternity.

The next day we drove over to the North Shore of Tahoe. An attorney there agreed to talk to us for a reasonable price. We were excited because this one attorney who agreed to see us was named Joseph Joynt. We paid our money up front and waited on pins and needles to ask him, "Could we go back into Nevada?"

He answered with one word: "Probably."

We drove directly to Nevada and spent the rest of our vacation there, knowing the entire time what it feels like to be an outlaw.

The Favor

ST. GERARD

Fred and I had struck out again on a Friday night, and we were leaving the bar. It was snowing lightly as we were walking to the car. As we passed two attractive females, I said, "Typical, we are walking out and two pretties are walking in." They chuckled and we struck up a nice conversation.

A few minutes later, the four of us were in Fred's snow-covered car, rolling a fatty. Suddenly, there was a flashlight banging on the window, knocking the snow off. A state trooper was ordering the four of us out of the car.

As he was getting ready to bust us on a minor possession charge, a car flew into the parking lot with a long-haired guy screaming, "Officers, there is a car hanging over the bridge up the street, there are people in it, and it looks like it's going to fall into the river!

The cops looked at each other, then at us, and then one said, "Look, get out of here, stay out of here, and never let me see this car around here again." With that, he put the pot in his pocket and sped off toward the bridge.

The long-hair looked at us and said, "You owe me one. Get out of here before he finds out I was fucking with him. If you ever see me on the side of the road, do me a return favor." With that, he was gone.

I looked at the two ladies and said, "Where should we go from here?" The one replied, "Straight to hell, asshole." It was another typical Friday night for Fred and me.

Busted

Fish Cops

We had planned a heavy recreational schedule that day, which included hiking, dinner out, and a Neil Young concert. It was the early 1980s, and money, not pleasure, was beginning to rule people's lives. That hadn't caught on with us yet, so we had rolled three or four joints to enhance our enjoyment of the day's activities.

We decided to stop by an out-of-the-way place we'd visited for just such an occasion many times before. It was an undeveloped area outside the sprawling city—no homes, businesses, or schools anywhere around. It was almost a mile-long walk on the unmarked trail from a county road to a quiet, wooded spot on the lakeshore. There was no one nearby, just some boats way out on the lake.

While we were indulging, I recalled a conversation I'd had with a coworker about law enforcement personnel, specifically conservation officers, who we referred to derogatorily as "Fish Cops." My coworker told me that CO's had more law enforcement authority than any other group: sheriffs, state police, city police—that is, they could arrest you at any time for anything. I was young and naïve in those days and mistakenly assumed the scope of their authority was hunting and fishing violations. This was news to me, and I was relaying the information to my companion while we smoked.

Before we finished inhaling, there was a noise in the woods behind us, and who should appear but two conservation officers. They promptly confiscated our small supply of medicinal herbs and arrested us for possession of marijuana. Bummer. While they were conducting the honors, one said, "So, just talking about us, huh?" Like Big Brother, they had been lurking nearby in the woods, listening to us the entire time. Serious bummer.

Who knows what they were doing there: looking for people fishing without a license, couples "doing it," or maybe dopers like us. We'd never encountered anyone else in the area during previous visits. It was a long, silent, humiliating walk back to the car with our new friends trailing behind us. Miraculously, they didn't search the car, which didn't matter since it was clean anyway. No doubt the story still circulates among drunken CO's at cop parties even to this day. It's easy to collar people who aren't going to fight back.

So, the major losses were all shreds of dignity, three joints, a nice roach clip, a good high and buoyant mood, and the $500 each we paid our lawyer to intervene on our behalf while appearing later before the local judge. He obtained for us one year of good-behavior probation and no conviction. And so we managed to be good and made sufficient reparation for the serious harm we inflicted upon society, that being appreciating the gifts of the Earth by sharing a joint in the woods, off the beaten path, bothering no one. Surprisingly, we have not become deranged dope fiends as depicted in *Reefer Madness* but remain "productive members of society," for what it's worth.

Most Likely to Succeed

Eleven nice plants in the ground. August, the late 1980s, 5:30 AM, Mendocino, California. The COMMET squad (County of Mendocino Marijuana Eradication Team) bursts into my house, waking me up from a sleep that still has four hours to go. They hold me at gunpoint as I pull on my trousers. A couple of their guys yell back to the house from the garden and confirm what the aerial photos had given them reason to suspect: This person is, indeed, a cultivator of marijuana.

As I listen to the swipes of their machetes putting an end to my short career as a dope farmer, I am told to sit at my dining room table and keep my hands where they can see them. They ask me to produce some identification. On the table in front of me is my high school yearbook, which I had been thumbing through the night before in anticipation of attending my twenty-fifth reunion a month later. I slide the book over and open it to the page that shows me in my blue-and-gold FFA (Future Farmers of America) jacket posing with the girl who, like me, had been voted "Most Likely to Succeed."

"There," I said, pointing to the picture. "That's me."

I think the deputy in charge of the bust cracked a tiny smile as she glanced at the photograph, but it was gone an instant later.

I was sentenced to ninety days. I did forty-seven of them and was released for good behavior and because the jail was overcrowded, largely because of arrests and convictions of other small growers and traffickers.

The part that hurts the most is that today, more than twenty years later, in a community I have served in many positive ways—as an artist, an educator, a worker for worthy causes—people still have a tendency to think of me first as "that guy who did some time for growing back in the '80s." And, sadly, no matter what I may do or accomplish in the years to come, that simple fact will probably never change.

A Tale of Two Busts

CHIC

In 1962, I was sitting in the lotus position in front of a large mirror trying to disappear, and Robin said, "Chic, someone's banging on my bedroom wall, and something is coming through the wall." I got up and went to the far wall of her room where there was a hole six inches in diameter that now had a bulging plastic bag beginning to protrude from it. I heard my neighbor yell, "Hey, man, hold on to this till the cops leave. They're coming in my front door!"

Meanwhile, Robin said, "Someone's banging on our door!" I quickly took three dime-bags of my personal herb stash, tossed them out the window to recover later, and answered the door. It was a policeman who said, "Are these apartments connected?" I said, "No," but he wanted to check anyway. He came into the kitchen and said, "What's that noise in there?"

"I don't know." Then he looked at the hole in the wall, saw the bag protruding, and then a hand came through, trying to cram the rest.

The cop said, "What is it?"

"I don't know."

"Pick it up!"

"Oh, no," I said. "You pick it up. It's all yours. I don't even know what it is." The cop grabbed the biggest bunch of it and disappeared back out to the storefront. Robin said, "There's still about two ounces on the floor. What are you going to do?"

"No choice. I have to go out there and watch the bust go down and act surprised."

I walked down the tile hall, through the large wood-and-glass door, down the corrugated iron steps where I stood by the banister, propped up by a couple of my Puerto Rican brothers who knew what was going down.

After the cops took away fellow members of the Living Theatre cast of *The Brig* and a couple of my other friends, I went back inside and wondered what to do about the grass remaining on the floor of Robin's bedroom. Little by little, we smoked it all. The cops never came back.

When I discovered that my three dime-bags were not where I had tossed them, I went out into the street and found one of my *hermanos*, Kimo, and asked him to put out the word that they were my bags. A half hour later, my friend Victor showed up with two $15 bags and said, "I'm sorry, Chico, I didn't know it was your stash. We thought it was ditched from the bust."

I said, *"No hay problema, amigo"* and gave him one of the bags. I loved my life on the Lower East Side. I loved our barrio. Good people.

Hash Police

In 1967, I was living in Hell's Kitchen. As an aspiring actor, I was compelled to sell grass, hash, and acid to augment my lifestyle. One day, three plainclothes police came to my door with a search warrant, seized my stash, and took me and a friend to the local precinct lockup for later transport to the Tombs.

After my initial interrogation, they knew I would tell them nothing they could use. They were angry, but they knew I wasn't a rat. The two older cops—one Irish, one Italian—left the room first, followed by the young Italian and myself. The young cop gestured with his eyes to the table in the room as we were leaving and said, "I didn't see anything."

I looked and saw a small piece of my hash just sitting there. I figured what the hell and picked it up and mashed it into the right hinge of my glasses and went to the holding cell to wait. I told my friend what happened and we were puzzled together.

Then the young cop walked by our cell and squeezed a horizontal bar and walked away snickering. He had stuck another piece of hash to the bars. I quickly molded my other hinge.

Later, when they took us to the Tombs, they gave us our own private cell away from the junkies and assholes, and we spent the whole night smoking little pieces of hash on a straight pin. I even managed to smuggle in a pen, and I wrote a song lyric on a piece of hanger cardboard.

Corrupting Minors
MAXIMUM TRAFFIC

I got a job and my first apartment when I was eighteen years old. Only weeks after moving into the place, the local cops came and forced in my door, knocking me on my butt. They tore the place apart, throwing all my clothes on the floor, overturning my bed. They looked in every nook and cranny. When they were done, they asked me if I wanted them to get a search warrant.

They found a full ounce of weed in my pocket and another ounce floating in the toilet. I had some friends visiting, and one of them—my best friend, Ray, who was only sixteen years old—had the presence of mind to try to flush one of the bags. Unfortunately, he emptied the bag into the toilet and flushed, but the damn thing never did flush very efficiently, and the weed was just swirling around and around.

One burly cop burst into the bathroom and yelled, "That's evidence! You fish that out of there!"

To my astonishment, my buddy Ray yelled right back, "If you want it so bad, *you* fish it out of there!"

Scared as I was, I had to fight back the laughter. They decided to leave the evidence.

The cops took us all to the city jail where they questioned us late into the night, trying to get us to rat on our friends. While sitting in the front office of the police station, Ray started to freak out. Even though he was only sixteen, he was a stocky kid, heavier than me. He never even touched any kind of dope, but his adrenaline suddenly kicked in.

He got up from the seat and started growling in a very menacing way. He walked over to the counter and started pounding on it. Instantly, the room was filled with cops. Ray was bellowing like a mad bull, and he was throwing the cops around like popcorn! It took a three-cop pileup to subdue and handcuff him. All the while the cops were screaming, "What kind of dope is he on?" No dope at all.

Well, when the dust settled, I was charged with corrupting minors because I was the only one who was eighteen and legally an adult. They later dropped the charges down to possession. I got thrown out of the apartment, lost my job, and got a year's probation and a $50 fine.

I was outraged. I knew that the revolution was here and that this kind of bullshit oppression was soon to be a thing of the past. Just goes to show you how wrong a person can be.

Serving Time

Escaping Reality

DENNIS SOBIN

Fortunately, when I was asked to make a contribution to this book, I was in an ideal place to get others more experienced than myself to write. Being in prison, I knew a lot of guys who had done lots of dope, both before and during their prison stays.

I wasted little time circulating the letter I had received asking for pot stories. Then a funny thing happened at the prison. The shit hit the fan, quite coincidentally. The factory here that makes license plates for the Florida Department of Highway Safety and Motor Vehicles got busted.

It seems that the inmates who worked there had a terrific scam going. They stole plates to ship to criminal contacts on the outside, people who would sell them to practicing libertarians who preferred not to register their cars with a government agency.

The payment these inmates received for their handiwork was pot. Everything was handled through the shipping and receiving department of the prison factory, staffed by clever inmates. Who knows what went wrong?

At any rate, the scheme got exposed about the time I started passing around the letter. As a result, paranoia was running high and a major source for pot stories closed up. Too bad, too. Prison is about the safest place to do dope since it's practically impossible to infiltrate by undercover cops.

The real trick is to get it in, but as long as people seek to escape reality—as they most surely do here—that will happen. Just the fact of using dope in prison seems pretty funny to me.

Lipton

FREDERIC BERTHOFF

I'm writing from the federal prison here in Miami, five years into a twenty-one-year sentence for hashish and marijuana trafficking. You hear a lot about drugs in jail, but at these new places, security is pretty tight, so there's not much around. I'd smell pot at night once in a while, but it was rare. So, when offered a joint for free, I should have known it was a gaff.

(A gaff is a hook used to land a big fish. You pull in the fish on the standard hook and line, but when it gets close to the boat, you reach out with a gaff hook and stick it in the side of the fish. The gaff hook is a big gnarly thing attached to the end of a three-foot pole. So, in the metaphorical sense, "setting the gaff" is when the predatory salesman gets the hook into his customer.)

Jose lived upstairs on the corner and was a cheerful little Puerto Rican who spoke English like he was born here. He was in charge of the only set of colored pencils on the block, so I knew him a little bit through that avenue. I used to borrow them sometimes and would give him cigarettes for the favor.

Like most of the wheeler-dealers on the block, Jose mixed it up pretty good and still had a black eye that had been healing for a couple of weeks. I had the colored pencils from the night before and was bringing them back to his room before we went out to recreation in the morning. In his cell, he pulled a wispy-thin jay-bar (joint) out from behind a protruding ear and gave a conspiratorial leer.

They say nothing's for nothing, especially in the can, but I liked the kid so I said, "All right, gimme the fucking thing" and took it. I brought a cigar and a lighter outside with me, looking forward to a good smoke despite the paranoia that I was way too old to enjoy anymore.

Outside, we had a choice of four cages to spend the hour in. The crowd from the cellblock divvied up mostly along age and color lines, but there was nothing formal or set about it. Each cage was a half court with a hoop, and that day I went over to the farthest one where Jose and the young kids of darker hues played.

So I lit up my El Producto and took a few puffs, taking a quick look around for the screws. Then out came the joint, looking pathetically small compared to the cigar, and I lit it, too. I took a couple of deep drags and let the sweet smoke out my nose like I always did to taste the quality. Old habits are hard to break.

I savored it like a wine steward wearing his little silver cup on a chain. It was sweet and kind of green tasting, but too dry for green pot, and yet it tasted familiar, like something from a long time ago. Smoke curled into the air and rolled indiscreetly downwind. Familiar, familiar.

I had a bamboo opium pipe that my mom bought in the Village back in the '40s as a souvenir. She'd given it to me when I was a teenybopper, and over the years I had smoked a little of everything in it, though it had never been degraded with "the rock." Banana peels and oregano, for starters, then later, several varieties of pot and hash, some opium psilocybin mushrooms, Sir Walter Raleigh Kentucky Burley, and one time, tea.

I was listening to a Simon & Garfunkel song about how they "smoke a pint of tea a day," and I knew they were talking about weed, but on a boring afternoon, I threw a pinch of Earl Grey into the little brass bowl and fired it up. A long, long time ago, but that day in the cage, there it was again. The taste of tea.

Bobby was a young black wise guy who'd just been booted out of Pilgrim County Jail for fighting and sent up to Littleton. He wore his hair in little twists on top of his head with the sides shaved, as was the style. We were talking about the past week when I was playing hoop barefoot, and he was laughing at me with his buddies. "Yo, look at this dude . . . " So he knew me and when he smelled the joint, he came hopping over, flashing his trademark troublemaker's grin.

"Hey, man, I smell that shit, man. Where'd you get that?"

It wouldn't have been cool to say just where, so I didn't and shrugged it off. "Somebody gave it to me."

"You pay for it?" He was laughing now just like he did when I was the dude playing hoop barefoot. "Never mind, I knows where you got it, man. Hey, yo, Lipton!" He was calling to my main man, my connection, Jose. "Hey, yo, Lipton!"

Jose came over from the game, knowing he was bagged (in trouble) and already looking at his shoes.

"Hey, yo, man, you still passin' that shit? You passin' that shit off on my man here?"

Jose—"Lipton"—looked so bad that I stuck up for him even though the jig was up. I said, "Well, Bobby, he gave it to me for nothing."

"That motherfucker passin' that shit out for weed, why you think he got a black eye? Motherfuckers caught him passin' that tea last week for money and fucked him up." Jose skulked back to the game and Bobby was hollering after him, "Hey, yo, Lipton! Lipton!"

It reminded me of the Eskimos I'd learned about in school. My anthropology teacher was a hands-on guy, and he went up to Alaska for an extended tour of field research with a primitive tribe up there. When one of the Eskimos got out of line, they punished him by assigning a derogatory name, related to the offense, for a specified period of time. A guy caught stealing someone else's kayak was called "Stealer of Kayak" for a full year.

So I guess these kids in prison had unknowingly adopted a universal code of behavior modification for their own use. They added a beating, which the Eskimos chose not to include. Call that the barbarian influence. Anyway, Lipton still had the pencils, and the gaff joint was for free, so after a couple of days of ball-breaking, I went back to calling him Jose. Bobby didn't let me forget so easily. He'd see me coming and say, "Hey yo, man, you smokin' any good reefer lately? Where's your boy, Lipton? Ha ha ha!"

Miscellaneous Joints

Good Vibes

STEPHEN GASKIN

One of the neatest hippie communes I ever lived in was a house in Stinson Beach on Highway 1 just north of San Francisco. It was a nice two-story house in a little ravine that went up Mount Tam behind the house. Off the left of the house, there was a grove of pine trees that was host to a swarm of monarch butterflies. On the other side of the house there was a river of nasturtiums whose flowers were the same colors as the butterflies.

It was a lovely hippie house and had three couples and a few single hippies living there. Paul and Pamela were an art student and a yogi. Charlie and Linda were the resident nonvegetarians. Linda had a liver condition and was under doctor's orders to eat meat. Charlie was much too loyal to let Linda be the only nonveggie. And there was Margaret and me.

I say wannabes because we would have done a better job of having some grass around if we were more serious hippies. We had been out for a while. One of the single men wasn't doing well at all without grass. He bitched and moaned and whined until we all said, "If you aren't going to do anything about it, just shut up."

Joe, the single man, admitted that he had some money and said, "Well, if none of you guys have enough gumption to do something about it, I will." And he took off for the city to buy a kilo of Acapulco Gold, which cost $250.

While Joe was gone, Linda told me that I didn't really understand her rat. I thought I did. I mean a rat is a rat. That was actually the attitude she was complaining about. She took me into the kitchen and got her rat out of the cage on top of the fridge.

"Look," she said, "notice his tail. There is not a scale or hair out of place. Look at his feet and claws, just perfect!"

As she showed me her rat, I saw that she was right. The rat was beautiful, intelligent, friendly, clean, and sweet smelling. He was an excellent rat. Linda and I got on well after I understood her rat.

That evening we saw the car Joe had taken to town coming up the drive. When Joe left the car, he had such a jaunty air and such a good vibe that we caught eyes with each other and lifted eyebrows. It must be really good stuff, we thought.

Joe came into the house.

"Well," we said, "where is it?"

"Where is what?" he asked.

"The pot!" we said.

"Oh, that. Well, I didn't actually get any."

We were confused. His good vibes seemed to persist.

"What happened?" we demanded.

"I got robbed."

We freaked out. "Wow, man, what a drag." We were mystified. His good vibes remained evident.

Joe said, "I met these guys and asked about dope and they took me in this alley and robbed me."

He continued to smile. We had to ask, "What the hell are you smiling about?"

"They didn't hurt me!"

Joe's good vibes and attitude adjustment lasted so long that we decided that he had gotten his money's worth out of his dope adventure. He might not have been so sweet for so long if he had actually scored.

Ms. Deal

DAWNA KAUFMANN

I've learned as a comedy writer in Hollywood, if ya wanna be a player, it helps to be a player, which is why my writer pal Jason's weekly poker game had for years been great for off-duty schmoozing with the TV elite. His regular group consists of an agent, a director, a producer, and a star, with an occasional drop-in. Whenever I'd try to wheedle an invitation, Jason would snipe that they "don't play with girls," which would cue my lecture on affirmative action.

After hearing this argument a zillion times, Jason finally relented and agreed to let me attend that coming Thursday's session, if, as he said, I could "cut it" Ha! Cut it? I can cut it, shuffle it, and deal it, I chortled, as I promised to show up at 7:30 PM. And bring cash 'cause they "don't take checks or credit cards"—as if I was gonna lose!

During the week, I bought a poker book, memorizing important things like the author's name, Scarne (which rhymes with Carney), and rules and strategy for the game. It reinforced my feeling that you can't fear high stakes—it's all relative, and winning is proportional to skill. Play your odds. Bet intelligently. Know when to fold 'em, know when to hold 'em. I felt "in the chips" already but bought a Kenny Rogers CD for extra inspiration.

It wasn't like I hadn't played before—I'd racked up hundreds of hours on my video poker for Windows program—I just hadn't played with humans. As long as I had my little card that says what beats what, and can keep straight which way is clockwise, I could reasonably take on these manly men. Besides, I've always been convinced of female supremacy, a point on which no male's ever agreed with me, and on behalf of sisterhood everywhere, I welcomed the challenge of pitting my shrewd intellect against their macho egoism. Prepare to die, scoundrels!

So, it's Thursday night and Jason introduces me to the crew. I come on strong, singing, from *Guys and Dolls*, "Where's the action, where's the game? Gotta have the game or we'll die from shame," but when they don't react, I figure they're not theater people. As we take our places around the table, the director wisely suggests that I watch the action a bit first. Right away I'm impressed with the speed of things. In the time it takes them to rotate around the table so that each player gets to select a dealer's choice game, I'd still be dealing one hand. Whew!

The producer mentions white chips are $1, reds are $5, and blues are $10, and while I rationally accept that, emotionally all I see is a patriotic pile of rent money in the middle of the table. The star hands me a beer in a can, and I'm glad he doesn't patronize me by asking if I want a glass like some sissy, although actually I would've liked one—so sue me. Despite their banter, there's a thickness in the air. I resist suggesting we turn on the nearby TV for *Friends*, fearing they might throw it, and me, out the window. Concentrate, concentrate, I beg myself.

You know that feeling you get when your instinct for survival is threatened and you're forced to rely on devious and drastic weapons to stay alive? Well, it occurs to me that I have one of the fattest joints in captivity in my purse, and not only is it a bomber, it's Maui Wowie. Certain that I'll have these clowns on their knees in moments, I light up, inhale deeply, and pass the joint to the guys. "No, thanks," they mutter and echo. They don't smoke dope? I'm screwed!

Not to seem a fool by putting it out now, I keep toking, each hit of the potent gold forming a cosmic key that unlocks corridors of mutinous brain cells which are, at this very moment, lining up single file and jumping like kamikaze parachutists out of my eyes and ears and into the poker chip quicksand. Whereas I originally couldn't wait to get into the game, my head's now so clogged I suspect someone's poured bacon grease in my ears.

An hour later, I know they're wondering when I'll join the game, a thought that crosses my mind, too. They play on, perfectly aware of the impact of each newly dealt card, knowing exactly which raise they're on, and how every hand's financial history is recorded—as I sit there, blitzed, pressing my body hard into the plastic of the kitchen chair, hoping that instead of me, they'll see just another orange daisy on the pattern.

How I wish I could astrally project myself home. What a perfect opportunity this would be to clean my oven; I'd been meaning to disengage that exploded baked potato residue from 1995. My enfeebled brain drifts back to their game, which is still vicious as ever. I'm not sure if it's a mean ruse to bilk me out of my humble life savings, but the agent speaks up to see if I'm ready to play. My senses prepare for red alert but my mouth settles for automatic pilot and I meekly mumble, "Any minute now . . . "

Nuts! Here's my chance to score points for feminism and I'm blowing it. What would Gloria Steinem do if she were here? And would she play with queens higher than kings? While contemplating this, I sense Jason's displeasure that I'm not in the game. After all, he promised these gung-ho gamblers a fellow Amarillo Slim, not some gutless lookie-loo with the canny aptitude of a blow-up doll. Plus Jason's losing—Lady Luck, I'm not. I try to steady my gaze and study their game, but it's no use. With cards flying at warp speed and chips clicking like a Saint Vitus flamenco dancer, my already pathetic attention span's in urgent need of new elastic.

Just then—miracle of miracles—my cell phone rings. I answer it: It's a wrong number, but I don't tell the fellas. "Hi," I lie into the receiver. "Oh, no! I'll be there in ten minutes!" With a whimper I announce that my father's in the hospital and I must go to him. They all understand— especially Jason, who attended my dad's funeral several years ago but, mercifully, keeps my secret.

As I head to the door, I state boldly, "Gentlemen," then weaken like a fist without bones. "I . . . I really planned to take all your money tonight, but, uh, now that I've watched you, I gotta admit I'm nowhere near your league. Unless you're willing to play open-handed till I catch up—like in 2023—it's better for me to just cut my losses and thank you for a most educational evening."

My embarrassment is cut short by a genuine release of tension, with laughter and good cheer replacing the formerly serious facades. They chatter about how much ahead they'd be if they were only smart like me, and Jason winks that he wants to borrow my cell phone. I make my escape, never mentioning the script I'd planned to pitch them, and head home to destroy my collection of Vegas junket brochures and immediate plans for world domination.

If there's a moral to this story—and I'm not sure there is—it's that poker and pot don't mix. At least for me, at least that night. But I'm happy to say video poker for Windows and pot mix just dandy, and that's what I did when I got home, and have done frequently since. There are just some pleasures one should not live without.

Smoking Pot in the White House

STEVE DIAMOND

Certain cities have a mystical aura, such as New York, Paris, Rome, Rio, Tokyo, and Washington, to name a few. In D.C., tourists stop and pose their families before the big iron fence in front of the White House and snap away. This phenomenon allows these visitors to take a little magic home and put it on their mantle.

It was 1977, and an early spring made D.C. a city of flowers. The traditional cherry blossoms, azaleas, tulips, and lilacs flowered in profusion, giving Washington the smell of an arboretum. I was working as executive director and lobbyist for a nationwide association of doctors headquartered in Washington, D.C.

The Carter administration was a group of likeable boobs. President Carter fanatically believed that if something was right, in a Biblical way, it would grow like mushrooms and become law. While this simple optimism worked in church, it would never do the job in Congress. Deals were made—"I'm for you, you're for me." Carter's lobbyists in Congress believed the same scripture.

Carter won in 1976 because he was considered an outsider. Gerald Ford, of course, spent over thirty years in the House of Representatives. Carter won because Ford pardoned Nixon. Ford was attempting to put the government, shaken by Nixon's fascist regime, back to normal. Ford was attempting to heal the war wounds of Watergate.

My Uncle Bunny, a veteran of World War II, was in the 82nd Airborne Division—a storied outfit that was on the front lines of the war, from Italy to the Battle of the Bulge and beyond. I remember something he once told me as we listened to a Cubs game on the radio.

"Stevie," he laughed and lamented, "near the end of World War II, we marched through Germany. As the inhabitants begged for cigarettes and chocolate, they all would say, 'Hitler was a bad man and I'm not a party member and I fought to overthrow him.' There wasn't a Nazi civilian in sight."

Similarly, in the mid-'70s, nobody in Washington had been a Nixon backer or even a Republican. They had no idea what Tricky Dick was doing in that consecrated White House to destroy our democracy.

Through my work, I often met for dinner with Don Harvey, Carter's health advisor. He was from South Carolina, had a country drawl, and wore Brooks Brothers suits. His prize possession was a roofless Corvair—the car Ralph Nader called a moving death trap.

Harvey invited me to do dinner in his closet-size office at the White House and tour the premises because only a few staffers worked past 10:00 PM. He was the tour leader, and we saw the offices of Dr. Peter Bourne (he had been dismissed because he proffered a prescription for quaaludes to a pretty, young secretary), Zbigniew Brzezinski, Burt Lance, and the whole sorry crew.

Unfortunately for his inexperienced administration, Carter and his majordomo, Hamilton Jordan, made the tough decisions. Carter hired many of his cronies from Georgia to fill policy-vetted sensitive positions.

Don's office was on the lower level of the building. It sported English windows three-quarters of the way up the wall and had no view, except of the Secret Service guards. Don and I walked up to the Rose Garden, planted by Jackie Kennedy Onassis, which was so small it made me sad.

Remember, this was precrack, and many of the '60s activists expected marijuana prohibition to end soon. Half the people in the country found it mildly relaxing and an appetite enhancer. They laughed at the movie *Reefer Madness*, directed by Louis Gasnier and adopted by Harry Anslinger and J. Edgar Hoover, the director of the FBI who denied that the Mafia ever existed.

Harvey made a small joke about this house being the safest place in America. He reached into the inside pocket of his made-to-measure suit and pulled out a huge reefer.

"You like the weed, don't you, Stevie?"

"Sure," I said, "but not here in the White House surrounded by cops, Secret Service, and executive-protection gumshoes."

Harvey asked, "Do you have a match?"

"No, but I've got a Bic lighter in my trench coat. You can keep it. Bob, I'm going home—thanks, but no thanks."

"Steve, you're a rookie in this town. Look up at the windows." I took off my glasses, which improved my astigmatic eyes, and I saw shoes moving back and forth next to the windows. "Relax, man. Do you see the shoes?"

"Yes, of course."

"Which way are the heels pointing?"

"Outward," I whispered.

"Steve, their job isn't to bust us. They never involve themselves in our business. They're looking out on that crowd of stalkers that could cause harm to the chief executive."

Scrabbled

MAXIMUM TRAFFIC

Whitey's house was shared by a half dozen guys—truck drivers and construction workers. They all smoked weed, a lot of weed. There were bags of weed all over the house. Everywhere there was an ashtray, there was a bag of weed. Little bags and big bags. They told me to smoke all I wanted. All these guys were a few years older than me, and most of them a hundred pounds heavier, and I was kind of nervous. They drank a whole lot of beer and smoked a whole lot of pot, and I got even more nervous.

There was a wired-up Mexican guy there who started hounding everyone to play Scrabble with him. They all just kept laughing at him and telling him that he couldn't spell in English anyway. He started getting really mad, so to cool him off, his buddies told him that I would play Scrabble with him. I could hardly refuse; actually I was afraid to refuse.

So I sat down at the kitchen table with this bad-tempered, wound-up, drunk Mexican construction worker and set up the Scrabble game. I had taken two years of Spanish in high school, so I asked the guy if he would like to play using Spanish words. He instantly became friendly to me. "*Hermano!* You know *Español!*"

He fired up another joint and we started to play. Well, the guy was a terrible Scrabble player and within a dozen plays I was miles ahead of him, even though we were playing in Spanish. It turned out that his friendly feelings toward me were very short-lived. He jumped up from his chair and threw the Scrabble board at my head, scattering pieces all over the room.

"You motherfucking cheater," he screamed at me. I ran for my life. His buddies all grabbed him and held him off me, but they were all laughing hysterically. The drunk Mexican didn't like it one bit. That was enough party for me. I told Whitey that I was tired and asked him where I could sleep. He took me to an unused attic room with a nice cot.

I was just starting to calm down when someone knocked on the door. It was a plain-looking girl, maybe ten years older than me. She walked in and sat on the cot. The guys downstairs had decided that they should provide me with a woman. I was seventeen years old and had never had my clothes off around a woman . . . and I didn't have the nerve to start with a total stranger. She was sweet and tried to talk me into it. A woman trying to talk me into sex—now *that* was a first.

So, you might imagine, this kind of experience changed my perspective on the world a bit. It made me feel a lot less "white bread and corn-fed." When I came back to my hometown, I felt that I belonged to a much bigger community than the one I had left behind. And that community was very fond of smoking dope.

Miracle Cure

ROBERT DELANCY

I am fifty-five years old. In 1986, when I was twenty-nine, I suffered a stroke. An aneurysm, to be exact. The doctors performed a right frontal lobotomy. The blood vessel they had clipped, the following day, let go. It broke. Needless to say, I suffered another stroke. Much more severe. They gave me less than a 1 percent chance of even making it to the operating table. They had already told my parents I was not going to make it.

As I am writing this, you can see that I survived. I was a vegetable for a while. It was like being born again. I had to learn to walk, talk, eat, think, and see. Just everything. Of all the visitors I'm told I had, I did not know anyone was even there. My sister tells me how I would just lay there looking right through her as the drool dripped from my mouth.

I was a nonfunctioning vegetable until about a week after the operation, when my good buddy George stopped in to see me. But first I must tell you that the doctors did say that I would definitely have some stroke effects—like a drooped mouth or the loss of function in one or more limbs—because of the severity of the stroke.

Anyway, my friend George comes walking in my room. He had no idea what kind of condition I was in. I had no idea that there was even anybody there. Not just yet. A little while later, I realized that he had asked me if I wanted a hit off his one-hitter. Somehow I understood and conveyed a yes. He lifted me up off the bed into my wheelchair and rolled me over to the window.

I took two hits back-to-back. Almost instantly, I snapped back to reality. I then remembered him coming into the room and what had followed. Instantly, I knew who he was and what he was saying. Instead of just drooling, I started communicating. At least the best that I could.

It was like, at that instant, my brain started functioning. I knew what was going on around me. I was actually thinking. Those two hits were absolutely a miracle for me. Since I have never heard of any other cases like mine, I thought that this might possibly be another area for the medical community to explore.

I truly believe, if not for those two hits, I would be a vegetable. It took me fourteen months to fully recover. I never had any stroke effects. At first, I was taking Dilantin to prevent seizures. But I still had a couple. When I was released, I was getting high and taking my Dilantin. After about three months, I stopped taking the pills.

I went about a year with no problems. Then a dry spell hit. No weed to be found. On my fifth dry day, I had a seizure, which was like a truck parking on my head, and my body shook profusely. A friend came through later that evening. And I have been high ever since. And never another seizure. I truly believe this is something that should be looked into. I believe it could possibly benefit other stroke victims.

Speaking of Talking

DAVID MCREYNOLDS

As a recovered (or recovering) alcoholic, I know there is one thing marijuana and vodka have in common—you get earthshaking insights when you get high. The huge difference between vodka and marijuana is that in the morning, when you are sober and dealing with the hangover from vodka, the insights are forgotten, buried under a wave of nausea, while even forty years later I can remember in detail the insights from my first encounter with marijuana.

It was in Ocean Park, California, the little bohemia by the sea where, as a UCLA student, I'd taken up residence in one of the cheap shacks. (Cheap? Hell, it didn't even have warm water or a shower.) A student friend, Bruce, a poet and a radical who had been expelled from Max Shachtman's Trotskyist Socialist Youth League for being queer, had asked if I wanted to try marijuana. I said sure.

We went to his shack and lit up. There were no hallucinations. I didn't feel light or think I was floating. But I did realize that as we talked I had the distinct impression that, just out of my line of sight to my right, was a golden wheat field in Kansas, viewed through an open window, while to my left, again just out of the line of sight, was a doorway leading downstairs to Le Club Tabu in Paris, which I'd visited on my first trip to Europe in 1951.

If I actually turned to the right, there was only the wall of Bruce's shack, with an art print tacked to it, and if I turned to the left, there was only another wall. Not a hallucination—just a simple certainty that, as I sat in that little room, I had Paris off to one side and Kansas to the other.

And I became aware that . . . I couldn't talk. I could see the words in my head drift off, assume shapes, become animals, sheep or cats, and wander into my unconscious. A simple sentence—such as "I find it hard to talk"—couldn't be completed because as soon as I stepped past "I find," the words had begun to drift away, and the next word, "it," refused to appear.

I was stranded on whatever word I had last spoken. I couldn't reach back, and I couldn't reach ahead. I couldn't even say, "I have forgotten what I was going to say." I got as far as "forgotten" and found I didn't know where that sentence had begun, nor where it was headed.

I became keenly aware of the fact that the mind was a time machine, that for a brief period of a few seconds, the past, present, and future co-existed absolutely. The only way any of us can talk is because we remember precisely the last words we spoke and because we know in advance precisely the words we are about to speak.

That which was objective reality only a moment earlier—my voice, which could have been recorded on tape, and which has, the instant I've finished speaking and the sound waves have faded and gone flat, ceased to have any objective reality—the words I have not yet spoken—are objectively real inside my brain.

That objective reality doesn't extend far in either direction. While I know what I've just said, with each passing moment the past becomes more variable and, barring a tape recording, memory becomes uncertain. And while I know what I'm about to say—for the next few instants—beyond that, the future also becomes variable.

My sentences may shift and change because of some event—a comment by Bruce, with whom I'm smoking dope, some outside event such as a dog barking, anything that might disrupt the direction in which my conversation had been headed.

However, for the brief period of a few seconds, what I have just said, what I am in the process of saying, and what I'm about to say, all coexist in the brain. Which makes the mind, not in some figurative sense, but in a real way, a time machine, in which dimensions that we thought could never meet, coexist.

Whether I've been able to explain this so that it makes sense to you, I don't know. But now, more than fifty years later, it is as clear to me as it was that night.

There are, of course, other experiences that I'm sure are common— music may make sense in new ways, making love becomes more pleasurable, more deeply involving. What marijuana is not good for is playing poker, where players can become more fascinated by the shapes and colors of their hand than by whether the five cards add up to anything that can win.

When I drank, I found I could play excellent poker up to the point I passed out. In social gatherings, alcohol is a social drug. A glass of wine and you relax, the group becomes more animated, more interactive. With marijuana, the group becomes less social as people drift into private worlds—in the words of Quentin Crisp, "Marijuana is a distancer."

Research Project

ROBERT ALTMAN

"Would you like to collaborate, Robert?"

This query was extended by my seatmate, Gene, as we were hurtling through space at seven hindred miles per hour. But let me backtrack a bit.

My great inner awakening began with certain consciousness-expanding drugs and, not atypically, the very first of all these was pot. Although I would never consider myself a "pothead," marijuana has, on occasion, been a part of my redemption.

Back to the plane.I was young, impetuous, and immortal, and I was seated with my dear friend on a cross-country charter plane heading toward one of those once-in-a-lifetime events, the Alternative Media Conference at Goddard College where we attended meetings at night and swam naked by day. Now, Gene was a medical doctor who found himself publishing medical advice columns and answering listeners' call-in questions on FM radio, the new town hall for the counterculture. He became the premiere medical "Dear Abby" for the young and the toothless.

Well, we had some time on our hands, as this was a cross-country flight, so Gene began opening his readers' mail. I snoozed beside him when I felt a tap on my shoulder.

"Would you like to see an interesting letter?"

"Sure, Gene."

It went something like this:

"Dear Dr. Gene: The enclosed substance fell into my hands through a neighborhood acquaintance. I have taken the liberty of rolling it into a joint with the hope you'll perform the necessary scientific research and chemical analysis. Thank you very much . . . "

Hmmmmm. Dr. Gene must have been reacting to a particularly fey moment. He invited me to share this extrinsic "research" by lighting a match. Well, I do recall embracing the occasion with a naughty gleam and a resounding chortle that only Lucifer could really appreciate.

Fortunately, the research turned out well. The substance was benign but powerful. It stimulated the good doctor with enough brashness and playfulness that he took over the plane's entire audio system. Since this was a charter flight, the stewardess winked at Dr. Gene as he sent raucous rock 'n' roll from his portable tape player through the plane's microphone, all to the delight of our fellow pilgrims.

Wasn't it Samuel Taylor Coleridge who opined, "He is the best physician who is the most ingenious inspirer"?

Digger

JOHN MCCLEARY

When you were with Digger, you didn't just smoke dope, you sat upon the tripod at Delphi, partook of the blood and body of Jesus Christ, or ascended the Himalayas to commune within the cave of an ascetic.

I never knew what he was going to call his dope. "Come over and have some tea, boo, leaf, reef, greens, shit, or sacrament."

His stuff never came from Fresno; it was always Maui Wowie, Kabul Gold, Nam Green, or Mendocino Mellow. Incense was as important as the lighting; music was supreme to the experience.

I never knew what he did to support his lifestyle. *Style* is perhaps the wrong word. His clothing was a Guatemalan shirt and nondescript faded jeans. Oh, and bare feet.

I never saw Digger outside of his place, although I have a photograph of him on his front doorstep, hiding behind an album cover of Frank Zappa in front of his face with his finger in Zappa's nose.

Digger lived in a small house with two cats, one that liked the smoke of burning marijuana and one that left the premises whenever it was lit. He lived on the alley behind my house and used to call me in as I walked by.

Entering his place was like stepping into a very well-appointed Dumpster or a library after the apocalypse, take your pick. The Oriental rug had the patina of a pizza place. His record collection overstepped bizarre. He had cannabis buds drying in the window on a wire coat hanger.

One afternoon, I emerged from my darkroom with prints to dry on the fence. "Come on over and smoke some boo," Digger said from his kitchen window. He slipped back into darkness as he closed the forest green terrycloth curtains. He lit three candles and a stick of musk incense. He put on the Fugs.

It was a water pipe that day. He was using sauterne instead of water.

He wore a New Year's Eve paper hat. I think I almost liked the Fugs that time.

At exactly 1:48 PM, Digger stopped om-ing and said he had to make a private phone call. I stumbled out. Almost back to the darkroom, I remembered my photographic tray left at Digger's. I slipped through his door and found the tray on the Oriental rug. Digger, hunched over his unbelievably cluttered desk, was saying into the phone, "Sell IBM and buy that new little company named after a fruit or something."

How Do You Spell Relief?

IRWIN GOOEN

Unlike any number of my acquaintances back in the '60s, I had never been paranoid or even overly concerned about smoking pot at least somewhat openly. I recall making a point of lighting up a joint when driving past the Center Street New York City Police Headquarters and having smoked (in a regular tobacco pipe) grass on a cross-country flight as well as on the streets of midtown Manhattan.

Eventually, when I moved to upstate New York at the end of the '60s, I smoked grass in the waiting room of a dental office, and once in the lobby of a movie house where Cheech & Chong's *Up in Smoke* was showing, and the ticket-seller scrunched her nose and remarked about the awful smell, something like rope burning. I told her that there were lotsa young people coming to see the film and whispered that some of them were no doubt smoking pot.

Anyway, back to New York City, where one day I was driving down Flatbush Avenue in Brooklyn and smoking away in my top-down sports car. Coming the other way was a police cruiser, which stopped parallel to me, and I saw the driving officer wave me over. I felt a flush in my face and thought that this was it, busted at last.

I put on the hand brake, crossed to the cruiser, and was about to say, "Hey, no—I wasn't smoking dope—just a skinny, roll-yourself cigarette," when the cop said, "Waddaya want?"

I said, "You waved me over."

He responded, "No, we're just stopping here, and I was waving on the traffic behind us."

"Oh," I smiled. "Sorry to bother you."

Good-bye, Reno, Good-bye

My friend Bob and I went up to the Sierras to ski for a few days. He thought it would be fun to go to a show called *Hello, Hollywood, Hello* at the MGM Grand Hotel in Reno. It was a dinner show, $50 a plate, and when we got there we found that (a) the only thing a vegetarian could eat was canned peas, (b) we were seated with an elderly couple from Canada, and (c) the show had nothing to do with Hollywood and everything to do with breasts (except for one scene, which was aimed at the gay bondage crowd).

The show was horrid, the food worse, and my embarrassment acute, but I was well raised and fifty bucks was a lot of money, so when Bob asked me, in the parking lot on our way back to the car, what I thought of the show, I said I'd never seen anything remotely like it, which was true.

We got into his Karmann Ghia and started back up over the mountains toward Incline Village. I wasn't saying much, and Bob decided to light up a joint. We smoked it, passing it from fingers to fingers in the light of the dashboard. It was good stuff, and presently we both had a good buzz on.

After a long silence, each with his own thoughts, I said, "God, that was good weed. It feels as if we're going five miles an hour. Wow!"

And Bob said, looking at the speedometer, "We are."

On the Border

Sometime in the '70s, a pal and I were in San Francisco and we were—well, pretty stoned, actually—stuck in North Beach with no cash and low stash. So naturally we decided to hitchhike to Mexico.

We made it out to Nineteenth Avenue and got picked up by a grungy-looking biker in a Ford van who had just come back from Mexico and had no intention of returning. He was headed north and picked us up assuming that we were, too, since we had been thumbing a ride on the wrong side of the street.

We discussed Mexico briefly, and he let us know that he was fucking heading for Oregon, that we were fucking going with him, that he would drop us off in fucking Sonoma County in time to see fucking Walt Disney with mommy and daddy, that we were staying the fuck out of his stash since it was a fucking bitch getting it across the fucking Mexican border, and that, by the way, we were fucking driving since he was fucking tired.

As soon as he fell asleep, my buddy broke into his stash, and I turned the van around and headed south.

We toked and drove like maniacs and made it to the border early the next morning. We were idling back in the line a bit, watching Governor Reagan's state troopers assist the border patrol by shaking down everyone under thirty who drove across from Mexico, and we were laughing and congratulating ourselves on being clever enough to be smuggling grass *into* Mexico, not out, when the biker woke up.

He had just slept for twelve hours in the back of a smelly van, after having been up for who-knows-how-long sweating his little score, so he probably wasn't thinking too clearly. He asked us where the fuck we were, and we told him we were at the Mexican border. He screamed like a wounded deer, grabbed the grocery bag with fourteen kilos of Mexican weed, kicked open the side door of the van, and hurled it all into the brush beside the highway.

My buddy and I took one look at each other and bolted out the front doors of the van. We crossed the highway, thumbed a ride with a dough-nut salesman, and got dropped off in Fresno, where my aunt lived, later that day. She gave us a good meal and bus fare back to Santa Rosa.

Biker Story

JAY LYNCH

Back in the days before the Summer of Love, I enjoyed smoking marijuana. I would hollow out a Winston cigarette and fill half of it with reefer.
This was called a "cocktail" back then. I used to smoke these things in
the school cafeteria, back when smoking was permitted in college. I
figured, on the off chance that people recognized the smell, I would
be down to the tobacco part of the Winston before they'd figure it was
coming from my table.

When the "legalize pot" protests began in the early days of the hippie
movement, I gave the stuff up. I didn't want to smoke pot to make a social
statement. I just wanted to get high and be left alone.

Back in 1965, most people just wanted to be left alone, including a
group of outlaw bikers I knew back then. True, many were dangerous
psychopaths, as I look back on it all. But I must admit that as a youth I
did appreciate their attitude—and I enjoyed their tales of life outside the
accepted social order.

There was Deviate, who was said to have killed a mailman in Milwaukee. He wore a vest, it was told, that his old lady made for him out of the
murdered postal worker's mail pouch.

There was Pony, who was able to turn into a werewolf. I had seen him
undergo this metamorphosis many times. He had a wife and kid on the
South Side. At home, he was a mild-mannered family man, known only
by the name he was born with. But he had a separate apartment, another
old lady, and an outlaw identity as Pony on the North Side. It was a Jekyll
and Hyde thing. In retrospect, I believe he had the power to cloud men's
minds. He would arrive looking like Wally Cox. Then he'd do a werewolf
take, grow a foot in stature, and sprout facial hair. Eventually, he got
divorced. Last I heard, he was an antiques dealer in Indiana.

And then here was Reno, who chronicled it all. In the saddlebag of his

Harley was his manuscript. Written in longhand on hundreds of sheets of school composition notebook paper, Reno had documented his ten years as a member of one of the Midwest's most notorious biker gangs. He was the Kerouac of the one percenters. Some day his book would be published. Some day his story, and the story of the fugitive culture to which he belonged, would be told. Reno was an outcast. He was a rebel. But his tattoos reflected primarily religious themes. He may have been abused and kicked around by life, but there was no question in his mind about who granted him that life. Reno believed in God!

Speed was this scribe's screwed-up drug of choice. Pot was not his scene at all. But at a biker party one night, we were all smoking reefer, including Reno. The talk was loose. Oaths, epithets, and curses flowed like cheap wine. And then somebody said (I forget in what context) the words that ignited something deep within Reno's inner psyche: "God damn it! God damn it!" The words pierced Reno's soul like a switchblade.

At first he looked flushed as he winced at the taking of the Lord's name in vain, but in seconds he turned red with some inexplicable kind of pot-induced perverse and misdirected rage.

"Yeah . . . God!" he snarled. "Let's talk about dear old God!"

With hate-filled eyes, Reno raised his gaze toward the ceiling. And, shaking his clenched, white-knuckled fist heavenward, he taunted his creator—daring the god, in whom he believed with every fiber of his being, to come down and take him on. Those in the crowd who knew him—and knew of his religious nature—were shocked. Here was a guy who believed in God, challenging Him to a here-and-now, kiss-my-ass fistfight. For Reno to defy God was as unbelievable as for Nixon to defy Eisenhower.

"This can't be happening," I thought. "This can't be real." But it was. His biker pals calmed him down and ushered him to a seat on the couch. Soon he chilled out. It was the reefer talking. It just couldn't have been Reno. Things mellowed out and the party wound down. Soon it was 4:00 AM, and a group of us, including Reno, split the scene and went outside. Out on the street, we noticed that Reno's bike was missing. We heard the distant roar of the Harley's motor. Looking down the block, in the direction of the sound, we saw the shadowy silhouette of a mystery rider mounted on Reno's bike. The cycle was weaving toward us in a crazy pattern.

It was Fith, the neighborhood idiot-boy, riding up to us on Reno's cycle. We stopped him, and Reno took his Harley back. The bikers tried to intimidate the moron child, but it had no effect on Fith. That's what the other neighborhood kids called him—Fith, an acronym for "Fucked in the head."

Reno looked in his saddlebag and flipped out. His manuscript was missing. Gone was the one and only copy of the book he had so painstakingly scrawled out in ballpoint, pencil, felt-tip—bit by bit, day by day—over the last decade of his life. Reno grabbed the idiot-boy by the front of his Dale Evans T-shirt.

"What did you do with my papers, you little piece of shit?" he shouted.

Fith didn't register fear. He just seemed confused. "Uhhh . . . I trew dem in da rivah," he replied.

The sun rose that dawn, casting a pallid light on the caravan of choppers heading south toward the Chicago River bridge on Wells where it crosses to Wacker Drive. The idiot-boy was riding shotgun on the lead cycle, babbling confused directions to its driver. In time, we found ourselves on the bridge at the Wells Street entrance to the Merchandise Mart, staring down fifty feet or so at the countless sheets of floating notebook paper that represented Reno's outlaw life. They were irretrievable. His book would never be published.

A few months later, Reno got married to a trade journal editor. On her urging, he quit his biker gang and got a job in construction.

It wasn't Reno's defiance of God that was his downfall so much as it was his *belief* in God. The forces that kept pot illegal likewise only have that power because we grant it to them by our belief in their authority over us. Instead of asking that marijuana be legalized, maybe it would just be better to just not acknowledge that the stuff is illegal—and just smoke it if you want to.

But, hey, what do I know? I have probably smoked seven or eight reefers in the last thirty-five years since people found out what it was. Pot . . . God . . . I don't know. I just want to be left alone.

Shooting Pot

REX WEINER

My friend Chris and I were at his house one afternoon, cutting school and looking to get high. All we had was some sorry Mexican weed and no rolling papers, so he says, "Let's shoot some grass!" So we cook up some grass tea, boiling it down to a dark green liquor.

Chris gets the spoon, pulls some cotton button-backing off his shirt, and I've got the spike. I fill up the works, trying to strain this swamp mixture through the cotton, but when I hold it up to the light, I can see leafy matter swimming around in there.

"What do you think?" I ask Chris.

He says, "What the hell" and bangs it into his arm.

Next it's my turn. I draw up some of the stuff and hold the works up to the light. There is a twig floating inside, but what the hell. I find the vein and shoot it in. The two of us sit around watching a stupid TV show, waiting and waiting and waiting. Nothing happens.

"I'm going home," I say. "My mom's cooking something special for dinner and I don't want to get in trouble."

Later, I'm sitting at the table with my dad, my little brother, and my mom, eating beef stroganoff, when I feel the blood drain out of my face and my stomach turning violent flip-flops.

"What's the matter?" my mom asks. "Don't you like the beef stroganoff? I made it especially for you."

My shithead brother, knowing I hate the food, says, "Hey, how come your face is green?"

I say that the food was great; I'm just feeling a little sick from something I ate at school.

I went to my room and was in bad shape for several days. Must have been that twig got stuck in my aorta. In any case, my mom never made beef stroganoff again.

Time Delay

A.J. PIRILLI

When I first came to Japan, I shared a rented house with six other people. One evening, while cruising the richer neighborhoods for usable trash—which is a popular pastime of foreigners in Japan on the night before the heavy trash is to be collected—I found a shortwave radio.

When I took it home and tried it out, I realized that it needed some sort of an antenna. While I was taking the steel strings off my guitar to fashion them into an outside antenna, one of my housemates came into my room with a friend of his who had just arrived from a Southeast Asian nation with a rather large lump of hashish concealed in his undershorts.

It was agreed that the three of us would try it out as I tried out my new radio, once the antenna was in place. He made his preparations and I made mine.

"I have no idea how good this stuff is," he said.

"Well, we'll soon find out," I answered back as I switched on the shortwave.

We puffed a bit and I fiddled with the dials, and suddenly we could hear a clear voice in English:

" . . . and . . . that . . . is . . . the . . . cur . . . rent . . . sit . . . ua . . . tion . . . on . . . Wall . . . "

I choked up some smoke to say, "Wow, this is some really good shit. Talk about getting spaced."

The three of us sat there, grinning and chuckling over our good fortune. Then the man on the radio said: "This . . . has . . . been . . . the . . . world . . . news . . . spoken . . . in . . . slow . . . English . . . for . . . foreign . . . listeners."

Roaches

But Who's Counting?

KIT SIBERT

As for pot stories, well, I got really paranoid once. Another time I couldn't stop laughing and thought that was like *hell*. And another time I got jumpy legs and had to put them straight out in front of me (I was sitting down) for about a hundred hours. And about 534 times I had to eat everything in the refrigerator. And about 341 times I got totally tired and went to sleep. And once I acted really stupid. I didn't cotton to pot much. Is that what you had in mind?

Problem Child

I'm a child-and-adolescent psychiatrist, and one day in the early 1980s these two parents drag their fourteen-year-old delinquent into the office, so I can treat his "dope" problem.

Their explanation was, "We don't care if he smokes pot, but you have to get him to stop copping *ours*."

Actual Dialogue

WILDMAN WEINER

"So, I'm over at Carole's . . . "

"Carole?"

"In Brentwood."

"I think I know her."

"I don't think you know her. I don't think *I* know her. I don't think she knows *herself*."

"Whattaya mean?"

"She's sitting on her couch weeping."

I hang up the phone.

"That's a nice fabric, Carole," I say.

"It should be," she barks. "It cost a mint!"

"Oh," I say. She returns to her weeping. "What's wrong?" I ask, and she sniffles.

"Everyone's always coming over here to get high and hang out all day and night and I can never get rid of them and I just want to be left alone! I've got so much to do!"

"Why don't you just throw them out?"

"I can't," she wails. "I'm the *dealer*!"

The Hole

HAL MUSKAT

There was that time I took a cube of hash off the serving tray in an Algerian café (down one alley, turn left at another alley, take a right and another right into yet another, smaller alley) and, as was the custom, brought it into the WC where, alone in the dark with the hole in the middle of the floor, I somehow found my chillum and got so stoned that I couldn't find my way out the door. I mean I couldn't find the *door*. That hole was the center of the universe. There was no out. Fuckin' joint stunk from colonial Algerian and hippie shit.

Moment of Truth

Four smugglers are sitting around a freezing apartment in Srinagar (imagine a place that adult human-size rabbits built, a warren three stories tall, hundreds of years old, no right angles), waiting for the best of the best to waft its way down from the Hindu Kush. They have been waiting for three months.

Whenever they ask their main man, Rashid, what's the status, he looks out the window, up and down the street, as if the shipment were just about at the front door. He turns to the gringos and says it's no problem. How reassuring. Business in Kashmiriville.

Smoking ten joints a day or so of the world's best hash, joints as thick as your forefinger, and now, now, they are running out of stash. The unthinkable. As the last joint is rolled, they all give each other a sly look, reach into various nooks and crannies, and come out with a kilo apiece that cach, thinking he is the only sane one of the bunch, the only one with foresight, had squirreled away.

Suddenly there are ten pounds of hash on the floor.

Choices

ERIC FURRY

When my friend Whitey and I first started smoking pot, he went into the drugstore and asked for a pack of rolling papers.

"Gummed or ungummed?" the clerk asked.

"Ungummed," Whitey replied quickly, not wanting to appear foolish.

Predictably, he was chastised when he returned home.

"Next time, just ask for a pack of Zig-Zags," a roommate remarked.

Needless to say, that's exactly what he did the next time.

"Wheat or rice?" asked the clerk.

"Gummed," Whitey responded.

Then there's the story of my stoned girlfriend being asked for her visa at Amsterdam's Centraal Station, to which she replied, "I don't have a Visa—is MasterCard okay?"

Brownie Baked

This has happened to three different parents. My friends leave brownies in the fridge and, not knowing they are loaded, their dad eats one or more. All three times the dad has sat down in front of the TV and laughs and smiles a lot more than usual. Two of the three dads then stayed up later than usual and fell asleep in their La-Z-Boys (not a normal thing for them to do). The next morning, they all said that they slept great and wanted more brownies.

Light Show

One evening after some relatively intense smoking, three friends of mine were out cruising when they happened to be pulled over by the Man. After checking the driver's ID, the cop shined his flashlight in the face of the very stoned person in the back seat, whose response was: "Strobe it, officer."

Evangelism

DAN NEWMAN

While hitchhiking in Oregon, I goofed and left my fanny pack on the side of the road. It contained the usual—including my wallet and my dope. Two weeks later, I received the fanny pack in the mail. Everything was returned, including the money, except for the dope. The Good Samaritan had replaced the pot with religious pamphlets.

About the Editor

Paul Krassner published *The Realist* (1958–2001). He was a cofounder of the Yippies. He blogs occasionally for The Huffington Post, Counter-Punch, and The Rag Blog. At the Cannabis Cup in Amsterdam, he was inducted into the Counterculture Hall of Fame. He is currently working on his first novel. In December 2010, the Oakland branch of the writers' organization PEN honored Krassner with their lifetime achievement award. It was a tough competition, but he finally beat out Justin Bieber, Levi Johnston, and Snooki.

Printed in the United States
by Baker & Taylor Publisher Services